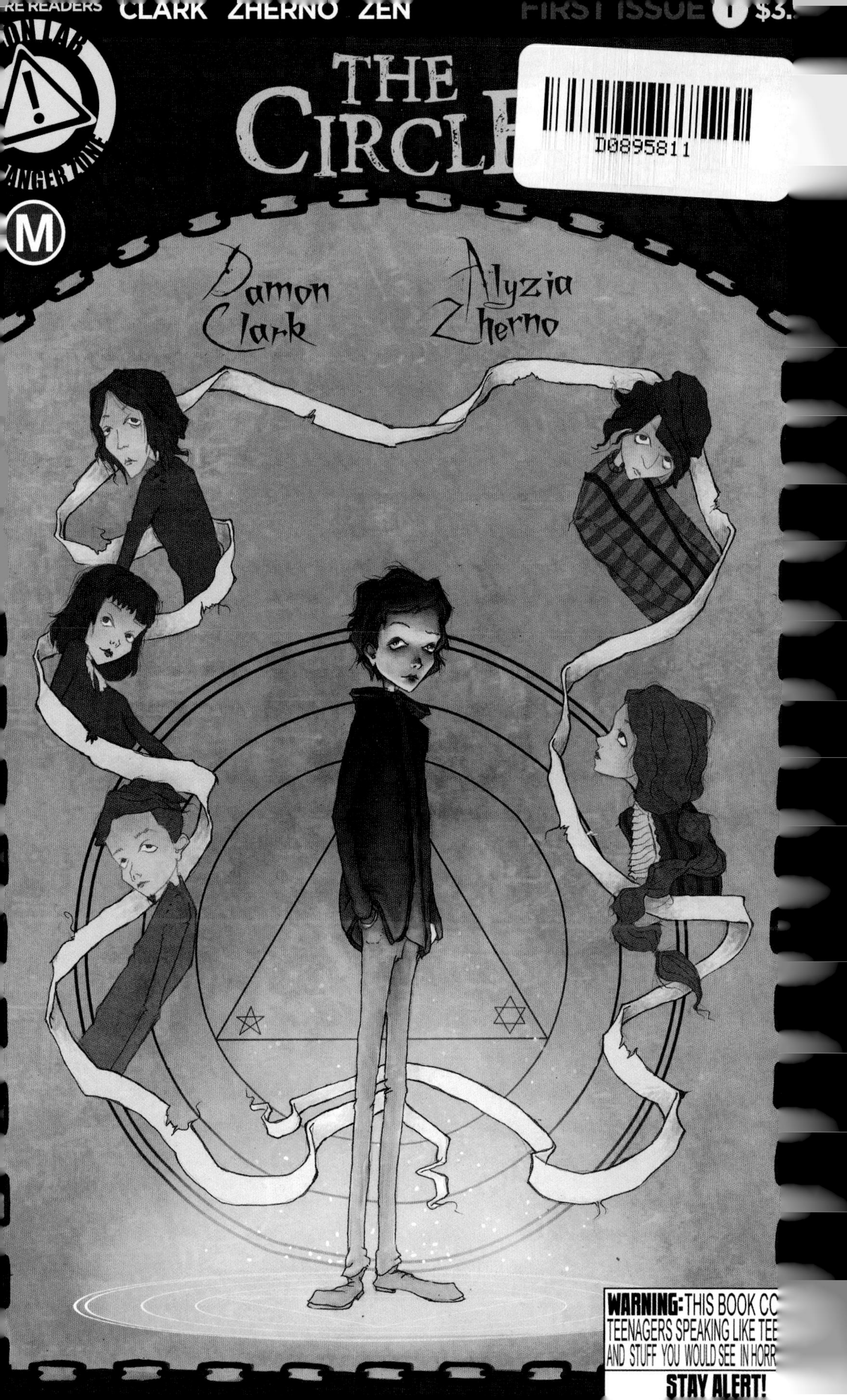
RE READERS
CLARK ZHERNO ZEN
FIRST ISSUE 1 $3.
THE CIRCLE
M
Damon Clark
Alyzia Zherno
WARNING: THIS BOOK CO
TEENAGERS SPEAKING LIKE TEE
AND STUFF YOU WOULD SEE IN HORR
STAY ALERT!

THE CIRCLE

WRITTEN BY

Damon Clark

ART & COLORS BY

Alyzia Zherno

EDITED & LETTERED BY

Zen

VARIANT COVER BY

Ivan Shavrin

JASON MARTIN - PUBLISHER
DAVE DWONCH - PRESIDENT
SHAWN GABBORIN - EDITOR IN CHIEF
JAMAL IGLE - VP OF MARKETING
JIM DIETZ - SOCIAL MEDIA DIRECTOR
NICOLE D'ANDRIA - SCRIPT EDITOR
COLLEEN BOYD - ASSOCIATE EDITOR

ACTIONLABCOMICS.COM

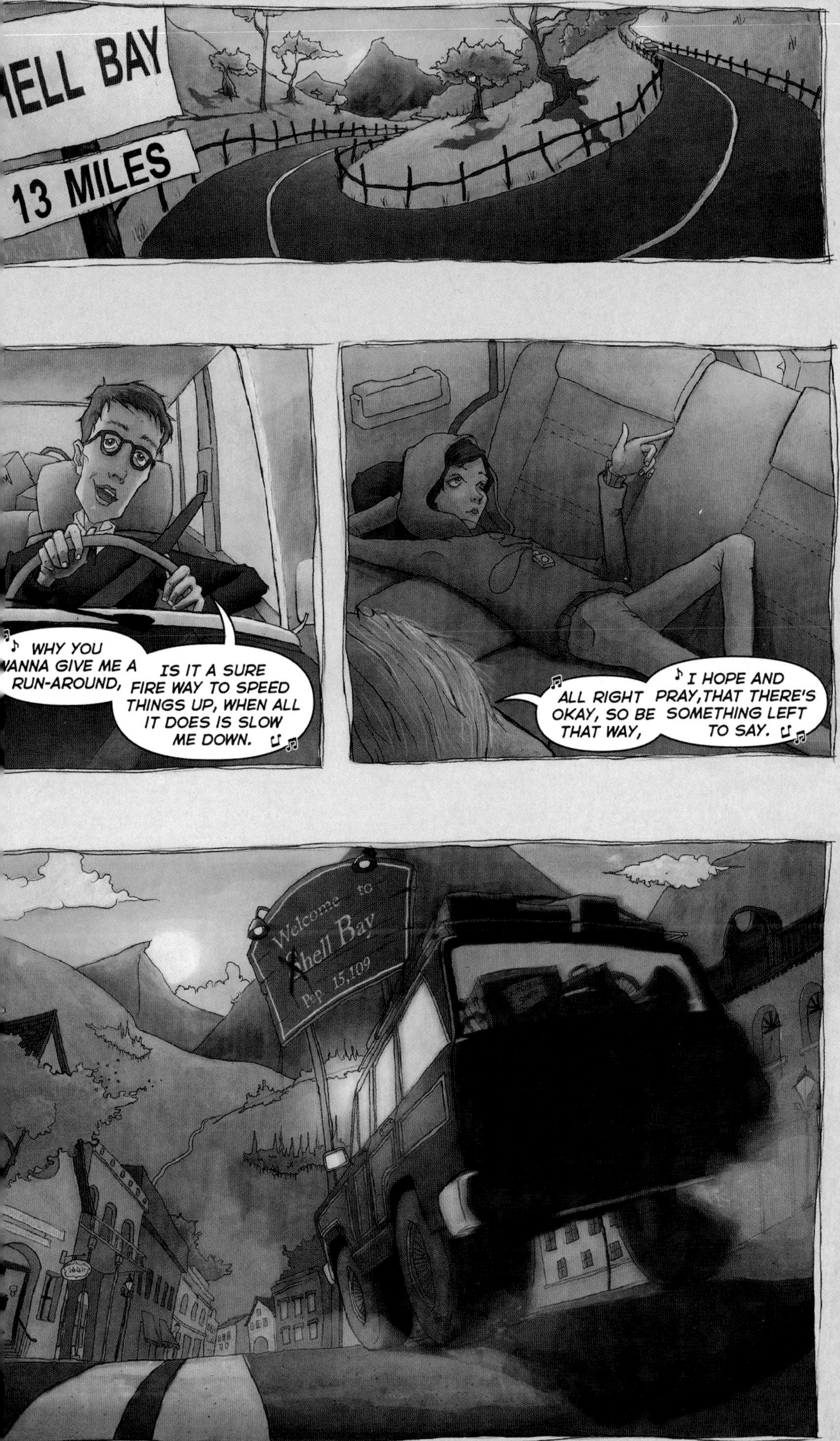
HELL BAY
13 MILES
WHY YOU WANNA GIVE ME A RUN-AROUND,
IS IT A SURE FIRE WAY TO SPEED THINGS UP, WHEN ALL IT DOES IS SLOW ME DOWN.
ALL RIGHT OKAY, SO BE THAT WAY,
I HOPE AND PRAY, THAT THERE'S SOMETHING LEFT TO SAY.
Welcome to Shell Bay
Pop 15,109

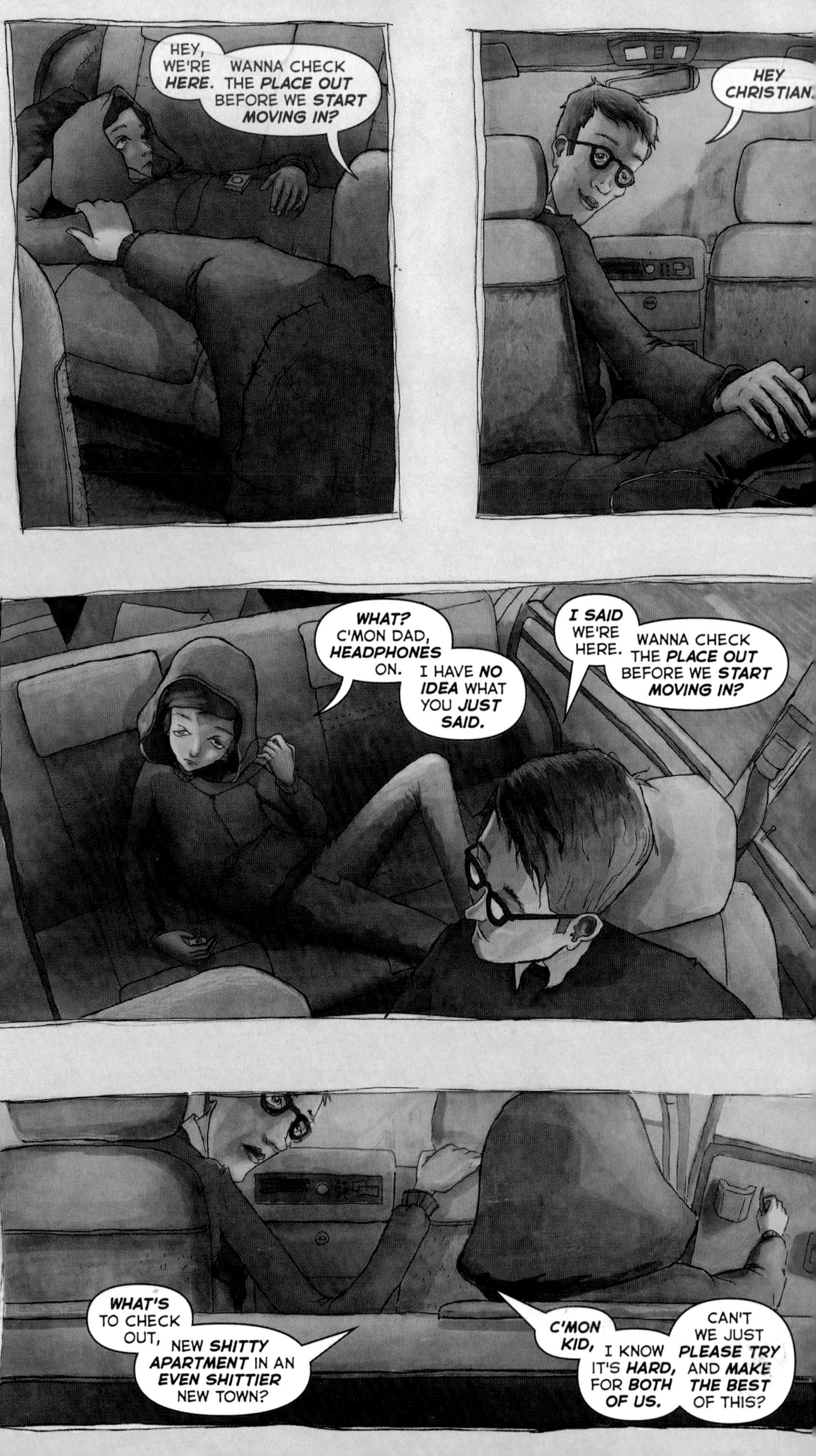
HEY, WE'RE HERE.
WANNA CHECK THE PLACE OUT BEFORE WE START MOVING IN?
HEY CHRISTIAN.
WHAT? C'MON DAD, HEADPHONES ON.
I HAVE NO IDEA WHAT YOU JUST SAID.
I SAID WE'RE HERE.
WANNA CHECK THE PLACE OUT BEFORE WE START MOVING IN?
WHAT'S TO CHECK OUT,
NEW SHITTY APARTMENT IN AN EVEN SHITTIER NEW TOWN?
C'MON KID,
I KNOW IT'S HARD, FOR BOTH OF US.
CAN'T WE JUST PLEASE TRY AND MAKE THE BEST OF THIS?

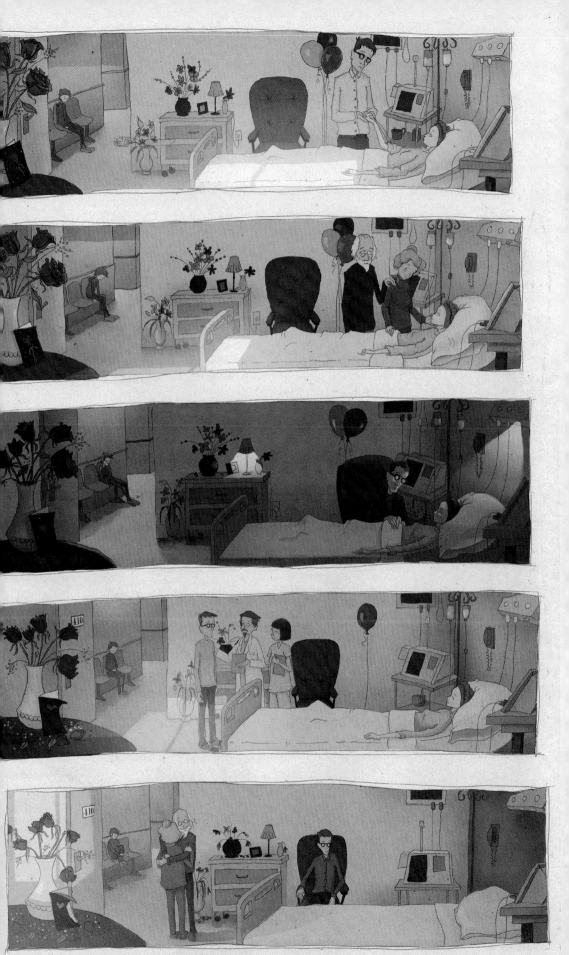

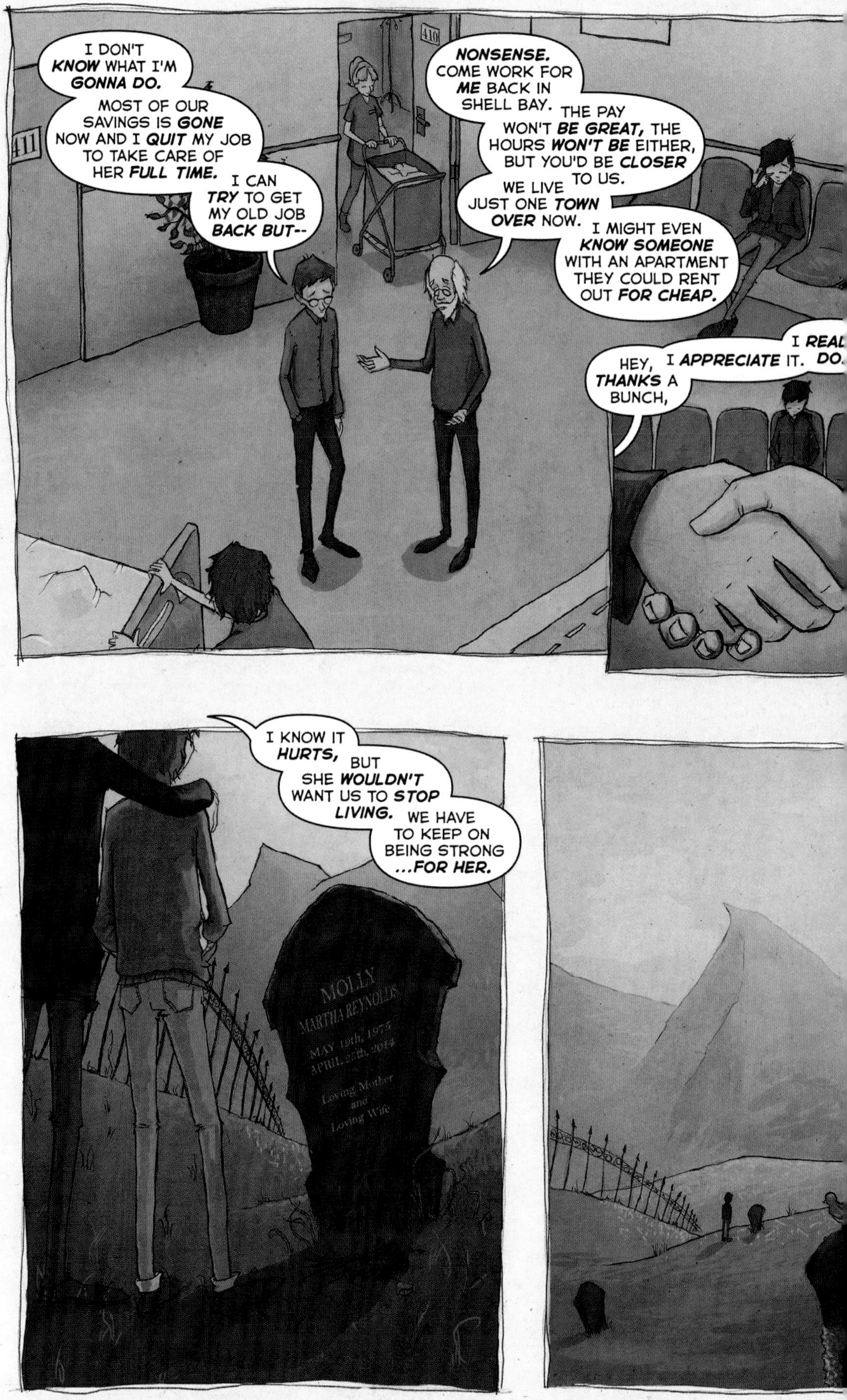
I DON'T KNOW WHAT I'M GONNA DO.
MOST OF OUR SAVINGS IS GONE NOW AND I QUIT MY JOB TO TAKE CARE OF HER FULL TIME.
I CAN TRY TO GET MY OLD JOB BACK BUT--
NONSENSE. COME WORK FOR ME BACK IN SHELL BAY.
THE PAY WON'T BE GREAT, THE HOURS WON'T BE EITHER, BUT YOU'D BE CLOSER TO US.
WE LIVE JUST ONE TOWN OVER NOW.
I MIGHT EVEN KNOW SOMEONE WITH AN APARTMENT THEY COULD RENT OUT FOR CHEAP.
HEY, THANKS A BUNCH,
I APPRECIATE IT.
I REAL
DO.
I KNOW IT HURTS,
BUT SHE WOULDN'T WANT US TO STOP LIVING.
WE HAVE TO KEEP ON BEING STRONG ...FOR HER.
MOLLY
MARTHA REYNOLDS
MAY 19th, 1975
APRIL 25th, 2014
Loving Mother
and
Loving Wife

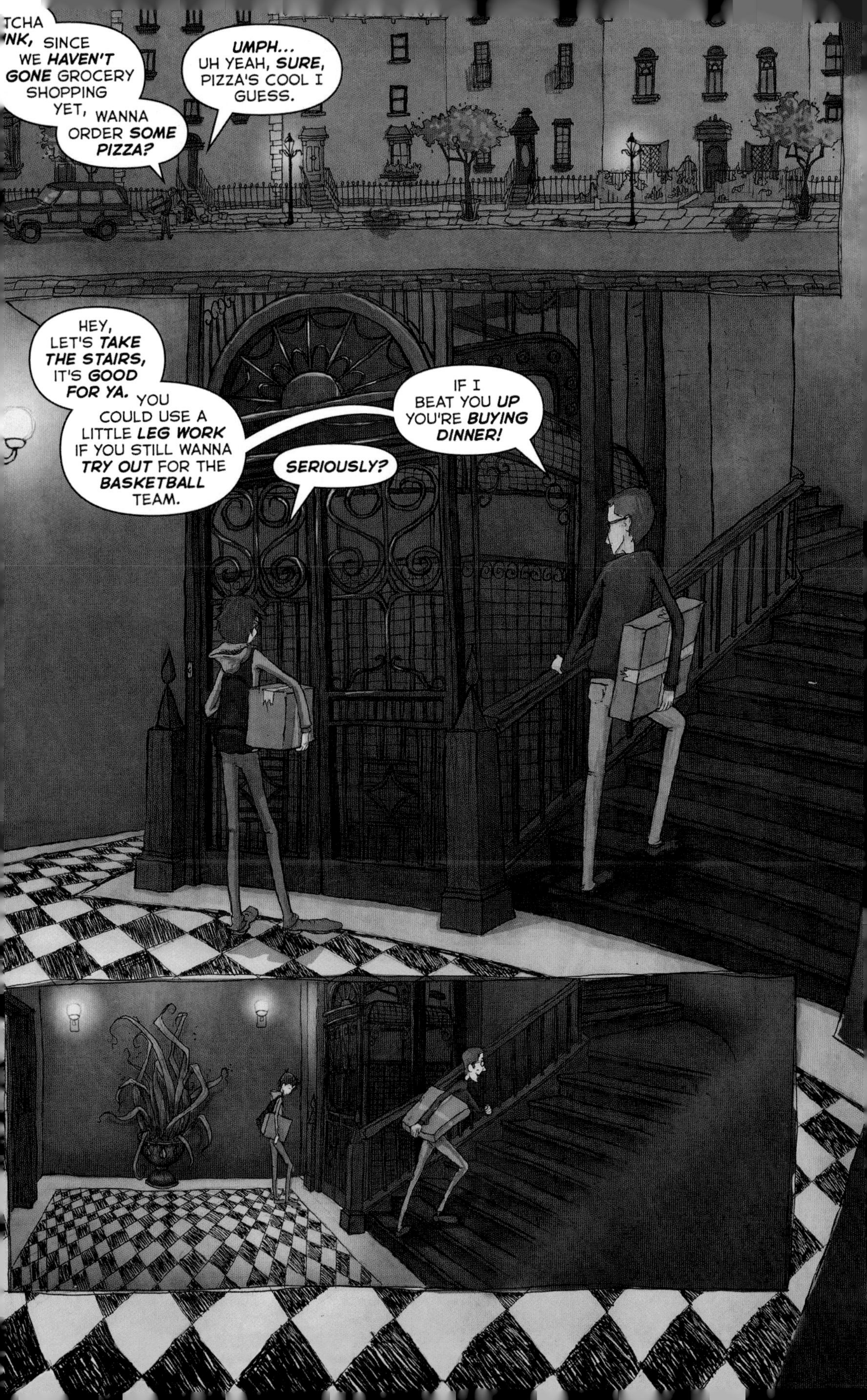
TCHA NK, SINCE WE HAVEN'T GONE GROCERY SHOPPING YET, WANNA ORDER SOME PIZZA?
UMPH... UH YEAH, SURE, PIZZA'S COOL I GUESS.
HEY, LET'S TAKE THE STAIRS, IT'S GOOD FOR YA.
YOU COULD USE A LITTLE LEG WORK IF YOU STILL WANNA TRY OUT FOR THE BASKETBALL TEAM.
SERIOUSLY?
IF I BEAT YOU UP YOU'RE BUYING DINNER!

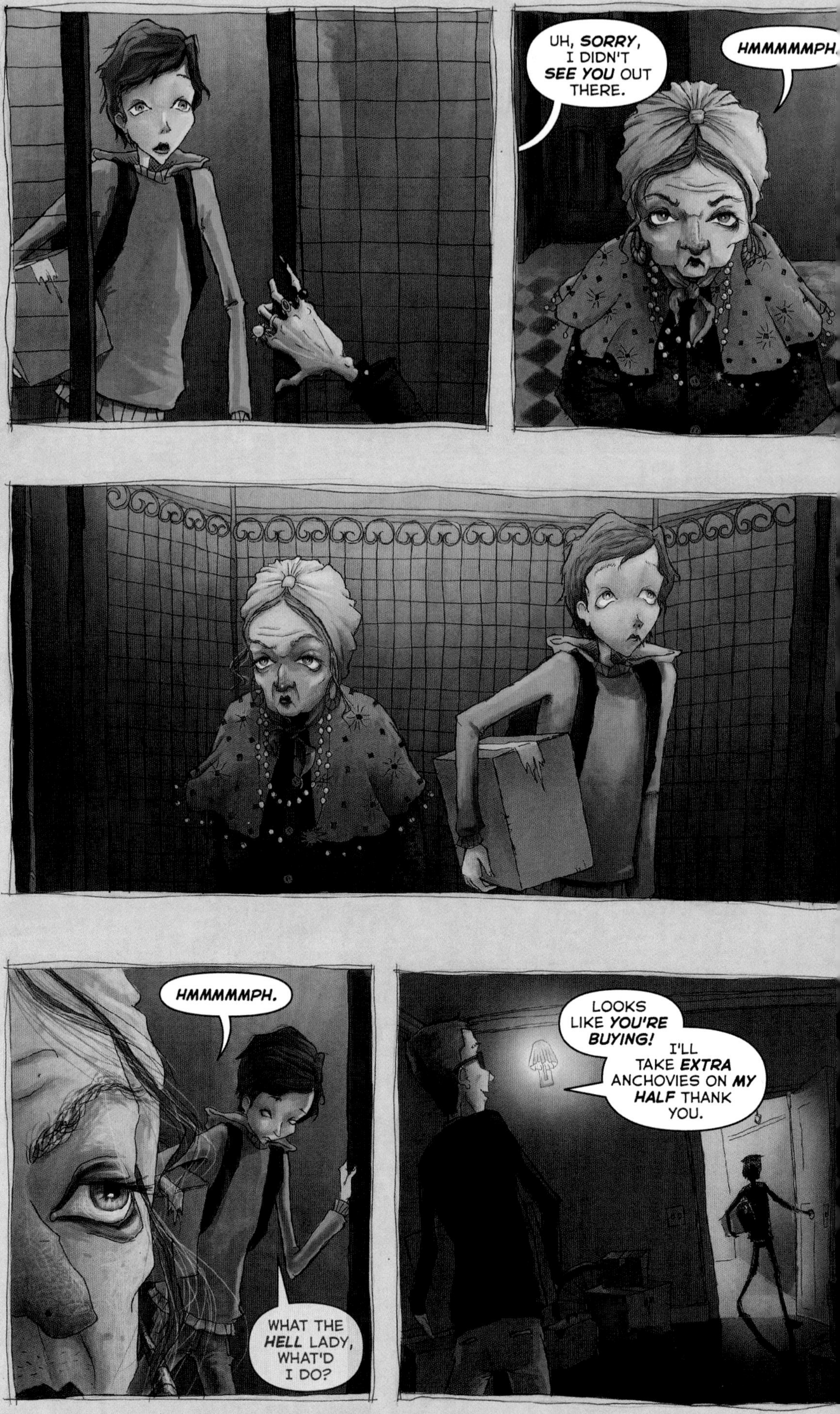
UH, SORRY, I DIDN'T SEE YOU OUT THERE.
HMMMMMPH.
HMMMMMPH.
WHAT THE HELL LADY, WHAT'D I DO?
LOOKS LIKE YOU'RE BUYING!
I'LL TAKE EXTRA ANCHOVIES ON MY HALF THANK YOU.

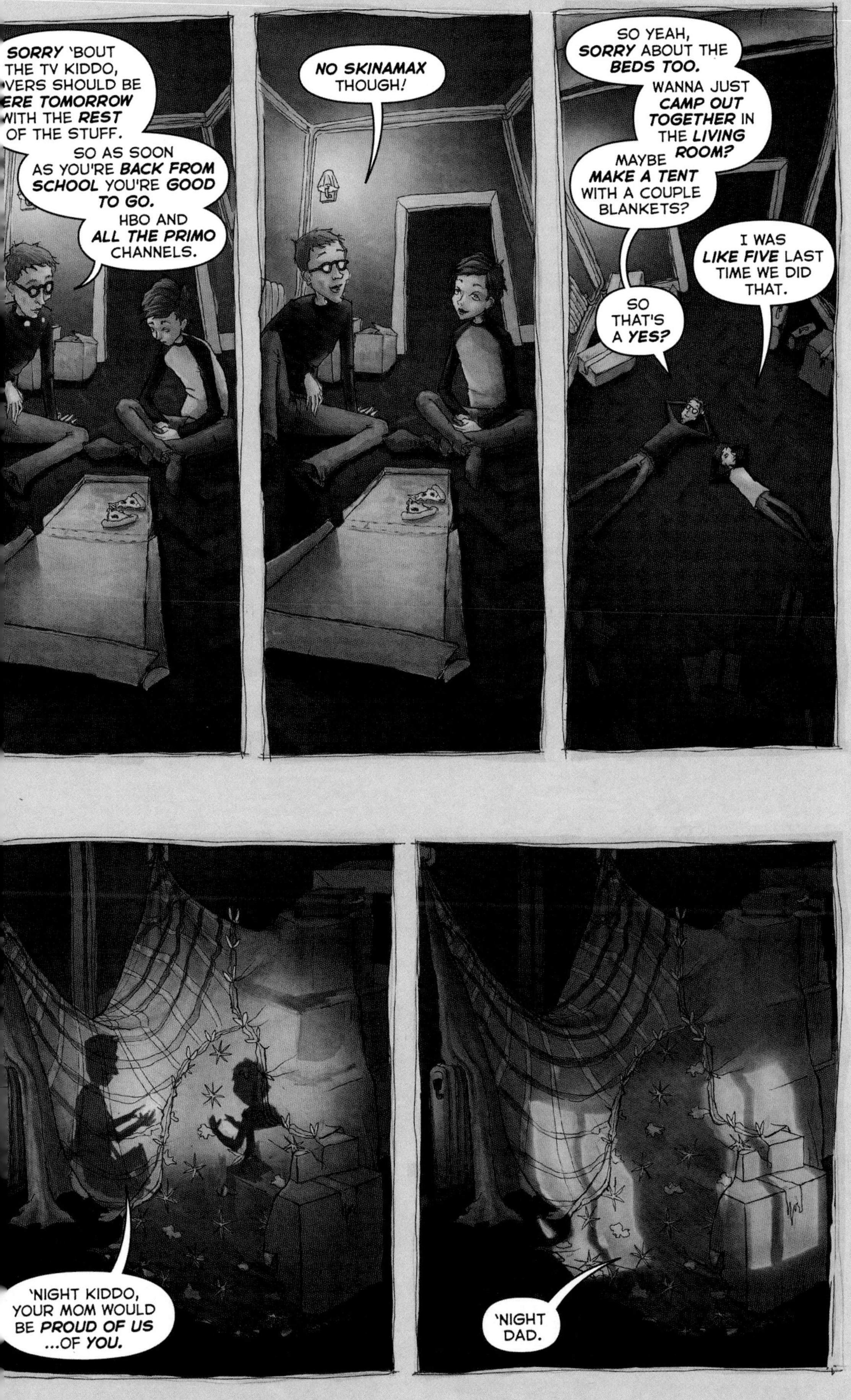
SORRY 'BOUT THE TV KIDDO, ...VERS SHOULD BE ...ERE TOMORROW WITH THE REST OF THE STUFF.
SO AS SOON AS YOU'RE BACK FROM SCHOOL YOU'RE GOOD TO GO.
HBO AND ALL THE PRIMO CHANNELS.
NO SKINAMAX THOUGH!
SO YEAH, SORRY ABOUT THE BEDS TOO.
WANNA JUST CAMP OUT TOGETHER IN THE LIVING ROOM?
MAYBE MAKE A TENT WITH A COUPLE BLANKETS?
I WAS LIKE FIVE LAST TIME WE DID THAT.
SO THAT'S A YES?
'NIGHT KIDDO, YOUR MOM WOULD BE PROUD OF US ...OF YOU.
'NIGHT DAD.

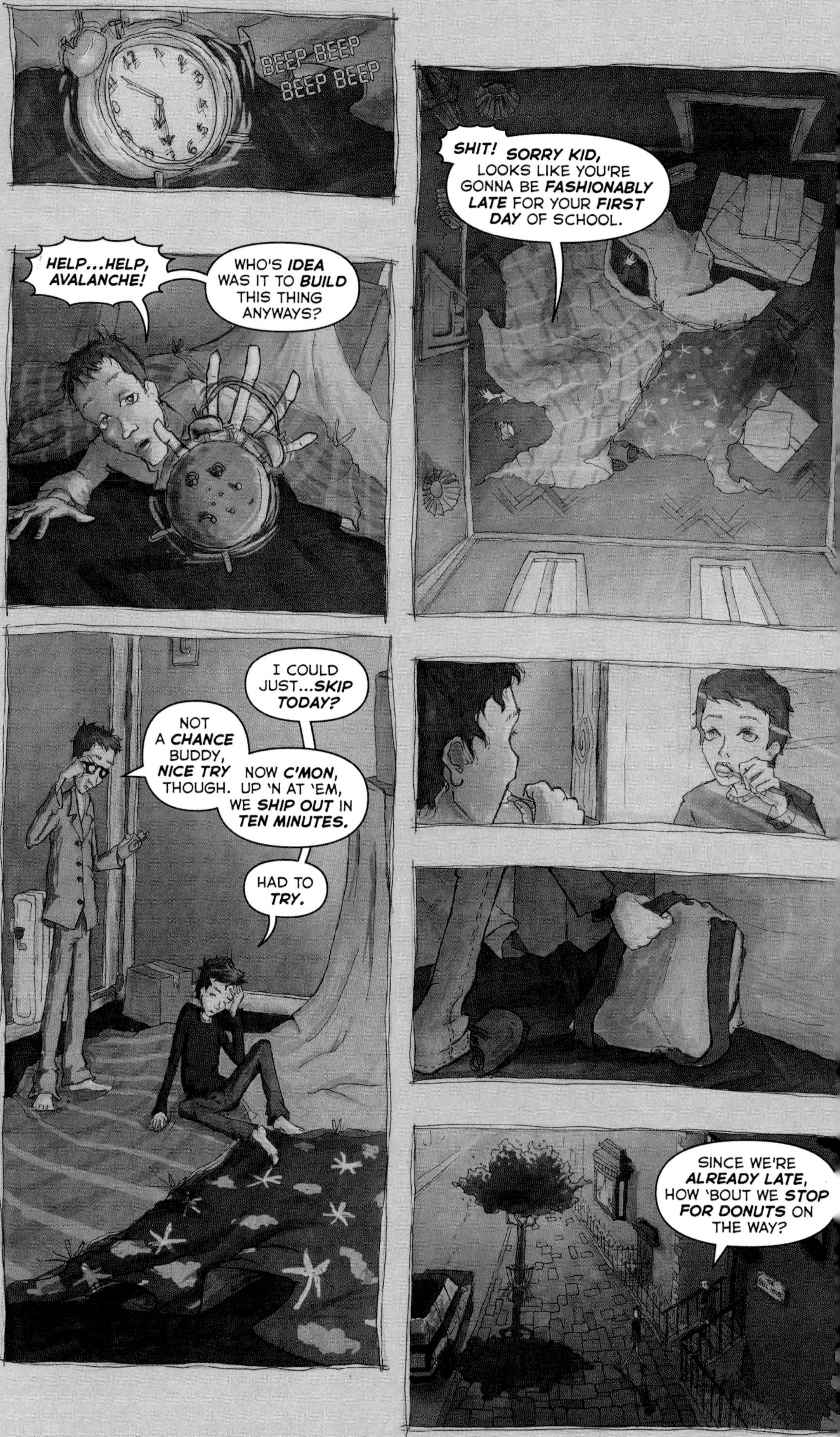
BEEP BEEP
BEEP BEEP
SHIT! SORRY KID, LOOKS LIKE YOU'RE GONNA BE FASHIONABLY LATE FOR YOUR FIRST DAY OF SCHOOL.
HELP...HELP, AVALANCHE!
WHO'S IDEA WAS IT TO BUILD THIS THING ANYWAYS?
I COULD JUST...SKIP TODAY?
NOT A CHANCE BUDDY, NICE TRY THOUGH.
NOW C'MON, UP 'N AT 'EM, WE SHIP OUT IN TEN MINUTES.
HAD TO TRY.
SINCE WE'RE ALREADY LATE, HOW 'BOUT WE STOP FOR DONUTS ON THE WAY?

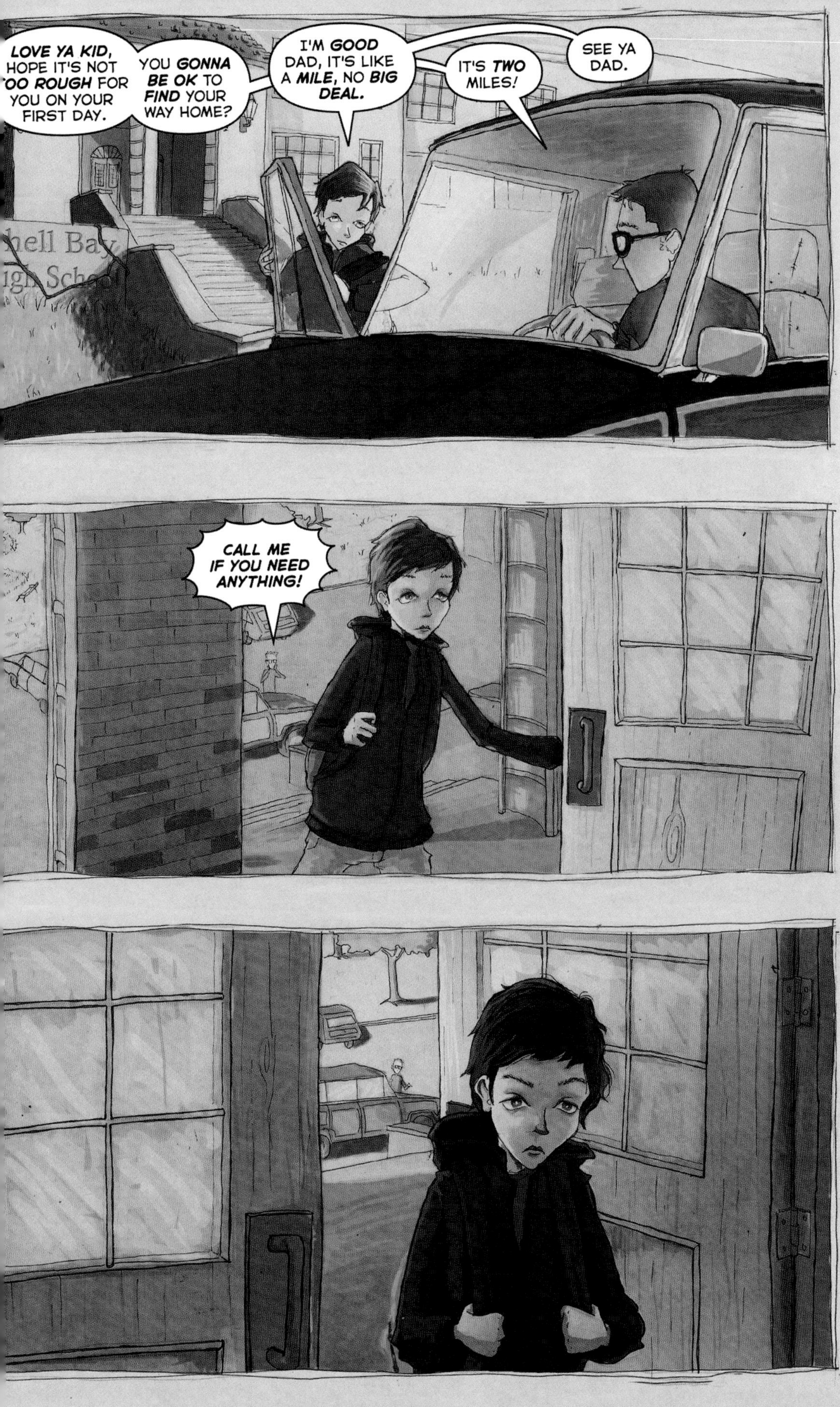
LOVE YA KID, HOPE IT'S NOT OO ROUGH FOR YOU ON YOUR FIRST DAY.
YOU GONNA BE OK TO FIND YOUR WAY HOME?
I'M GOOD DAD, IT'S LIKE A MILE, NO BIG DEAL.
IT'S TWO MILES!
SEE YA DAD.
CALL ME IF YOU NEED ANYTHING!

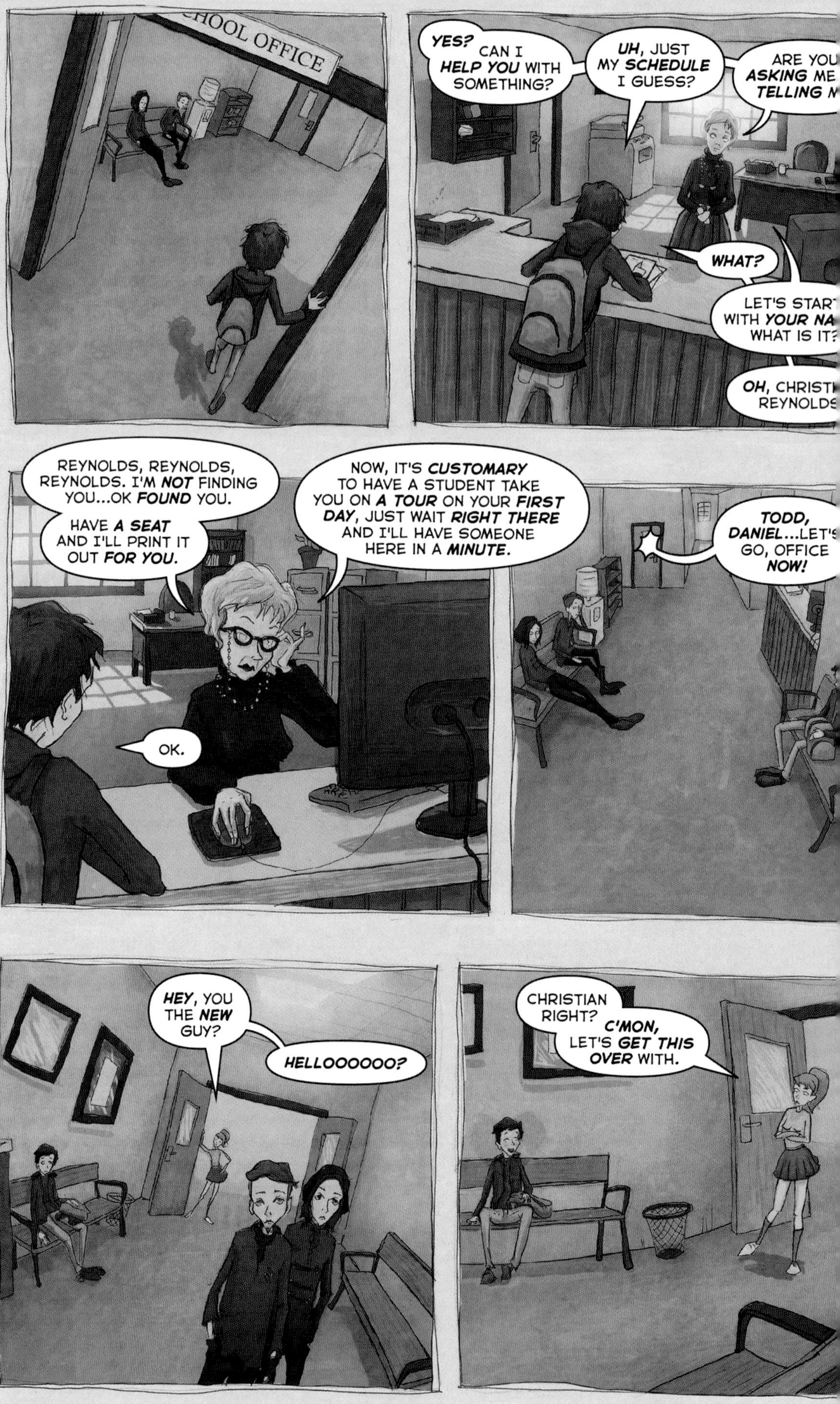
SCHOOL OFFICE
YES? CAN I HELP YOU WITH SOMETHING?
UH, JUST MY SCHEDULE I GUESS?
ARE YOU ASKING ME TELLING M
WHAT?
LET'S START WITH YOUR NA WHAT IS IT?
OH, CHRIST REYNOLDS
REYNOLDS, REYNOLDS, REYNOLDS. I'M NOT FINDING YOU...OK FOUND YOU.
HAVE A SEAT AND I'LL PRINT IT OUT FOR YOU.
OK.
NOW, IT'S CUSTOMARY TO HAVE A STUDENT TAKE YOU ON A TOUR ON YOUR FIRST DAY, JUST WAIT RIGHT THERE AND I'LL HAVE SOMEONE HERE IN A MINUTE.
TODD, DANIEL...LET'S GO, OFFICE NOW!
HEY, YOU THE NEW GUY?
HELLOOOOOO?
CHRISTIAN RIGHT? C'MON, LET'S GET THIS OVER WITH.

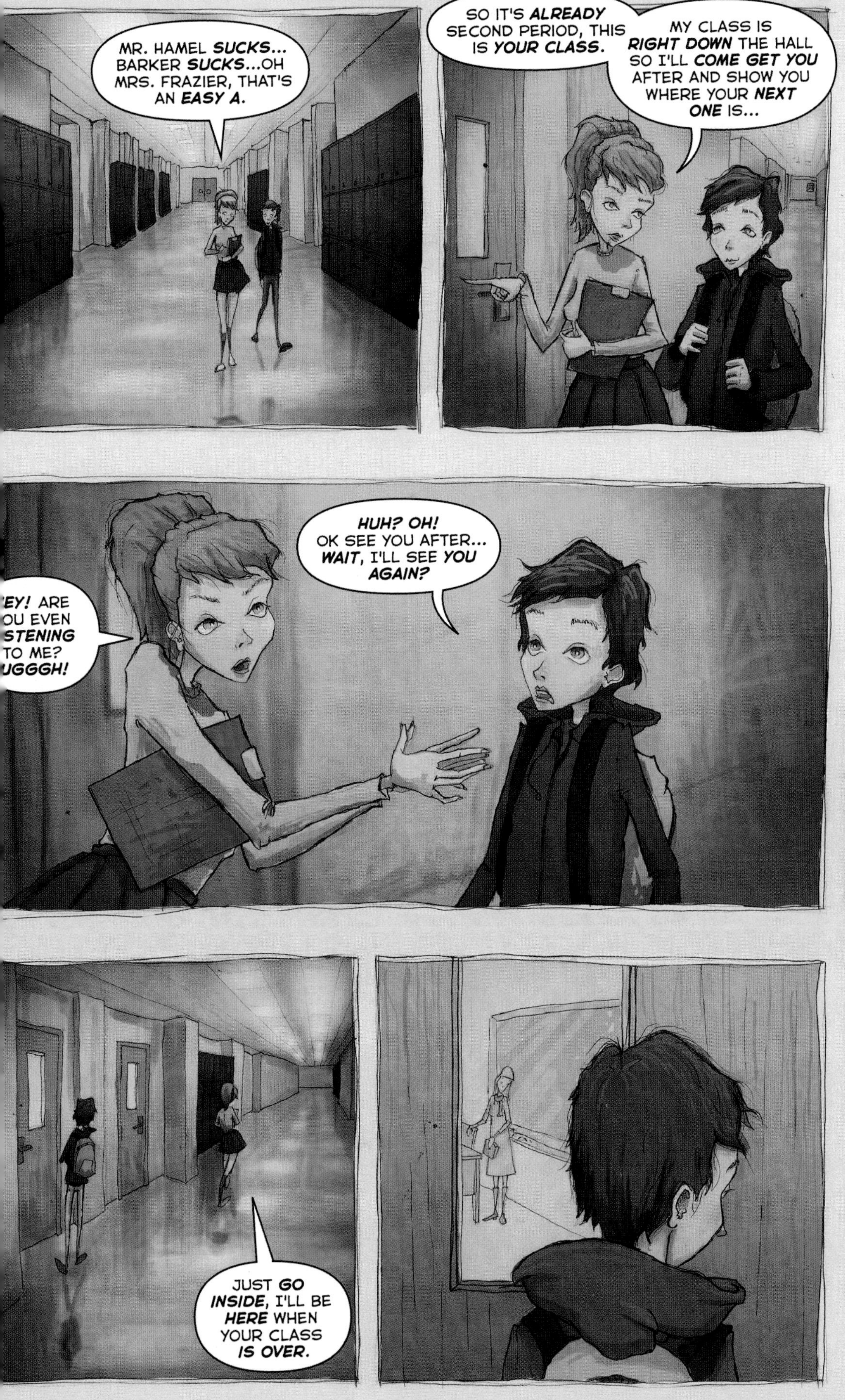
MR. HAMEL SUCKS... BARKER SUCKS...OH MRS. FRAZIER, THAT'S AN EASY A.
SO IT'S ALREADY SECOND PERIOD, THIS IS YOUR CLASS.
MY CLASS IS RIGHT DOWN THE HALL SO I'LL COME GET YOU AFTER AND SHOW YOU WHERE YOUR NEXT ONE IS...
EY! ARE OU EVEN STENING TO ME? UGGGH!
HUH? OH! OK SEE YOU AFTER... WAIT, I'LL SEE YOU AGAIN?
JUST GO INSIDE, I'LL BE HERE WHEN YOUR CLASS IS OVER.

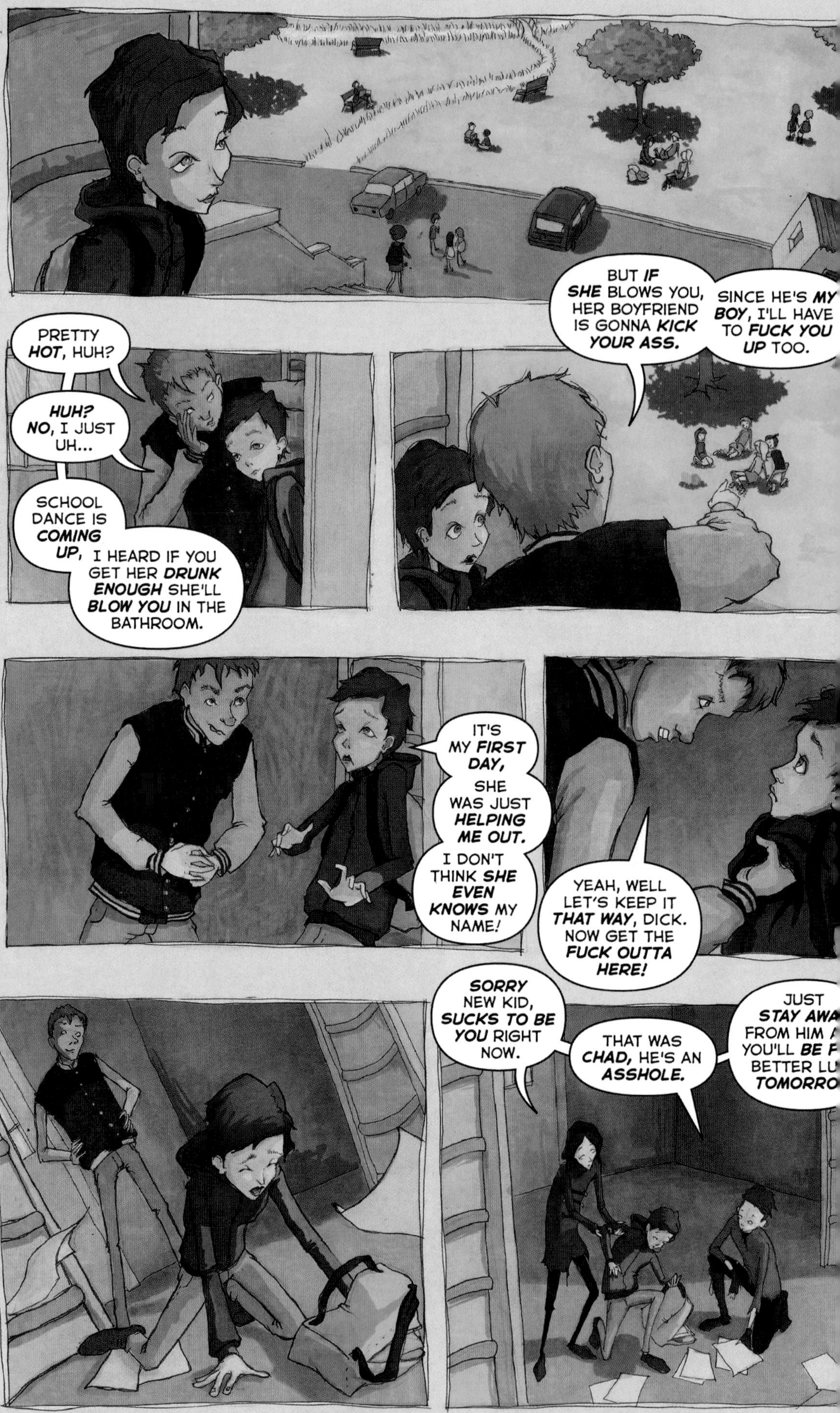
PRETTY HOT, HUH?
HUH? NO, I JUST UH...
SCHOOL DANCE IS COMING UP, I HEARD IF YOU GET HER DRUNK ENOUGH SHE'LL BLOW YOU IN THE BATHROOM.
BUT IF SHE BLOWS YOU, HER BOYFRIEND IS GONNA KICK YOUR ASS.
SINCE HE'S MY BOY, I'LL HAVE TO FUCK YOU UP TOO.
IT'S MY FIRST DAY,
SHE WAS JUST HELPING ME OUT.
I DON'T THINK SHE EVEN KNOWS MY NAME!
YEAH, WELL LET'S KEEP IT THAT WAY, DICK. NOW GET THE FUCK OUTTA HERE!
SORRY NEW KID, SUCKS TO BE YOU RIGHT NOW.
THAT WAS CHAD, HE'S AN ASSHOLE.

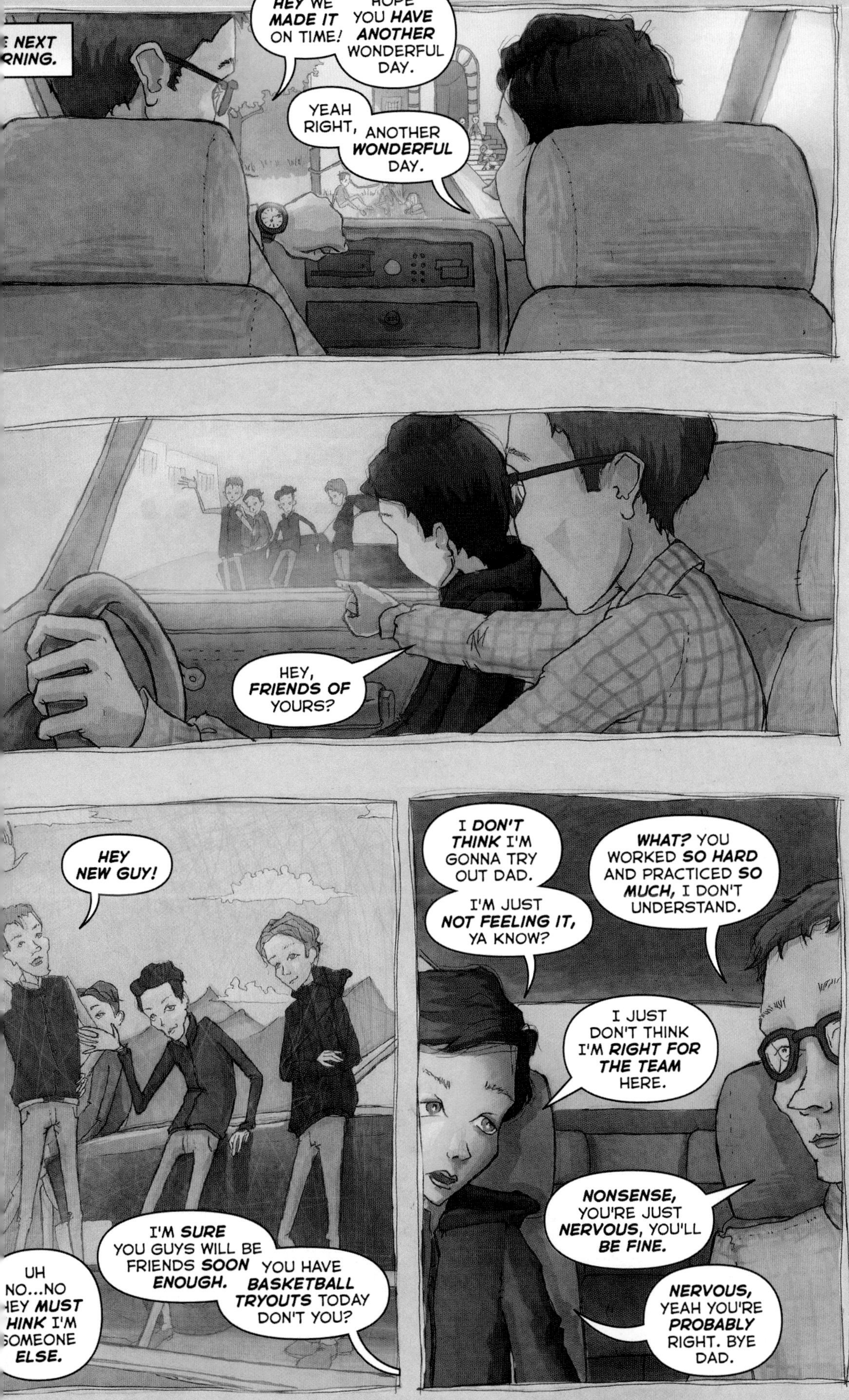
E NEXT RNING.
HEY WE MADE IT ON TIME!
HOPE YOU HAVE ANOTHER WONDERFUL DAY.
YEAH RIGHT, ANOTHER WONDERFUL DAY.
HEY, FRIENDS OF YOURS?
HEY NEW GUY!
UH NO...NO HEY MUST HINK I'M OMEONE ELSE.
I'M SURE YOU GUYS WILL BE FRIENDS SOON ENOUGH.
YOU HAVE BASKETBALL TRYOUTS TODAY DON'T YOU?
I DON'T THINK I'M GONNA TRY OUT DAD.
I'M JUST NOT FEELING IT, YA KNOW?
WHAT? YOU WORKED SO HARD AND PRACTICED SO MUCH, I DON'T UNDERSTAND.
I JUST DON'T THINK I'M RIGHT FOR THE TEAM HERE.
NONSENSE, YOU'RE JUST NERVOUS, YOU'LL BE FINE.
NERVOUS, YEAH YOU'RE PROBABLY RIGHT. BYE DAD.

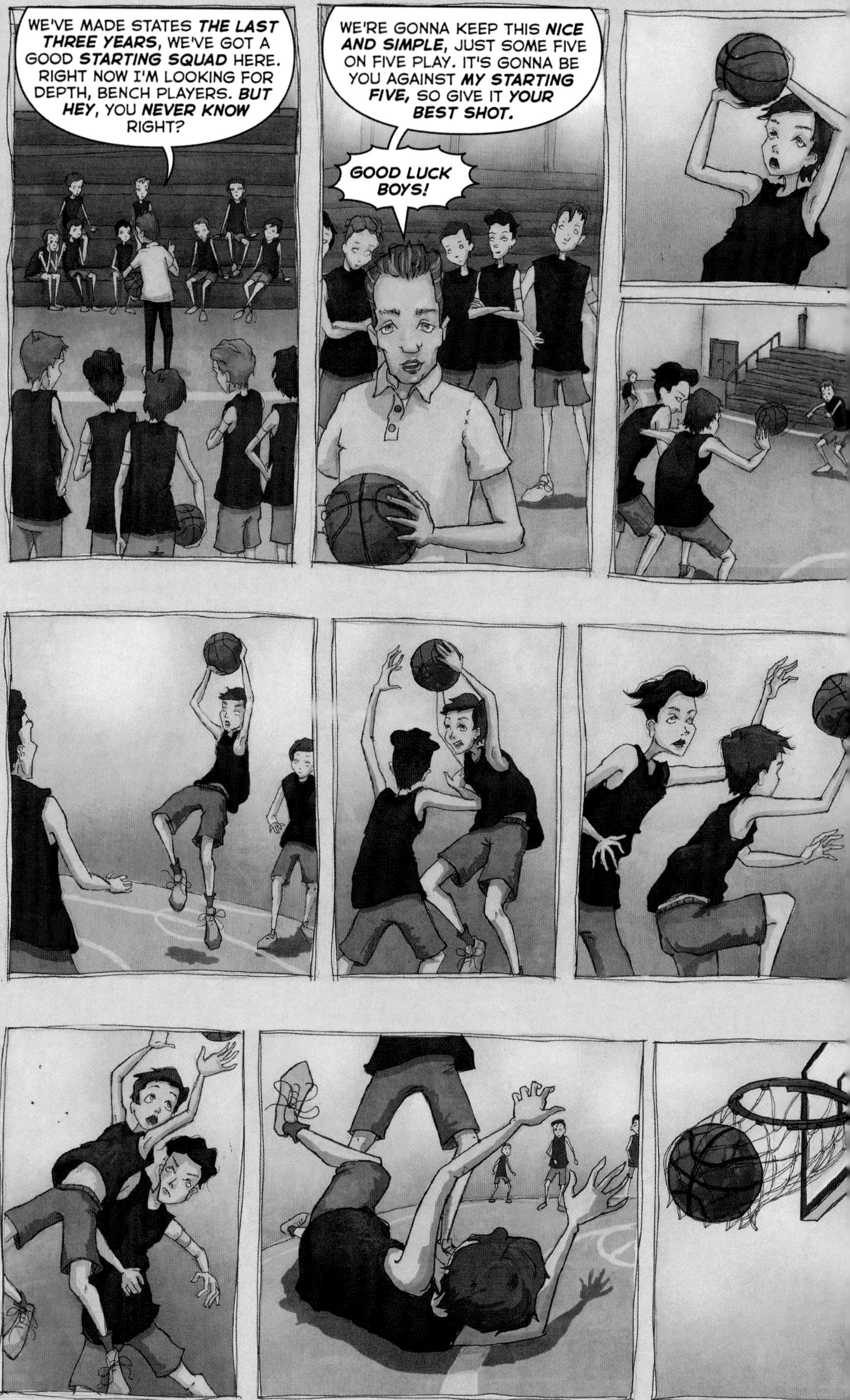
WE'VE MADE STATES THE LAST THREE YEARS, WE'VE GOT A GOOD STARTING SQUAD HERE. RIGHT NOW I'M LOOKING FOR DEPTH, BENCH PLAYERS. BUT HEY, YOU NEVER KNOW RIGHT?
WE'RE GONNA KEEP THIS NICE AND SIMPLE, JUST SOME FIVE ON FIVE PLAY. IT'S GONNA BE YOU AGAINST MY STARTING FIVE, SO GIVE IT YOUR BEST SHOT.
GOOD LUCK BOYS!

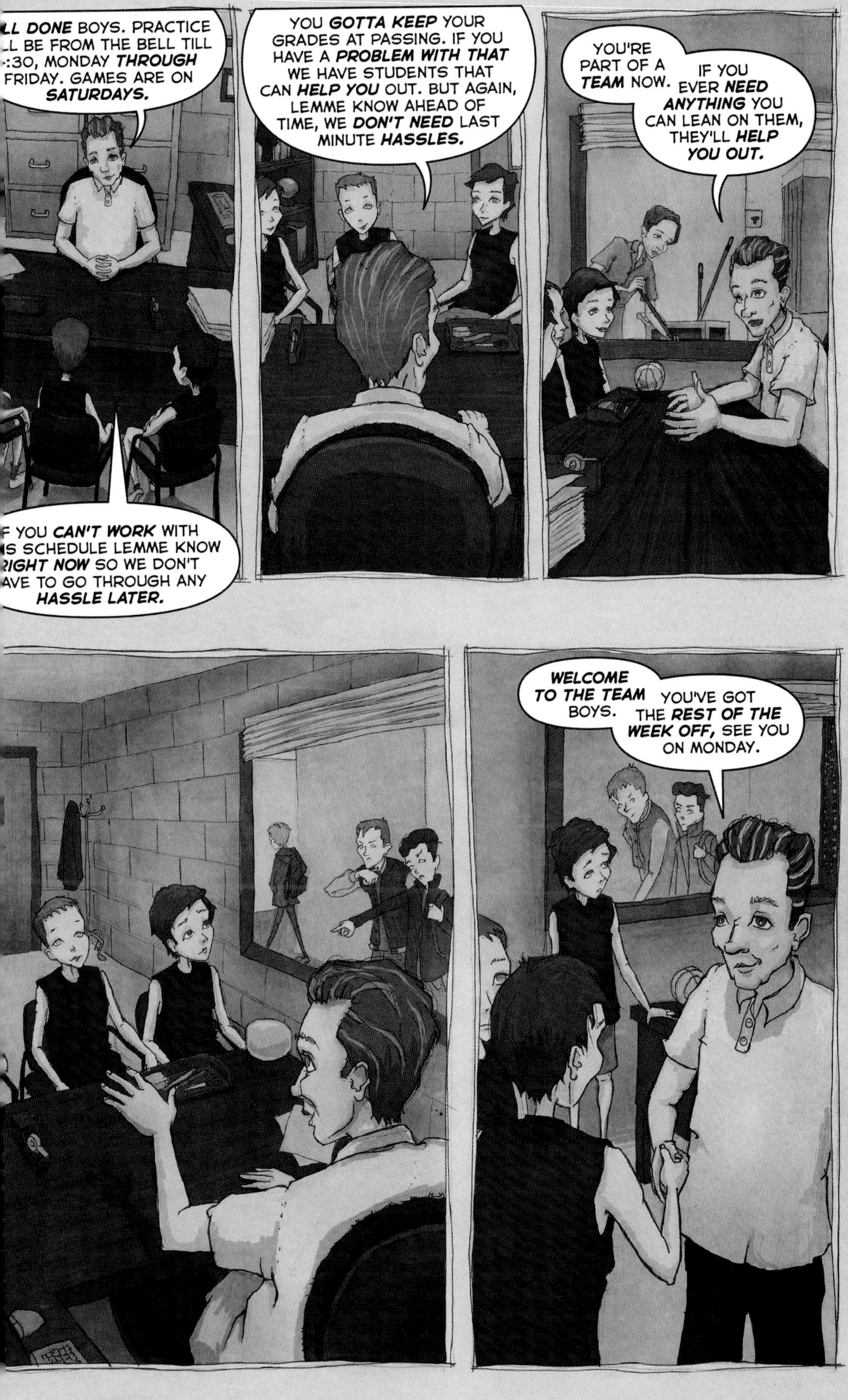
LL DONE BOYS. PRACTICE LL BE FROM THE BELL TILL :30, MONDAY THROUGH FRIDAY. GAMES ARE ON SATURDAYS.
F YOU CAN'T WORK WITH S SCHEDULE LEMME KNOW RIGHT NOW SO WE DON'T AVE TO GO THROUGH ANY HASSLE LATER.
YOU GOTTA KEEP YOUR GRADES AT PASSING. IF YOU HAVE A PROBLEM WITH THAT WE HAVE STUDENTS THAT CAN HELP YOU OUT. BUT AGAIN, LEMME KNOW AHEAD OF TIME, WE DON'T NEED LAST MINUTE HASSLES.
YOU'RE PART OF A TEAM NOW.
IF YOU EVER NEED ANYTHING YOU CAN LEAN ON THEM, THEY'LL HELP YOU OUT.
WELCOME TO THE TEAM BOYS.
YOU'VE GOT THE REST OF THE WEEK OFF, SEE YOU ON MONDAY.

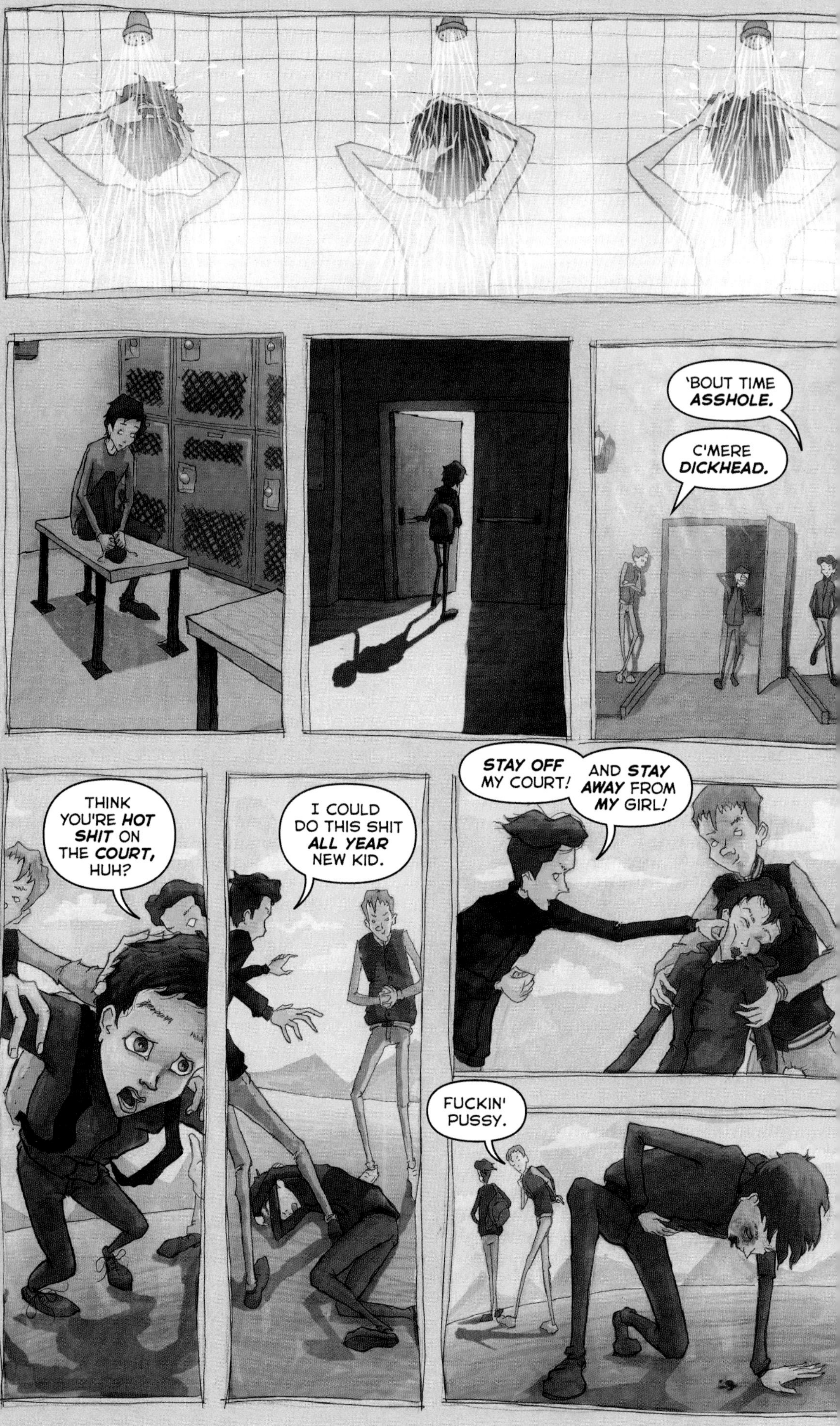
'BOUT TIME ASSHOLE.
C'MERE DICKHEAD.
THINK YOU'RE HOT SHIT ON THE COURT, HUH?
I COULD DO THIS SHIT ALL YEAR NEW KID.
STAY OFF MY COURT!
AND STAY AWAY FROM MY GIRL!
FUCKIN' PUSSY.

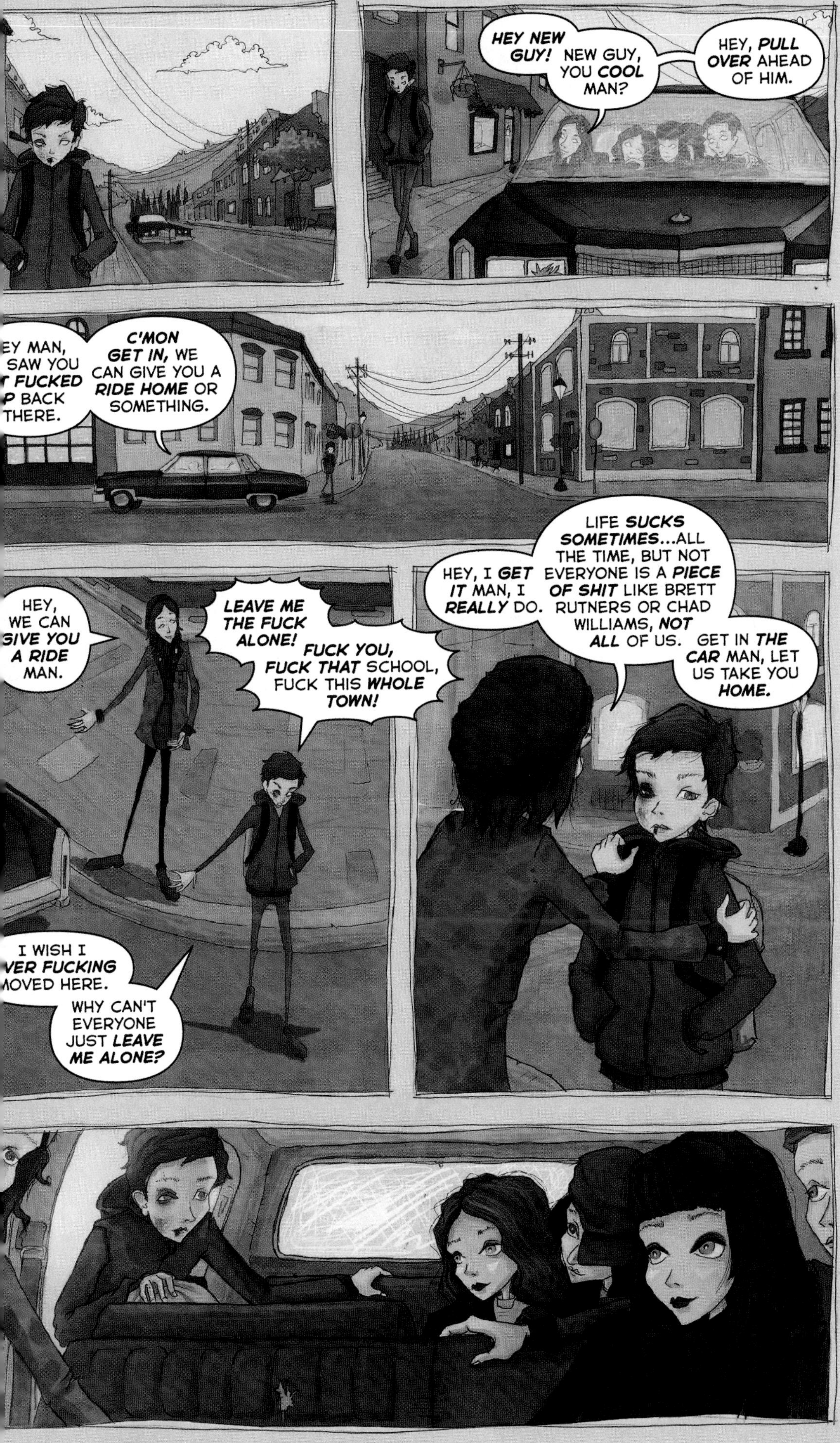
HEY NEW GUY! NEW GUY, YOU COOL MAN?
HEY, PULL OVER AHEAD OF HIM.
EY MAN, SAW YOU FUCKED BACK THERE.
C'MON GET IN, WE CAN GIVE YOU A RIDE HOME OR SOMETHING.
HEY, WE CAN A RIDE MAN.
LEAVE ME THE FUCK ALONE!
FUCK YOU, FUCK THAT SCHOOL, FUCK THIS WHOLE TOWN!
I WISH I MOVED HERE.
WHY CAN'T EVERYONE JUST LEAVE ME ALONE?
HEY, I GET IT MAN, I REALLY DO.
LIFE SUCKS SOMETIMES...ALL THE TIME, BUT NOT EVERYONE IS A PIECE OF SHIT LIKE BRETT RUTNERS OR CHAD WILLIAMS, NOT ALL OF US.
GET IN THE CAR MAN, LET US TAKE YOU HOME.

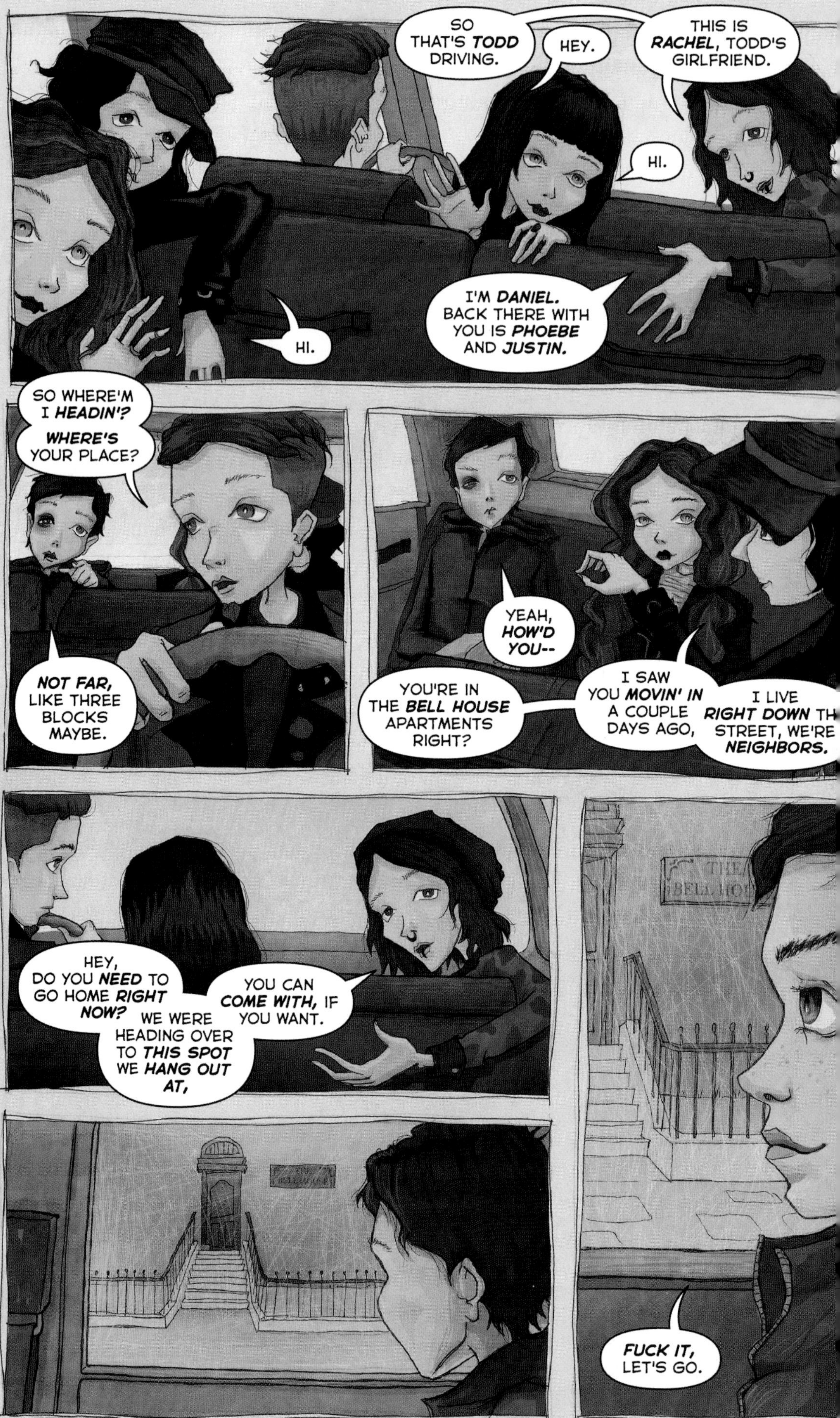
SO THAT'S TODD DRIVING.
HEY.
THIS IS RACHEL, TODD'S GIRLFRIEND.
HI.
I'M DANIEL. BACK THERE WITH YOU IS PHOEBE AND JUSTIN.
HI.
SO WHERE'M I HEADIN'?
WHERE'S YOUR PLACE?
NOT FAR, LIKE THREE BLOCKS MAYBE.
YOU'RE IN THE BELL HOUSE APARTMENTS RIGHT?
YEAH, HOW'D YOU--
I SAW YOU MOVIN' IN A COUPLE DAYS AGO,
I LIVE RIGHT DOWN TH STREET, WE'RE NEIGHBORS.
HEY, DO YOU NEED TO GO HOME RIGHT NOW?
WE WERE HEADING OVER TO THIS SPOT WE HANG OUT AT,
YOU CAN COME WITH, IF YOU WANT.
FUCK IT, LET'S GO.

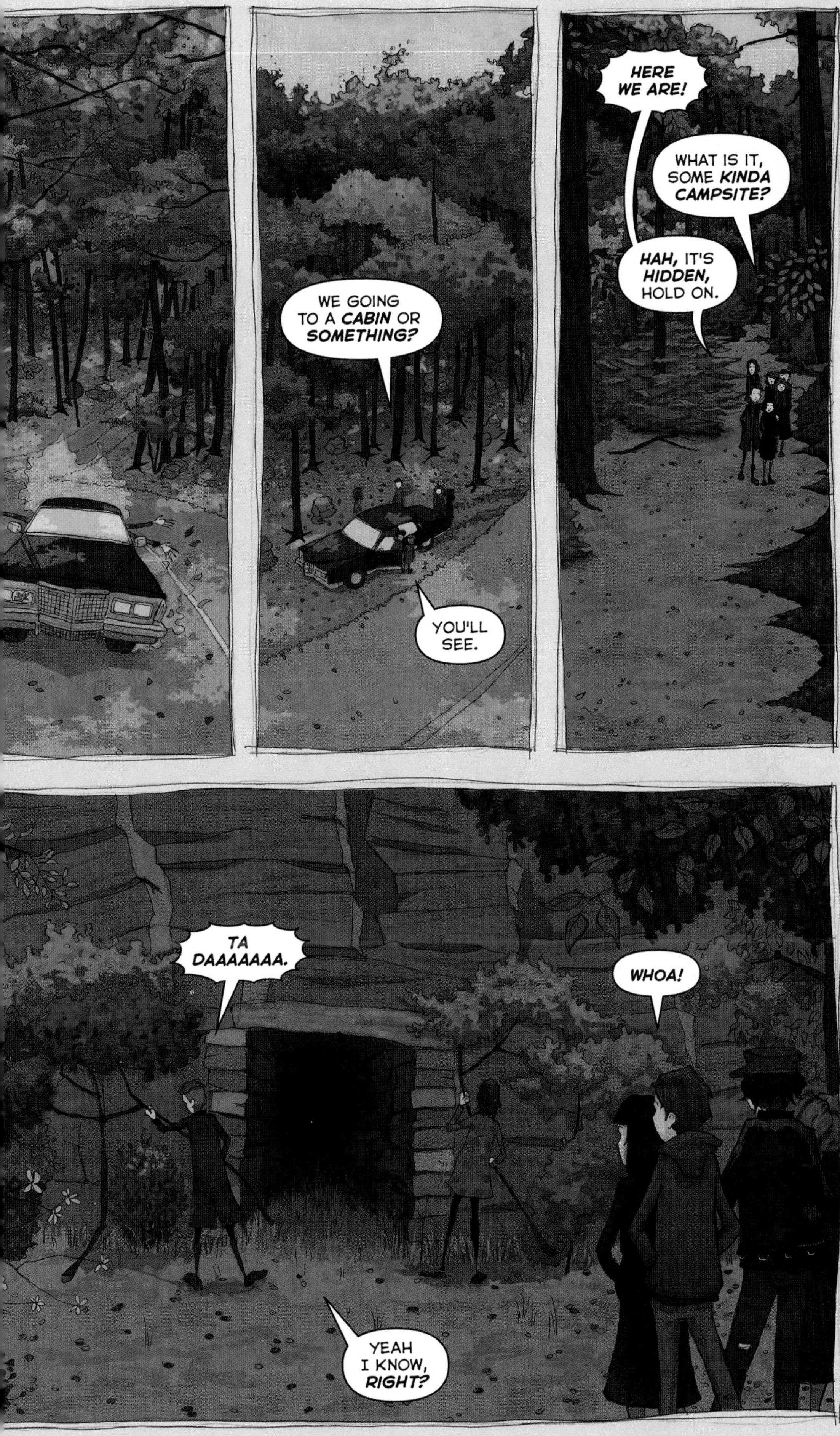
WE GOING TO A CABIN OR SOMETHING?
YOU'LL SEE.
HERE WE ARE!
WHAT IS IT, SOME KINDA CAMPSITE?
HAH, IT'S HIDDEN, HOLD ON.
TA DAAAAAAA.
WHOA!
YEAH I KNOW, RIGHT?

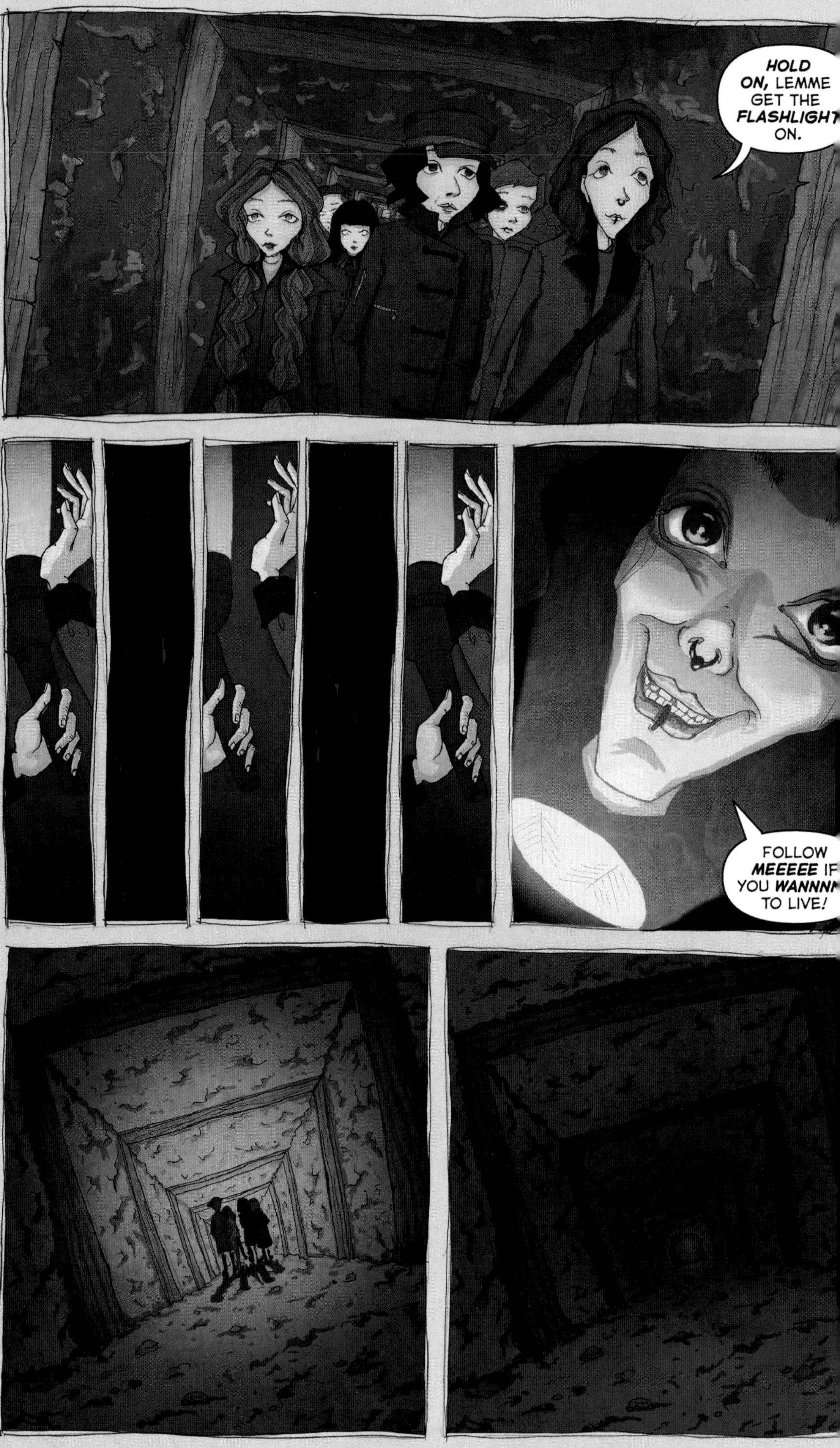
HOLD ON, LEMME GET THE FLASHLIGH ON.
FOLLOW MEEEEE IF YOU WANNN TO LIVE!

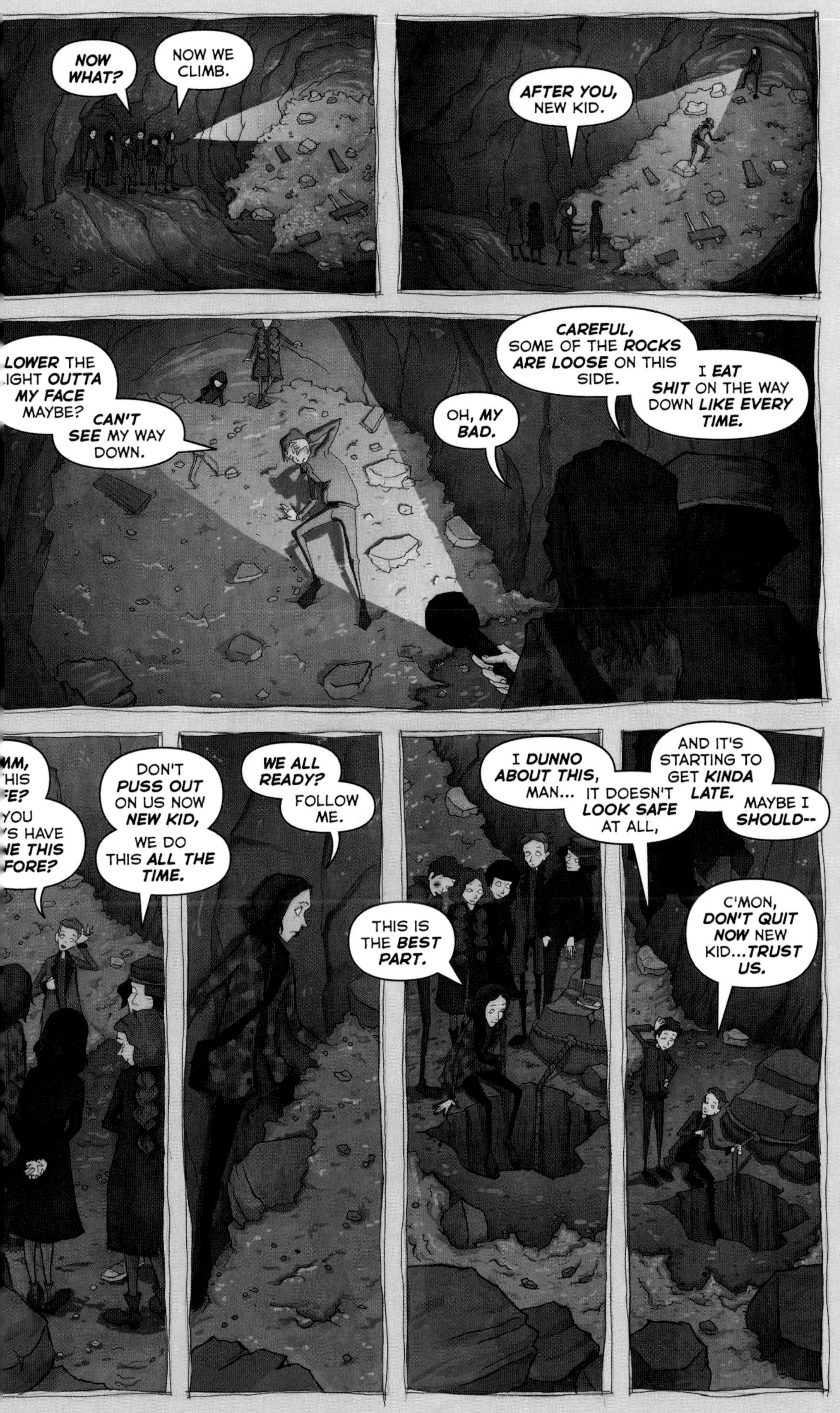
NOW WHAT?
NOW WE CLIMB.
AFTER YOU, NEW KID.
LOWER THE IGHT OUTTA MY FACE MAYBE?
CAN'T SEE MY WAY DOWN.
OH, MY BAD.
CAREFUL, SOME OF THE ROCKS ARE LOOSE ON THIS SIDE.
I EAT SHIT ON THE WAY DOWN LIKE EVERY TIME.
MM, HIS E? YOU 'S HAVE E THIS FORE?
DON'T PUSS OUT ON US NOW NEW KID,
WE DO THIS ALL THE TIME.
WE ALL READY?
FOLLOW ME.
I DUNNO ABOUT THIS, MAN...
IT DOESN'T LOOK SAFE AT ALL,
AND IT'S STARTING TO GET KINDA LATE.
MAYBE I SHOULD--
THIS IS THE BEST PART.
C'MON, DON'T QUIT NOW NEW KID...TRUST US.

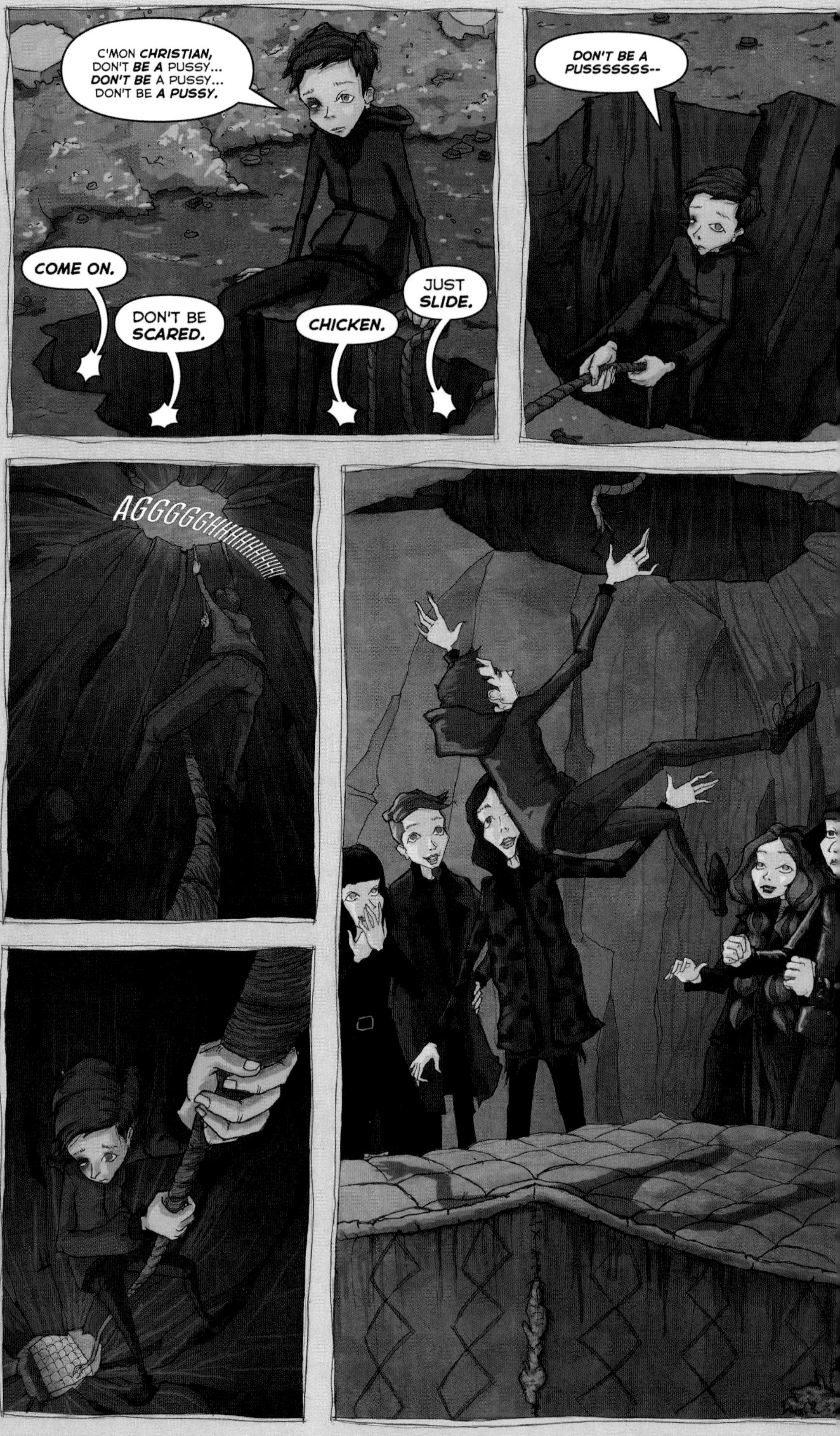
C'MON CHRISTIAN, DON'T BE A PUSSY... DON'T BE A PUSSY... DON'T BE A PUSSY.
COME ON.
DON'T BE SCARED.
CHICKEN.
JUST SLIDE.
DON'T BE A PUSSSSSSS--
AGGGGGGHHHHHHHHHHHH

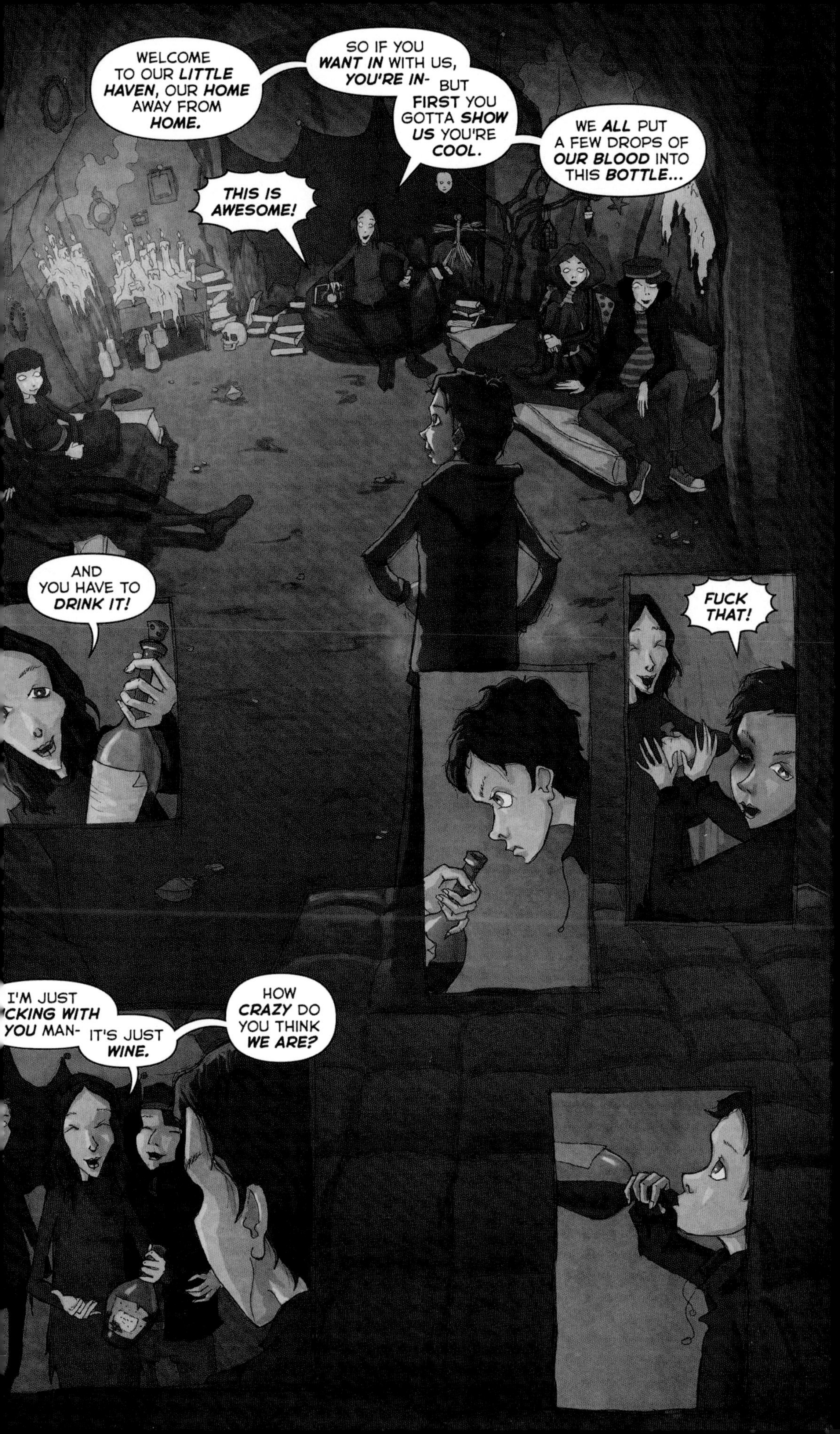
WELCOME TO OUR LITTLE HAVEN, OUR HOME AWAY FROM HOME.
SO IF YOU WANT IN WITH US, YOU'RE IN-
BUT FIRST YOU GOTTA SHOW US YOU'RE COOL.
WE ALL PUT A FEW DROPS OF OUR BLOOD INTO THIS BOTTLE...
THIS IS AWESOME!
AND YOU HAVE TO DRINK IT!
FUCK THAT!
I'M JUST CKING WITH YOU MAN-
IT'S JUST WINE.
HOW CRAZY DO YOU THINK WE ARE?

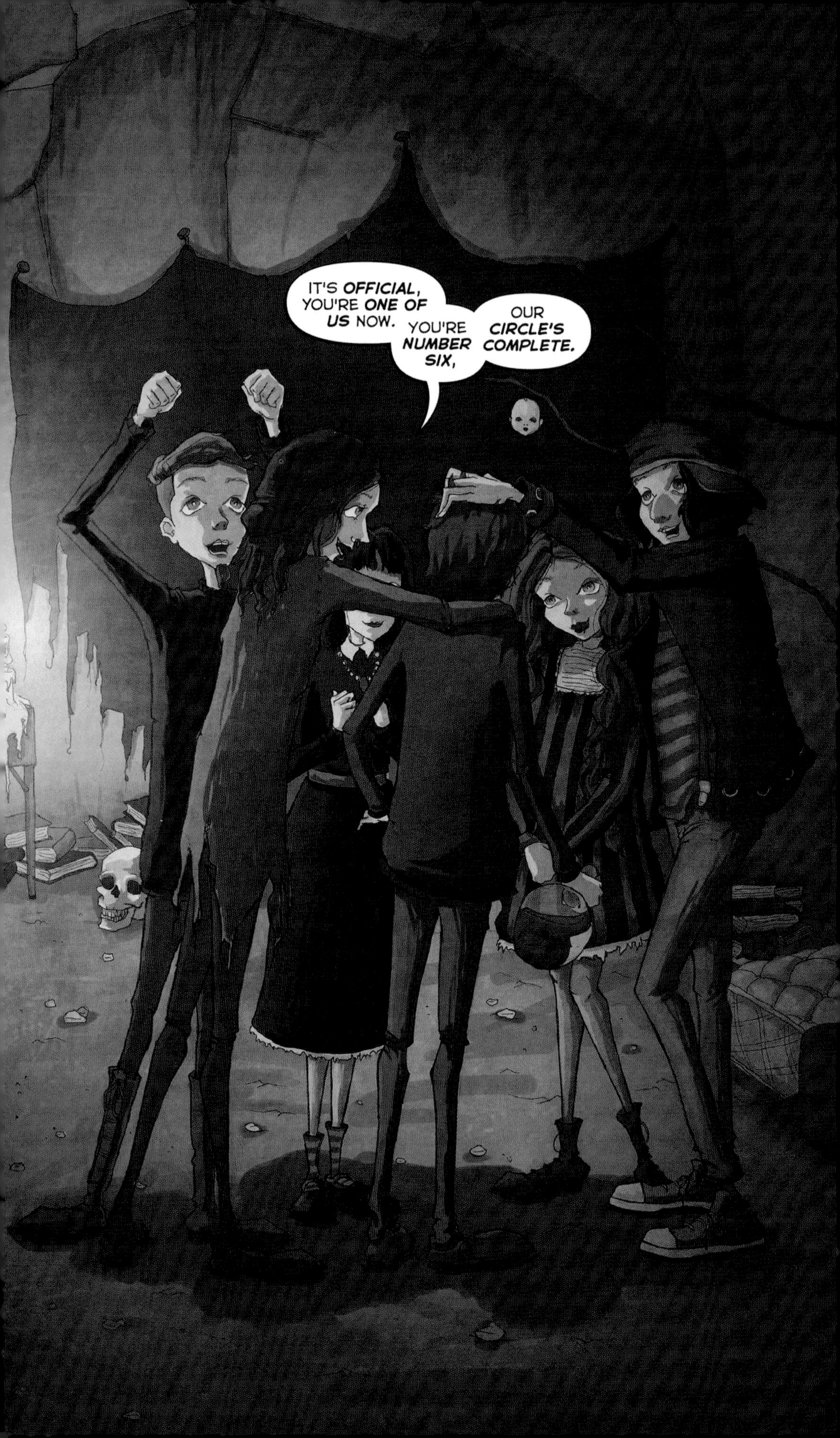
IT'S **OFFICIAL**, YOU'RE **ONE OF US** NOW.
YOU'RE **NUMBER SIX**,
OUR **CIRCLE'S COMPLETE.**

IN THE NEXT OVER-SIZED ISSUE OF

THE CIRCLE

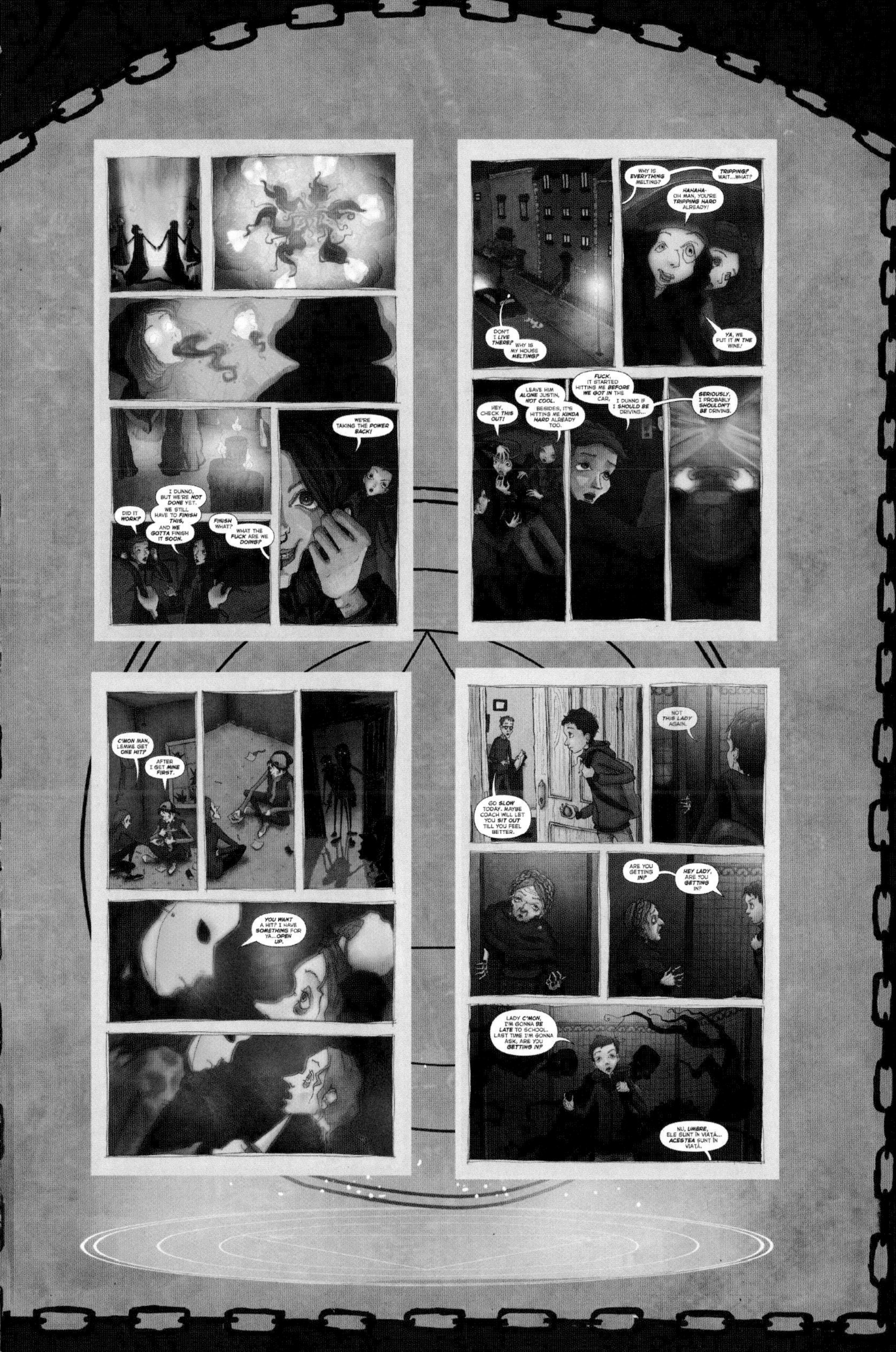

DID IT WORK?
I DUNNO, BUT WE'RE NOT DONE YET.
WE STILL HAVE TO FINISH THIS,
AND WE GOTTA FINISH IT SOON.
FINISH WHAT?
WHAT THE FUCK ARE WE DOING?
WE'RE TAKING THE POWER BACK!
DON'T I LIVE THERE?
WHY IS MY HOUSE MELTING?
WHY IS EVERYTHING MELTING?
TRIPPING? WAIT...WHAT?
HAHAHA- OH MAN, YOU'RE TRIPPING HARD ALREADY!
YA, WE PUT IT IN THE WINE!
HEY, CHECK THIS OUT!
LEAVE HIM ALONE JUSTIN, NOT COOL.
BESIDES, IT'S HITTING ME KINDA HARD ALREADY TOO.
FUCK, IT STARTED HITTING ME BEFORE WE GOT IN THE CAR,
I DUNNO IF I SHOULD BE DRIVING...
SERIOUSLY, I PROBABLY SHOULDN'T BE DRIVING.
C'MON MAN, LEMME GET ONE HIT?
AFTER I GET MINE FIRST.
YOU WANT A HIT? I HAVE SOMETHING FOR YA...OPEN UP.
GO SLOW TODAY. MAYBE COACH WILL LET YOU SIT OUT TILL YOU FEEL BETTER.
NOT THIS LADY AGAIN.
ARE YOU GETTING IN?
HEY LADY, ARE YOU GETTING IN?
LADY C'MON, I'M GONNA BE LATE TO SCHOOL. LAST TIME I'M GONNA ASK, ARE YOU GETTING IN?
NU, UMBRE, ELE SUNT ÎN VIAȚĂ... ACESTEA SUNT ÎN VIAȚĂ.

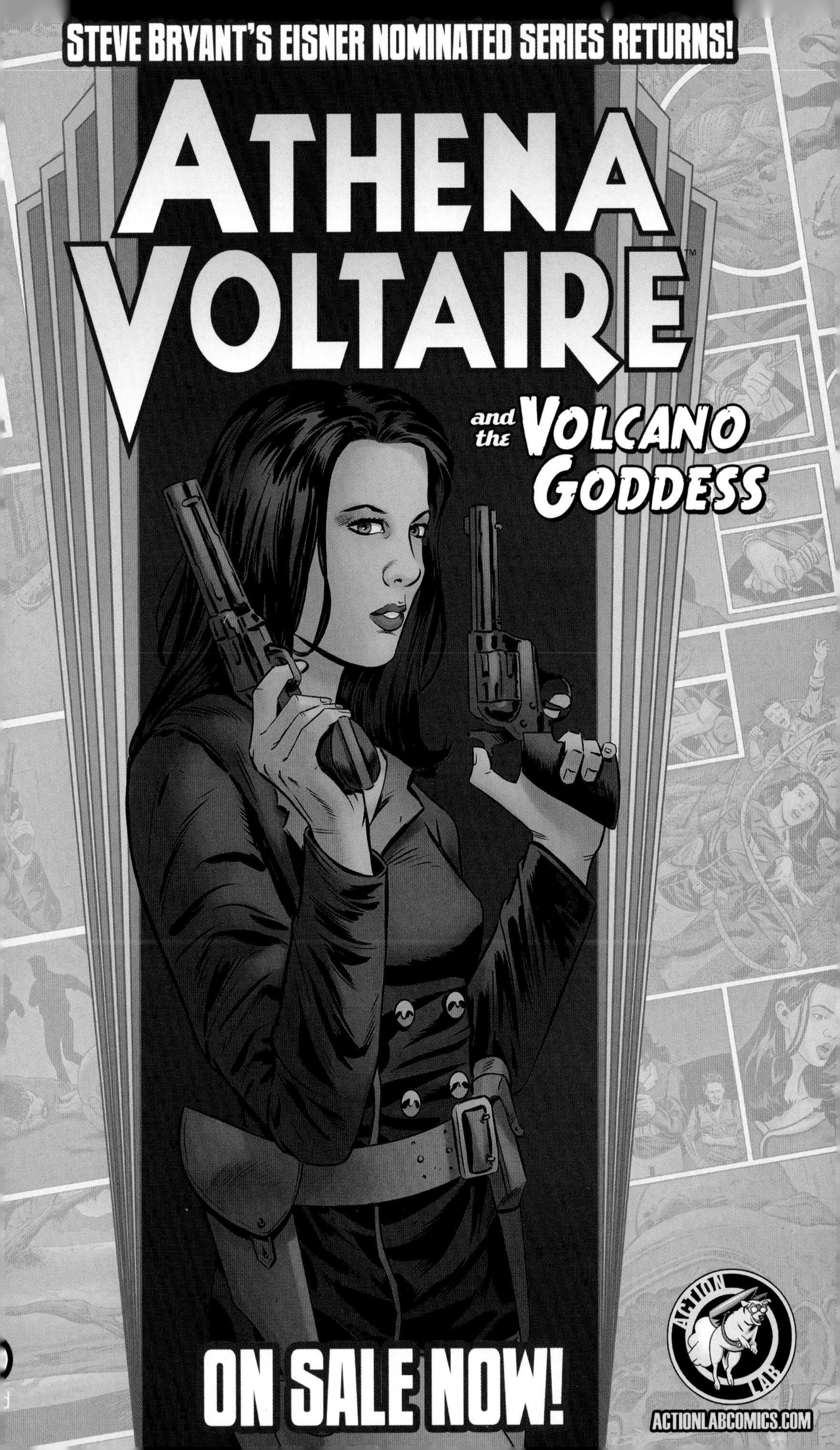
STEVE BRYANT'S EISNER NOMINATED SERIES RETURNS!
ATHENA VOLTAIRE™
and the VOLCANO GODDESS
ON SALE NOW!
ACTION LAB
ACTIONLABCOMICS.COM

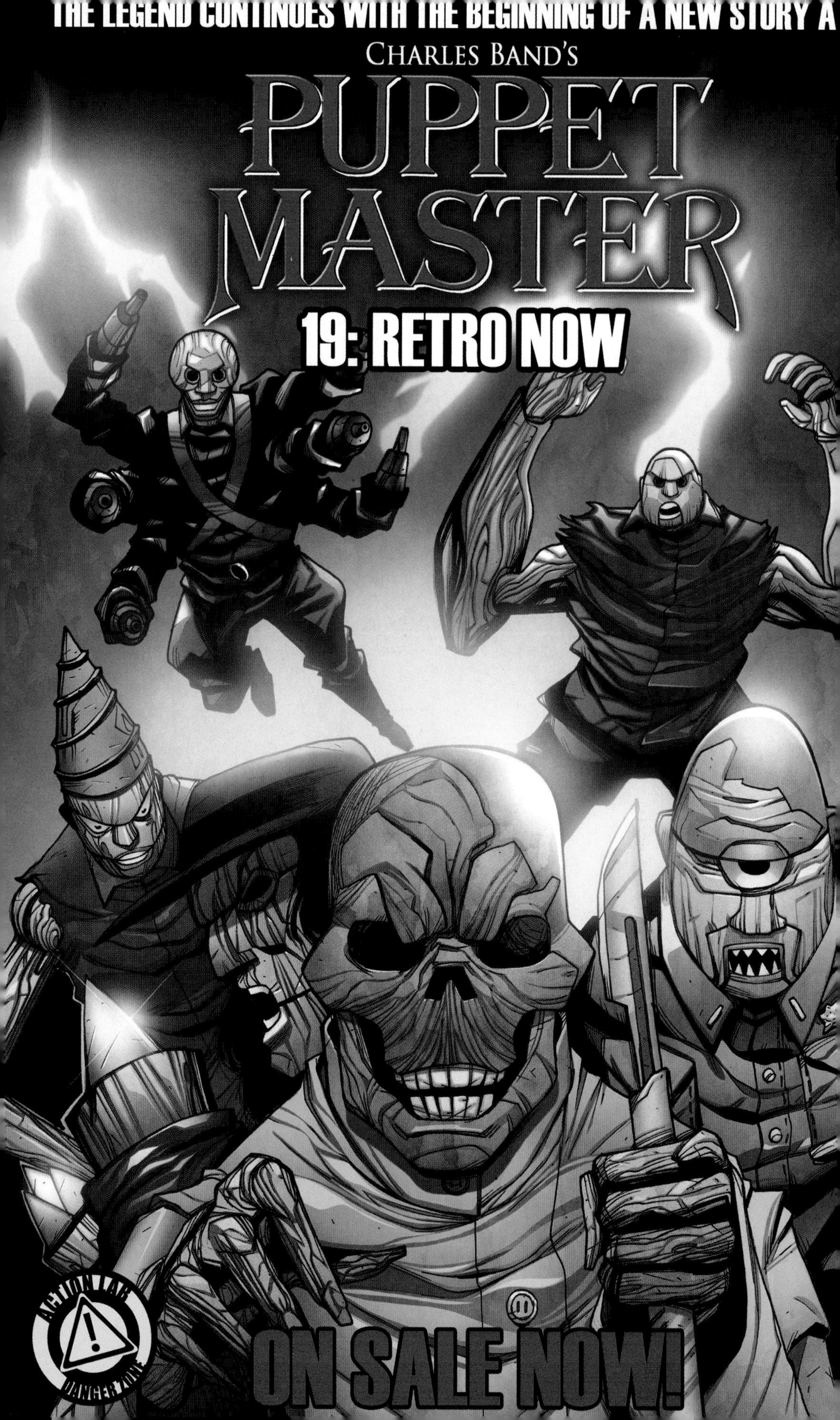
THE LEGEND CONTINUES WITH THE BEGINNING OF A NEW STORY A
CHARLES BAND'S
PUPPET MASTER
19: RETRO NOW
ACTION LAB DANGER ZONE
ON SALE NOW!

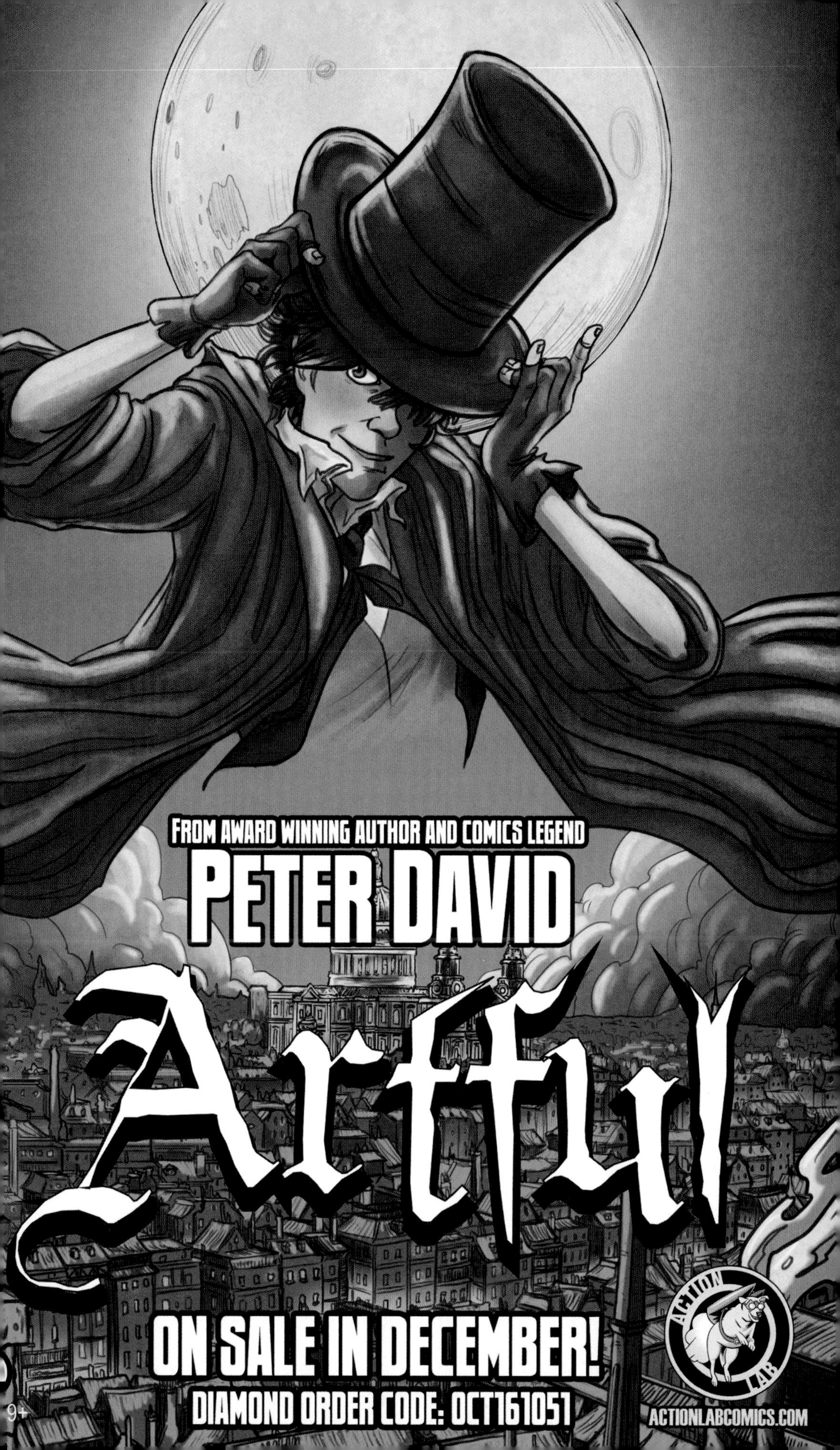

FROM AWARD WINNING AUTHOR AND COMICS LEGEND
PETER DAVID
Artful
ON SALE IN DECEMBER!
DIAMOND ORDER CODE: OCT161051
ACTION LAB
ACTIONLABCOMICS.COM
9+

ACTION LAB

DANGER ZONE

READ MORE NOW

The Circle - Danger Zone
www.actionlabcomics.com

7 02382 69148 6 00111

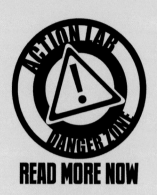

ACTIONLABCOMICS.COM

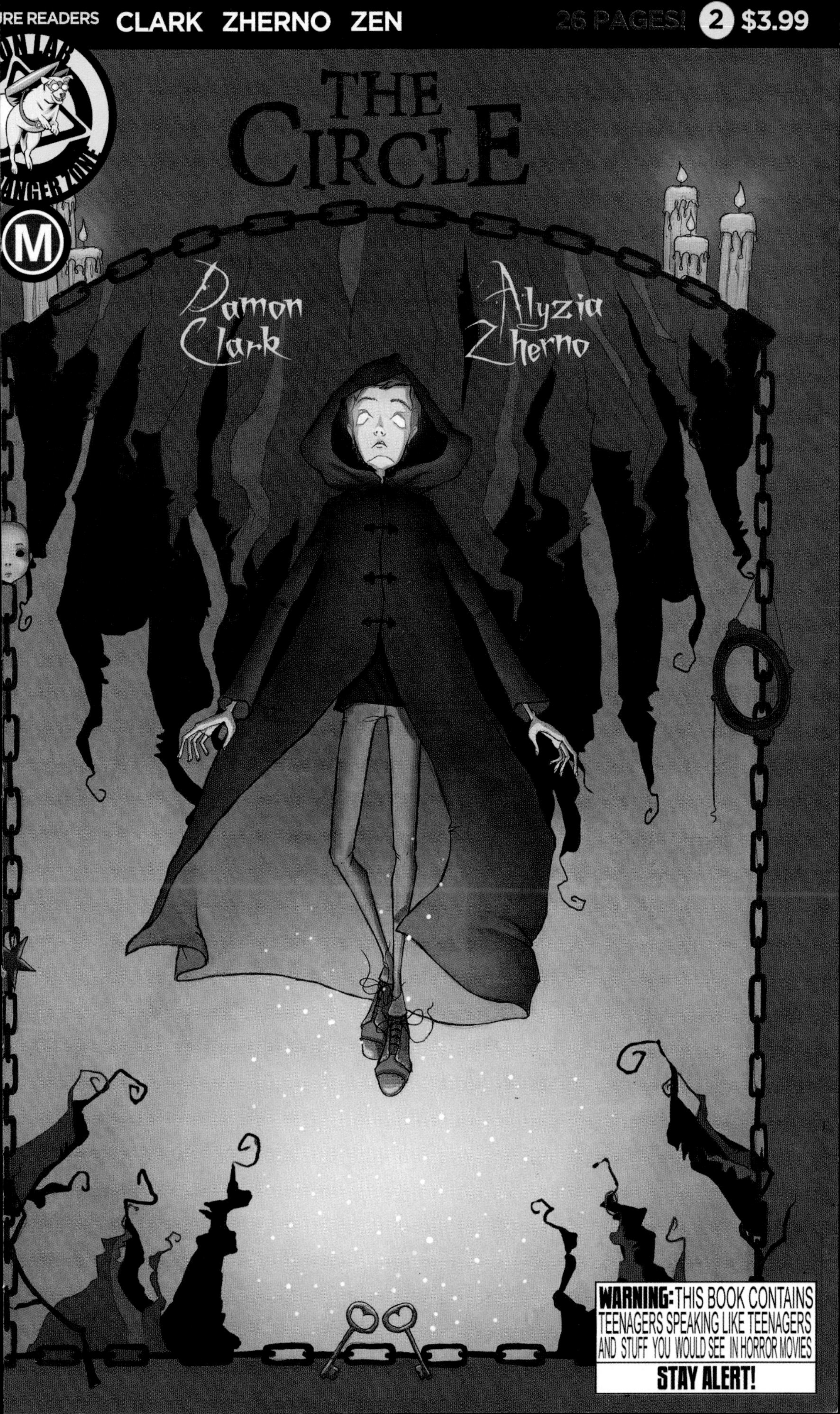

RE READERS
CLARK ZHERNO ZEN
26 PAGES! 2 $3.99
M
THE CIRCLE
Damon Clark
Alyzia Zherno
WARNING: THIS BOOK CONTAINS TEENAGERS SPEAKING LIKE TEENAGERS AND STUFF YOU WOULD SEE IN HORROR MOVIES
STAY ALERT!

ACTION LAB: DANGER ZONE PRESENTS

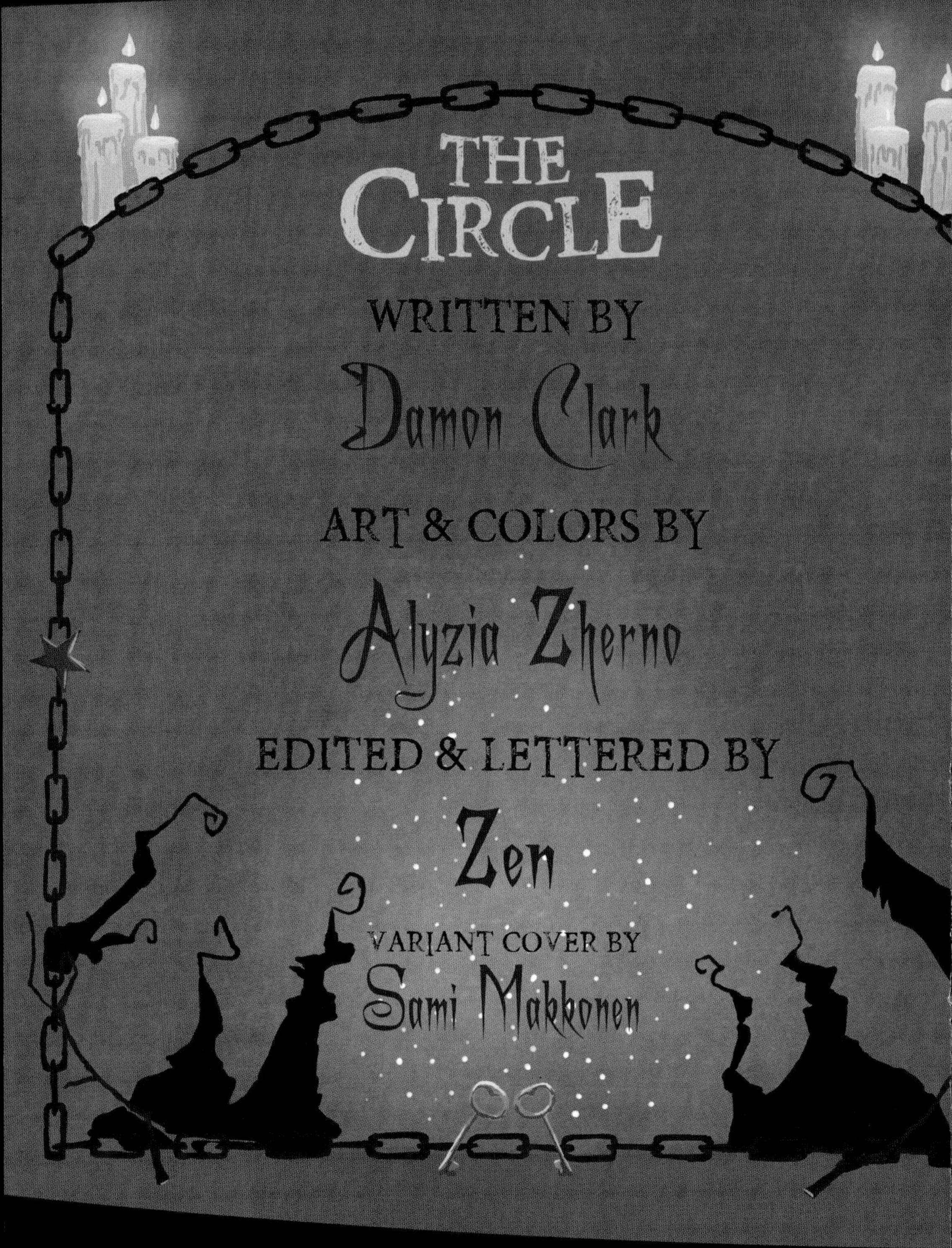
THE CIRCLE
WRITTEN BY
Damon Clark
ART & COLORS BY
Alyzia Zherno
EDITED & LETTERED BY
Zen
VARIANT COVER BY
Sami Makkonen

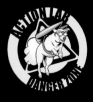

JASON MARTIN - PUBLISHER
DAVE DWONCH - PRESIDENT OF MARKETING
SHAWN GABBORIN - EDITOR IN CHIEF
NICOLE D'ANDRIA - MARKETING DIRECTOR/EDITOR
JIM DIETZ - SOCIAL MEDIA MANAGER
SCOTT BRADLEY - CFO
BRYAN SEATON - CEO

THE CIRCLE #2. January 2016.

Published by Action Lab Comics.

Printed in Canada.
First printing.

ACTIONLABCOMICS.COM

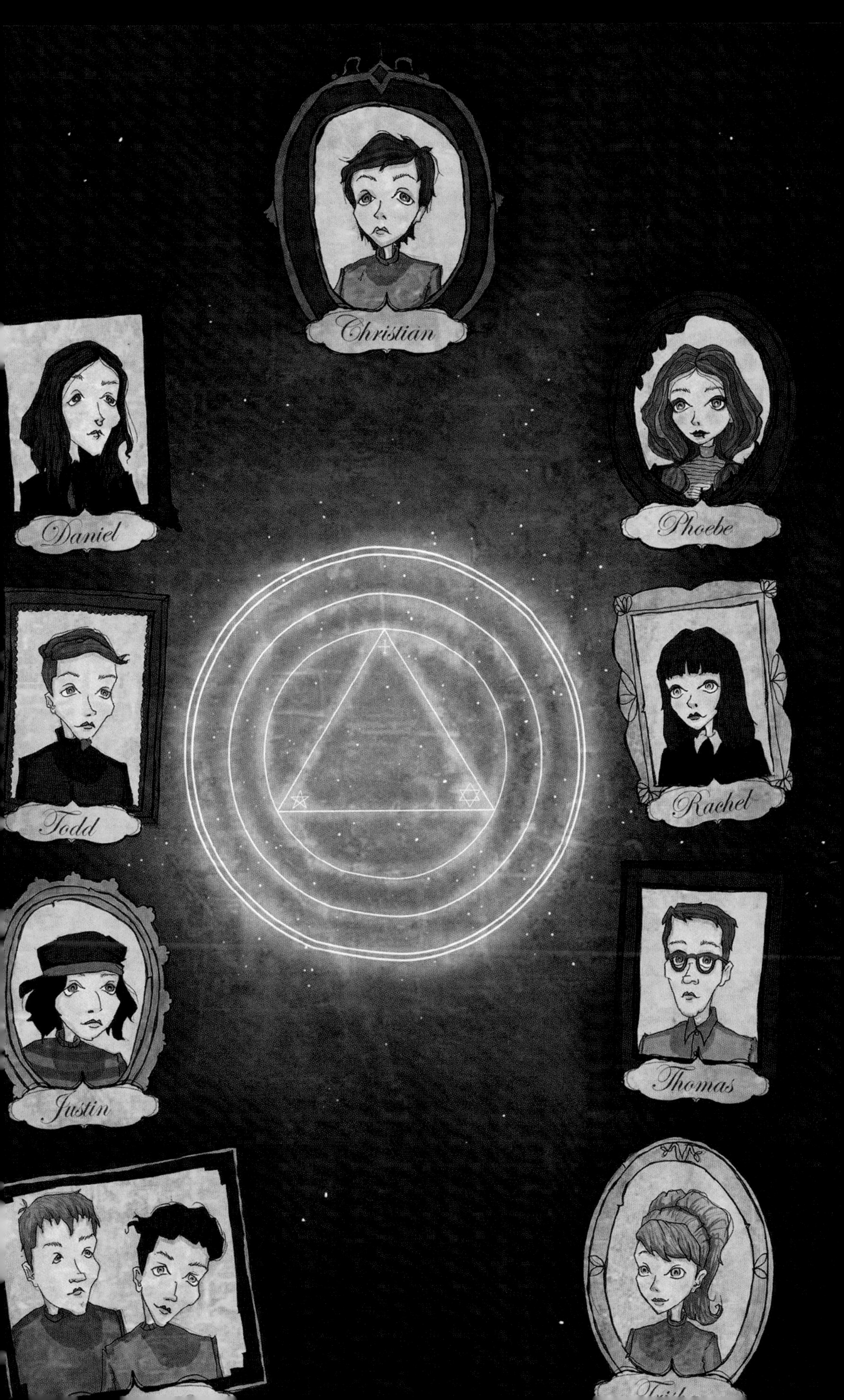
Christian
Daniel
Phoebe
Todd
Rachel
Justin
Thomas

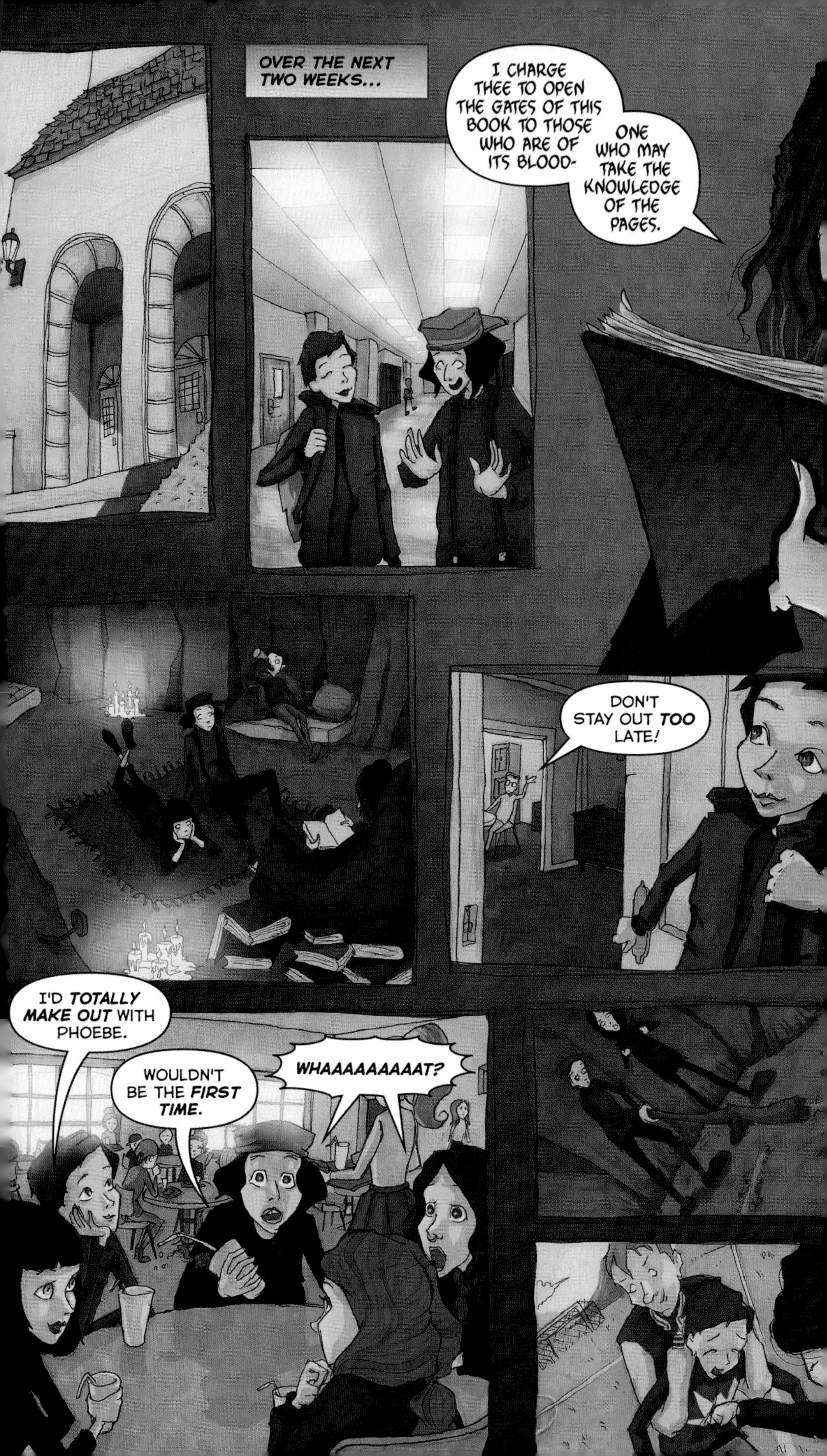
OVER THE NEXT TWO WEEKS...
I CHARGE THEE TO OPEN THE GATES OF THIS BOOK TO THOSE WHO ARE OF ITS BLOOD-
ONE WHO MAY TAKE THE KNOWLEDGE OF THE PAGES.
DON'T STAY OUT *TOO* LATE!
I'D ***TOTALLY MAKE OUT*** WITH PHOEBE.
WOULDN'T BE THE ***FIRST TIME.***
WHAAAAAAAAAT?

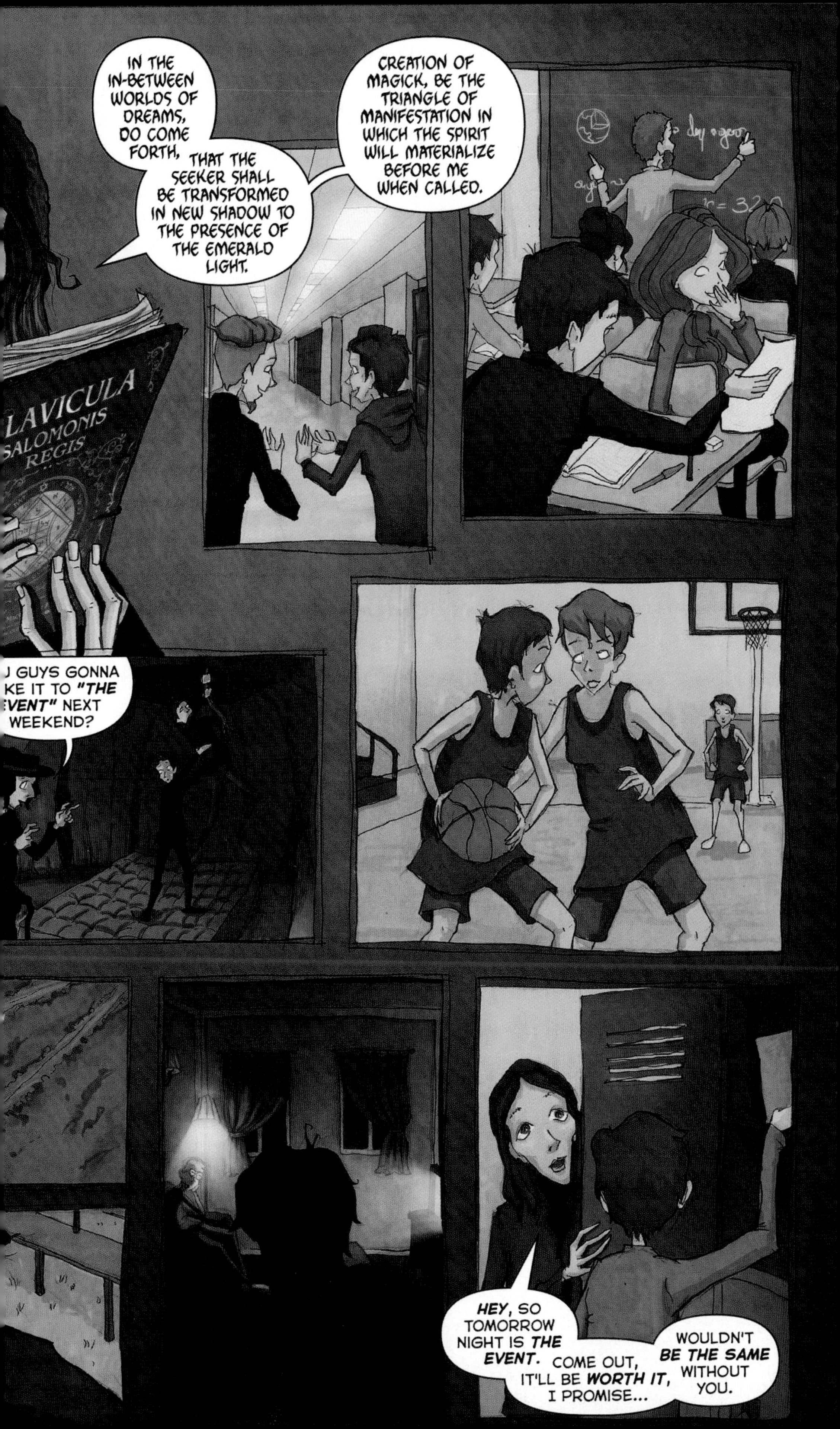

IN THE IN-BETWEEN WORLDS OF DREAMS, DO COME FORTH,
THAT THE SEEKER SHALL BE TRANSFORMED IN NEW SHADOW TO THE PRESENCE OF THE EMERALD LIGHT.
CREATION OF MAGICK, BE THE TRIANGLE OF MANIFESTATION IN WHICH THE SPIRIT WILL MATERIALIZE BEFORE ME WHEN CALLED.
LAVICULA SALOMONIS REGIS
U GUYS GONNA KE IT TO "THE VENT" NEXT WEEKEND?
HEY, SO TOMORROW NIGHT IS THE EVENT.
COME OUT, IT'LL BE WORTH IT, I PROMISE...
WOULDN'T BE THE SAME WITHOUT YOU.

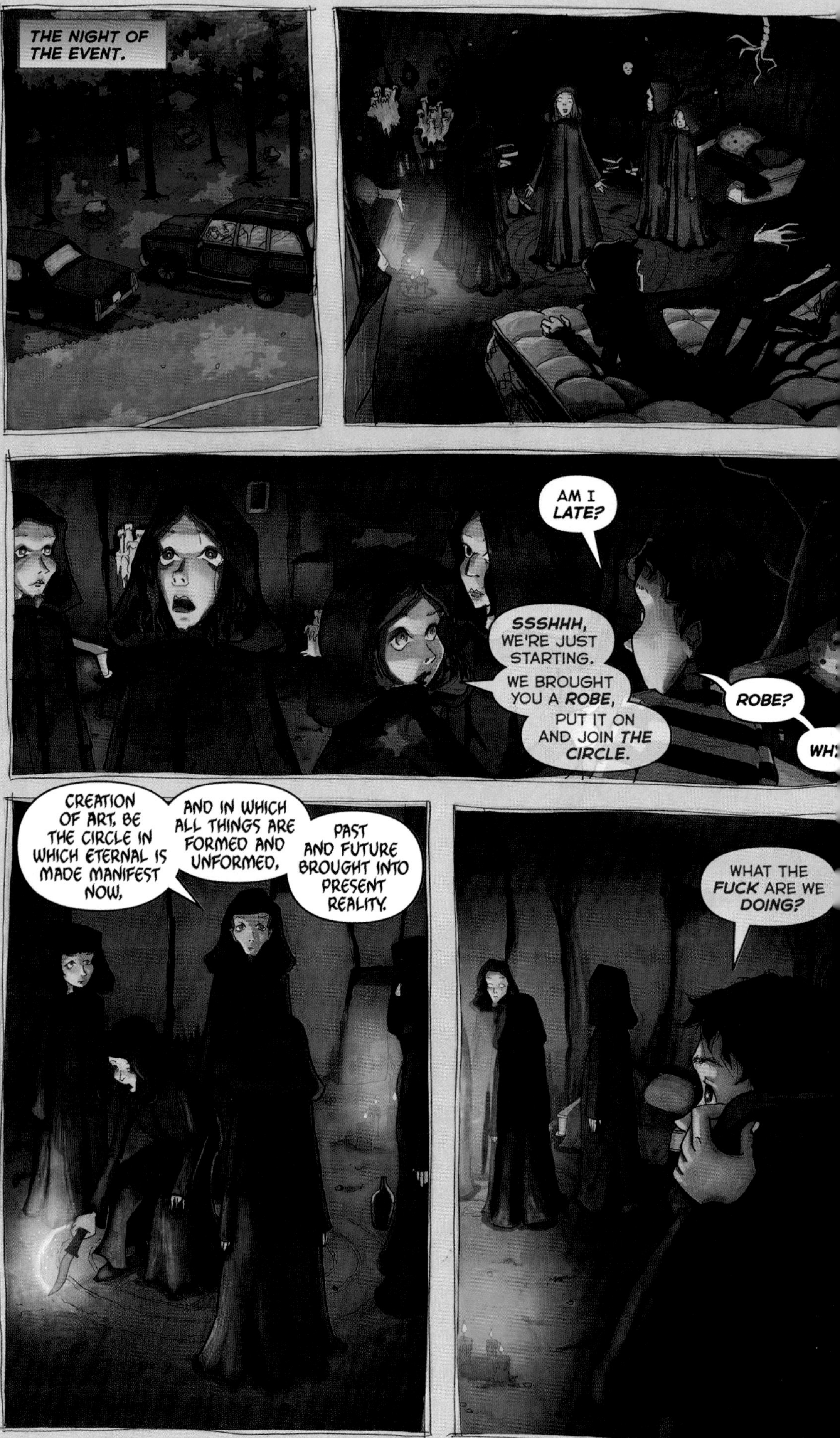
THE NIGHT OF THE EVENT.
AM I LATE?
SSSHHH, WE'RE JUST STARTING.
WE BROUGHT YOU A ROBE,
PUT IT ON AND JOIN THE CIRCLE.
ROBE?
CREATION OF ART, BE THE CIRCLE IN WHICH ETERNAL IS MADE MANIFEST NOW,
AND IN WHICH ALL THINGS ARE FORMED AND UNFORMED,
PAST AND FUTURE BROUGHT INTO PRESENT REALITY.
WHAT THE FUCK ARE WE DOING?

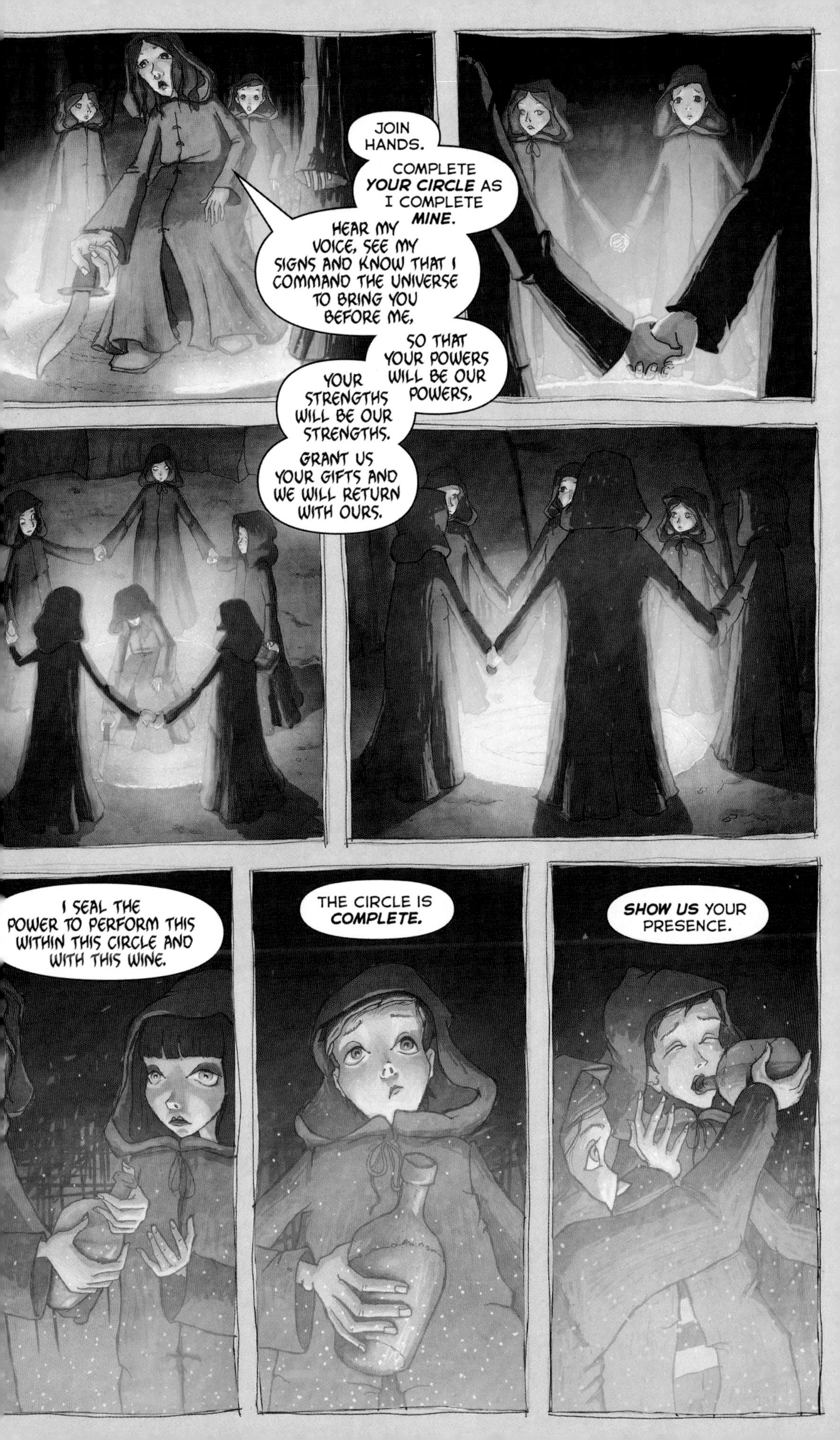
JOIN HANDS.
COMPLETE YOUR CIRCLE AS I COMPLETE MINE.
HEAR MY VOICE, SEE MY SIGNS AND KNOW THAT I COMMAND THE UNIVERSE TO BRING YOU BEFORE ME,
SO THAT YOUR POWERS WILL BE OUR POWERS,
YOUR STRENGTHS WILL BE OUR STRENGTHS.
GRANT US YOUR GIFTS AND WE WILL RETURN WITH OURS.
I SEAL THE POWER TO PERFORM THIS WITHIN THIS CIRCLE AND WITH THIS WINE.
THE CIRCLE IS COMPLETE.
SHOW US YOUR PRESENCE.

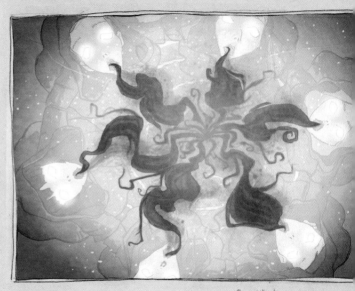

WE'RE TAKING THE POWE BACK!

I DUNNO, BUT WE'RE *NOT DONE* YET.

WE STILL HAVE TO *FINISH THIS,* AND *WE GOTTA* FINISH IT *SOON.*

DID IT *WORK?*

FINISH WHAT?

WHAT THE *FUCK* ARE WE *DOING?*

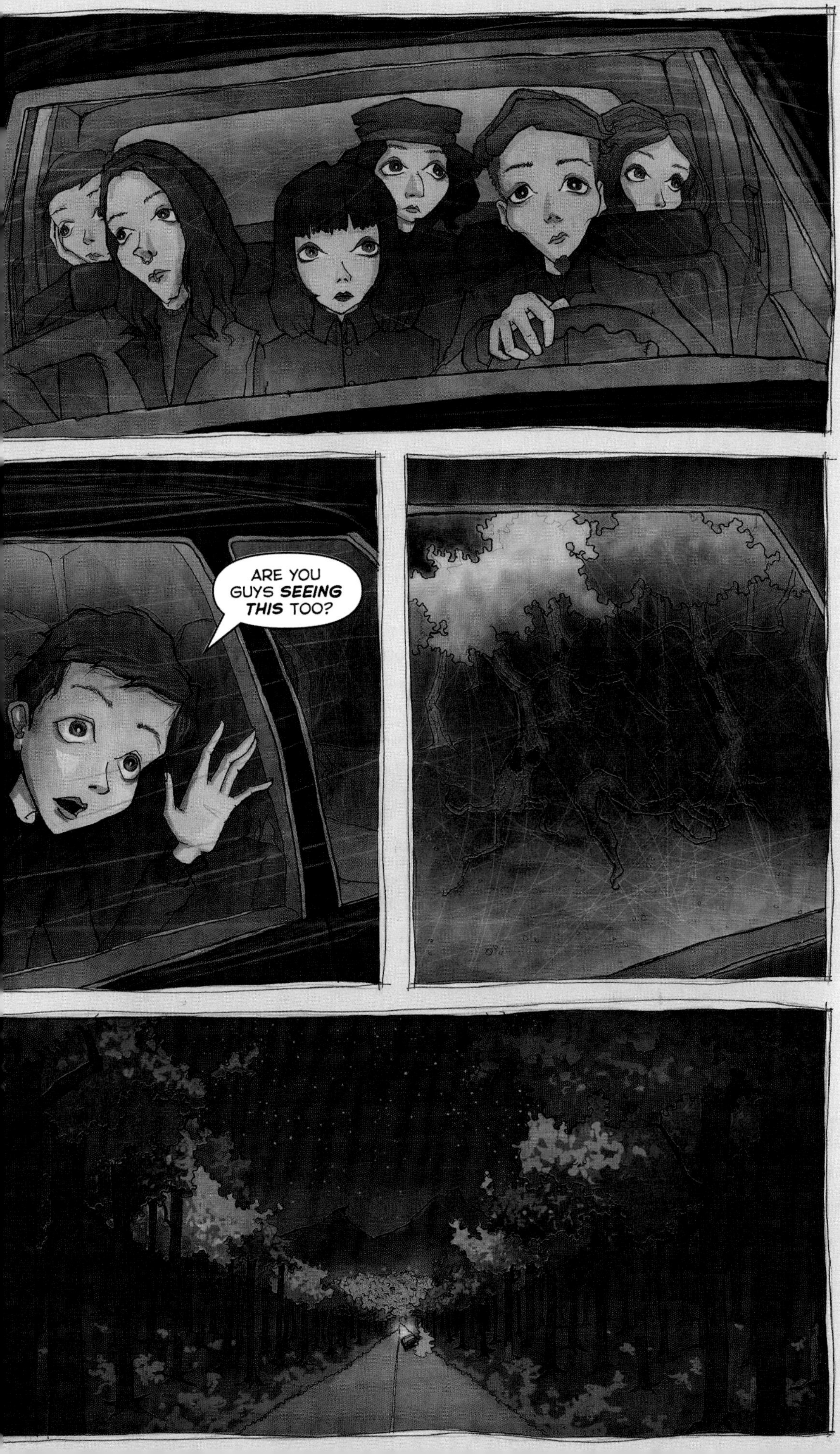
ARE YOU GUYS **SEEING THIS** TOO?

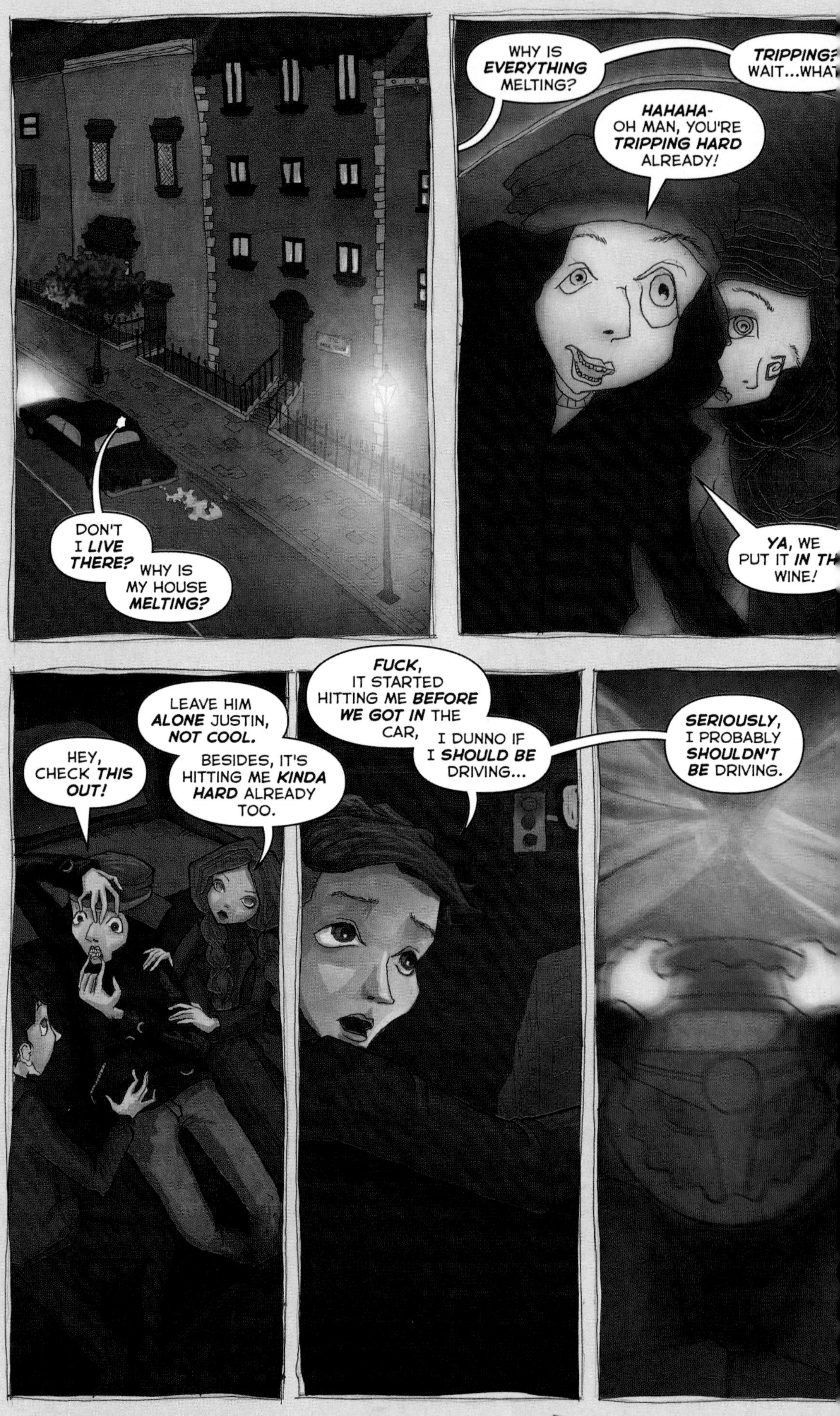
DON'T I LIVE THERE?
WHY IS MY HOUSE MELTING?
WHY IS EVERYTHING MELTING?
TRIPPING? WAIT...WHAT
HAHAHA- OH MAN, YOU'RE TRIPPING HARD ALREADY!
YA, WE PUT IT IN TH WINE!
HEY, CHECK THIS OUT!
LEAVE HIM ALONE JUSTIN, NOT COOL.
BESIDES, IT'S HITTING ME KINDA HARD ALREADY TOO.
FUCK, IT STARTED HITTING ME BEFORE WE GOT IN THE CAR,
I DUNNO IF I SHOULD BE DRIVING...
SERIOUSLY, I PROBABLY SHOULDN'T BE DRIVING.

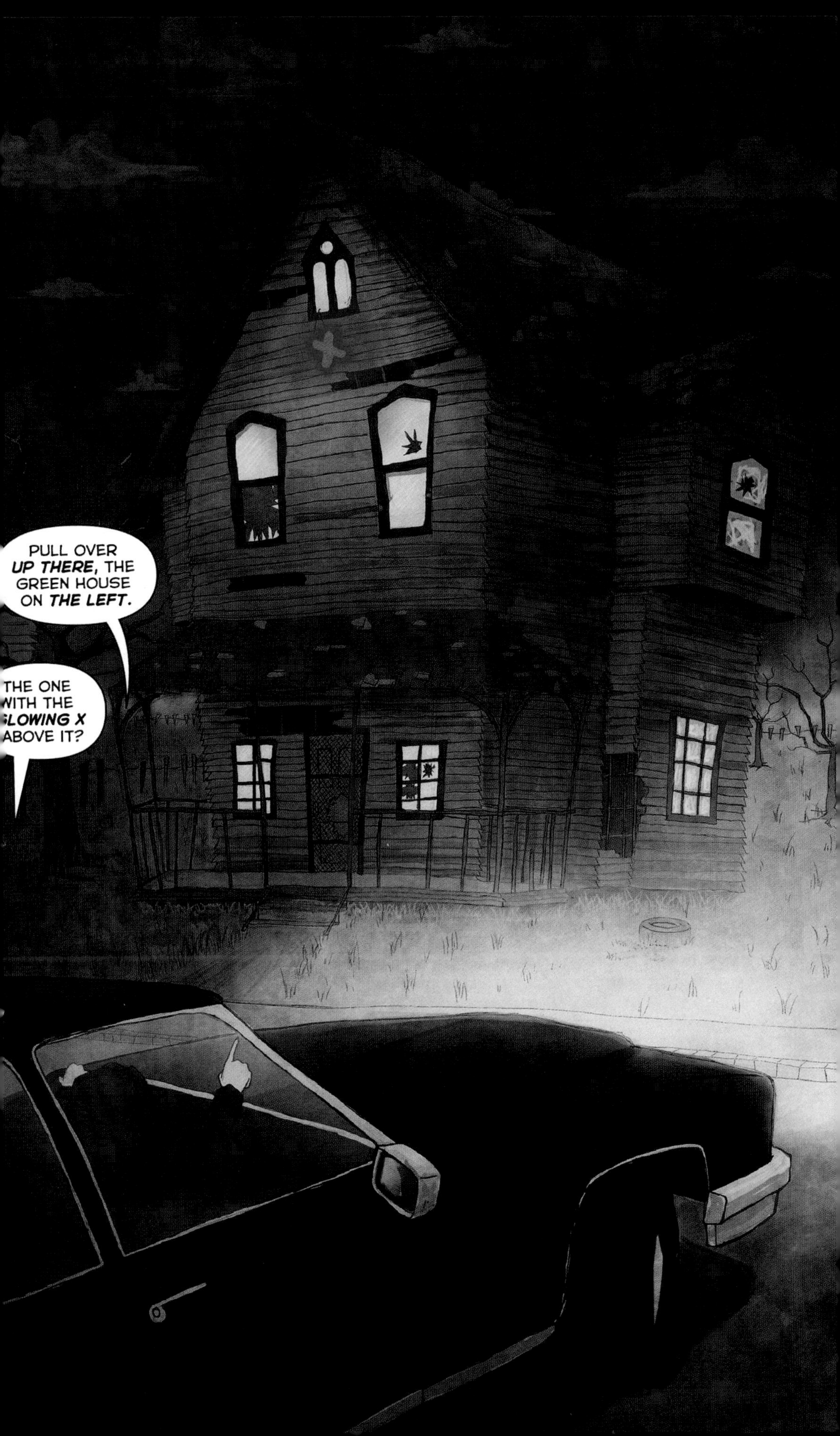
PULL OVER *UP THERE*, THE GREEN HOUSE ON *THE LEFT*.
THE ONE WITH THE *GLOWING X* ABOVE IT?

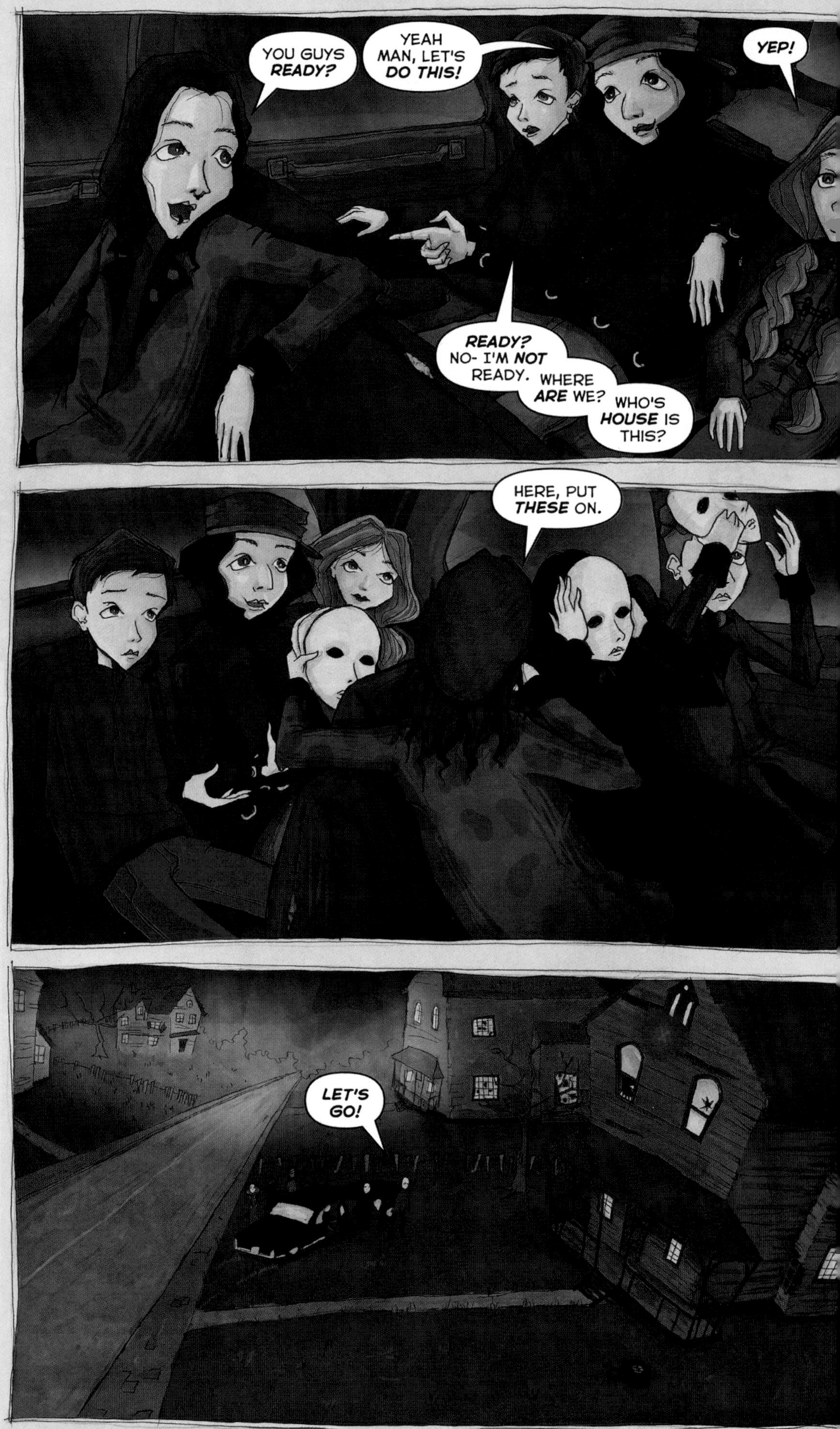
YOU GUYS READY?
YEAH MAN, LET'S DO THIS!
YEP!
READY? NO- I'M NOT READY. WHERE ARE WE? WHO'S HOUSE IS THIS?
HERE, PUT THESE ON.
LET'S GO!

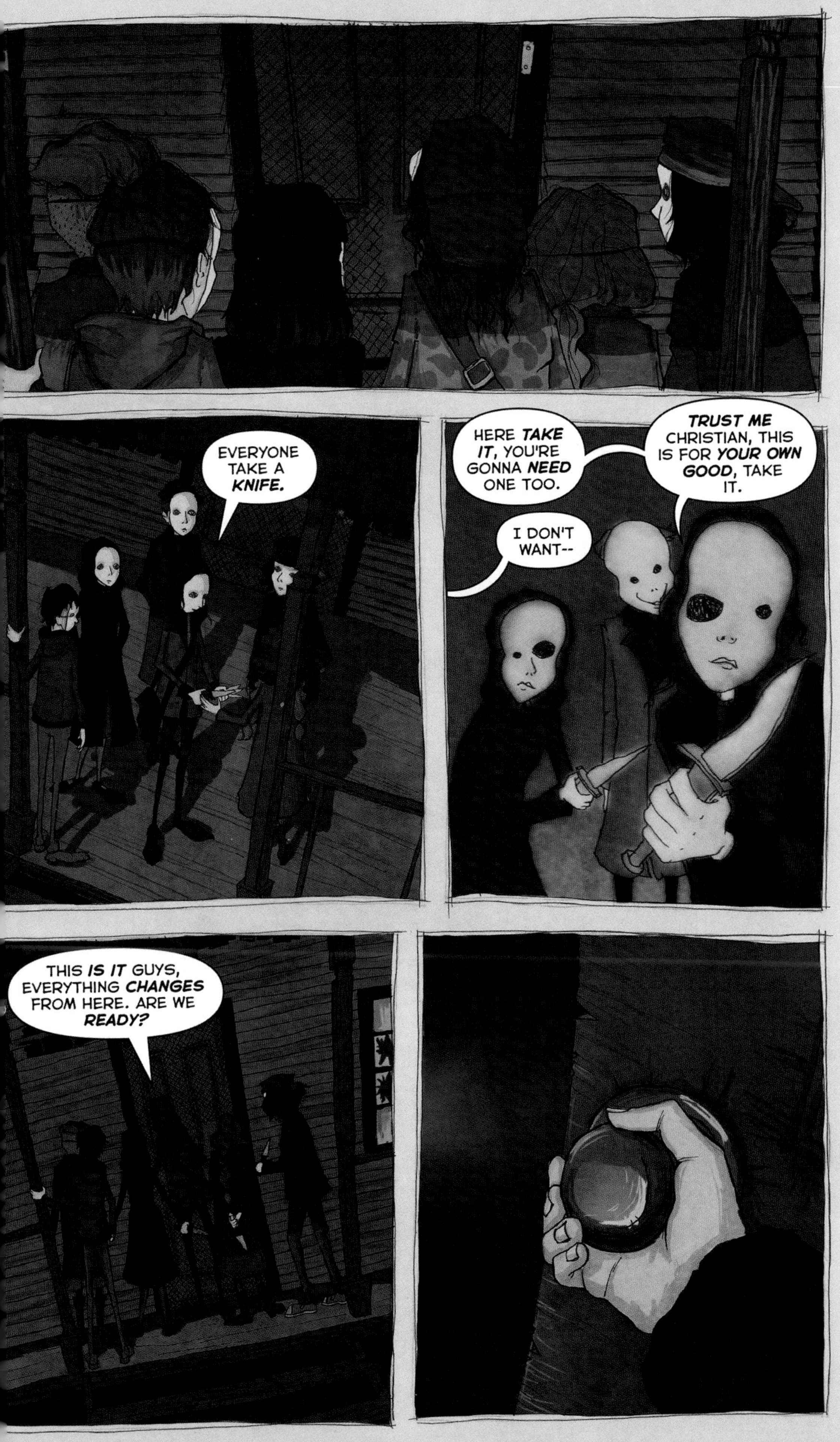
EVERYONE TAKE A *KNIFE.*
HERE *TAKE IT*, YOU'RE GONNA *NEED* ONE TOO.
TRUST ME CHRISTIAN, THIS IS FOR *YOUR OWN GOOD*, TAKE IT.
I DON'T WANT--
THIS *IS IT* GUYS, EVERYTHING *CHANGES* FROM HERE. ARE WE *READY?*

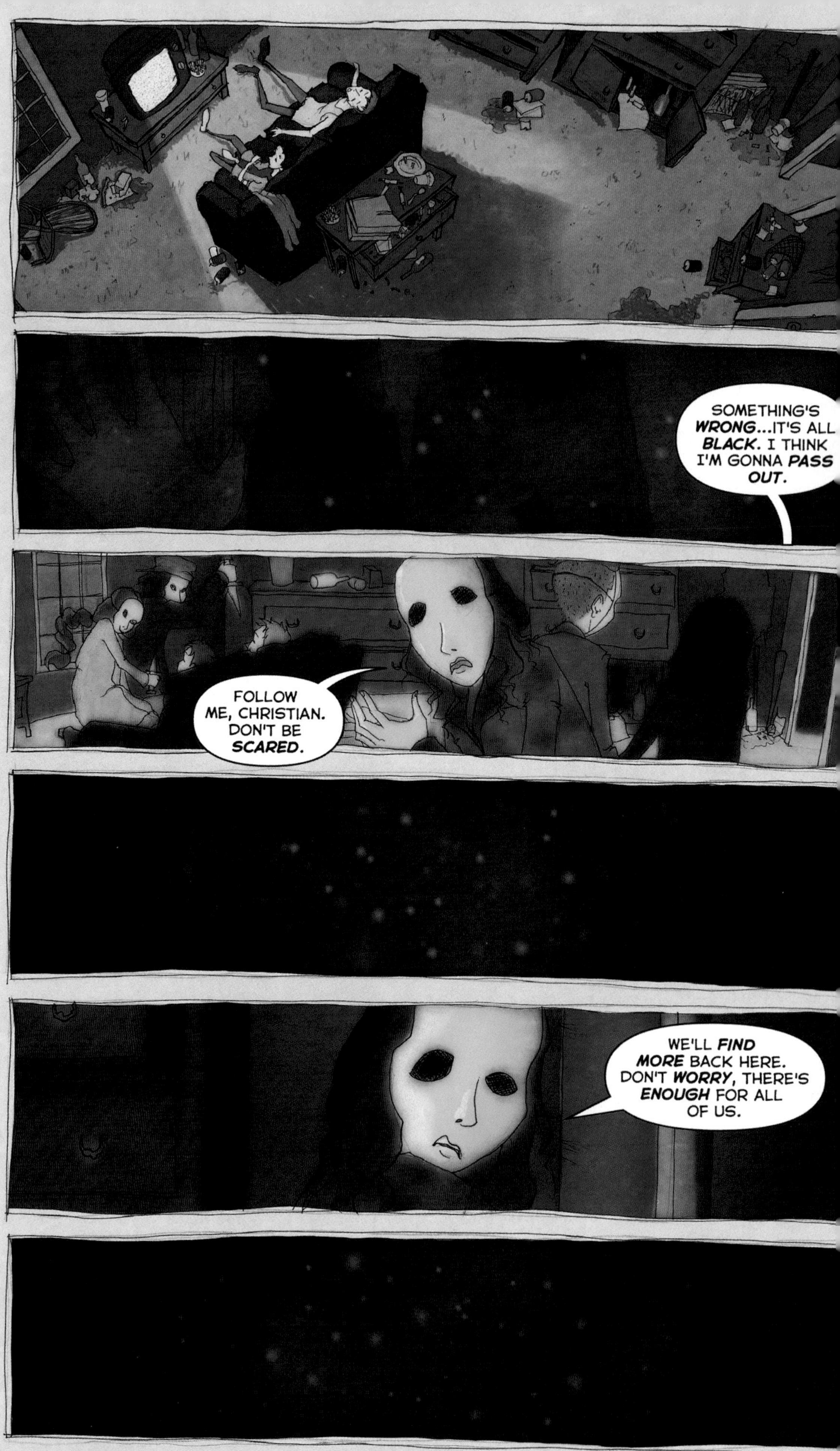
SOMETHING'S WRONG...IT'S ALL BLACK. I THINK I'M GONNA PASS OUT.
FOLLOW ME, CHRISTIAN. DON'T BE SCARED.
WE'LL FIND MORE BACK HERE. DON'T WORRY, THERE'S ENOUGH FOR ALL OF US.

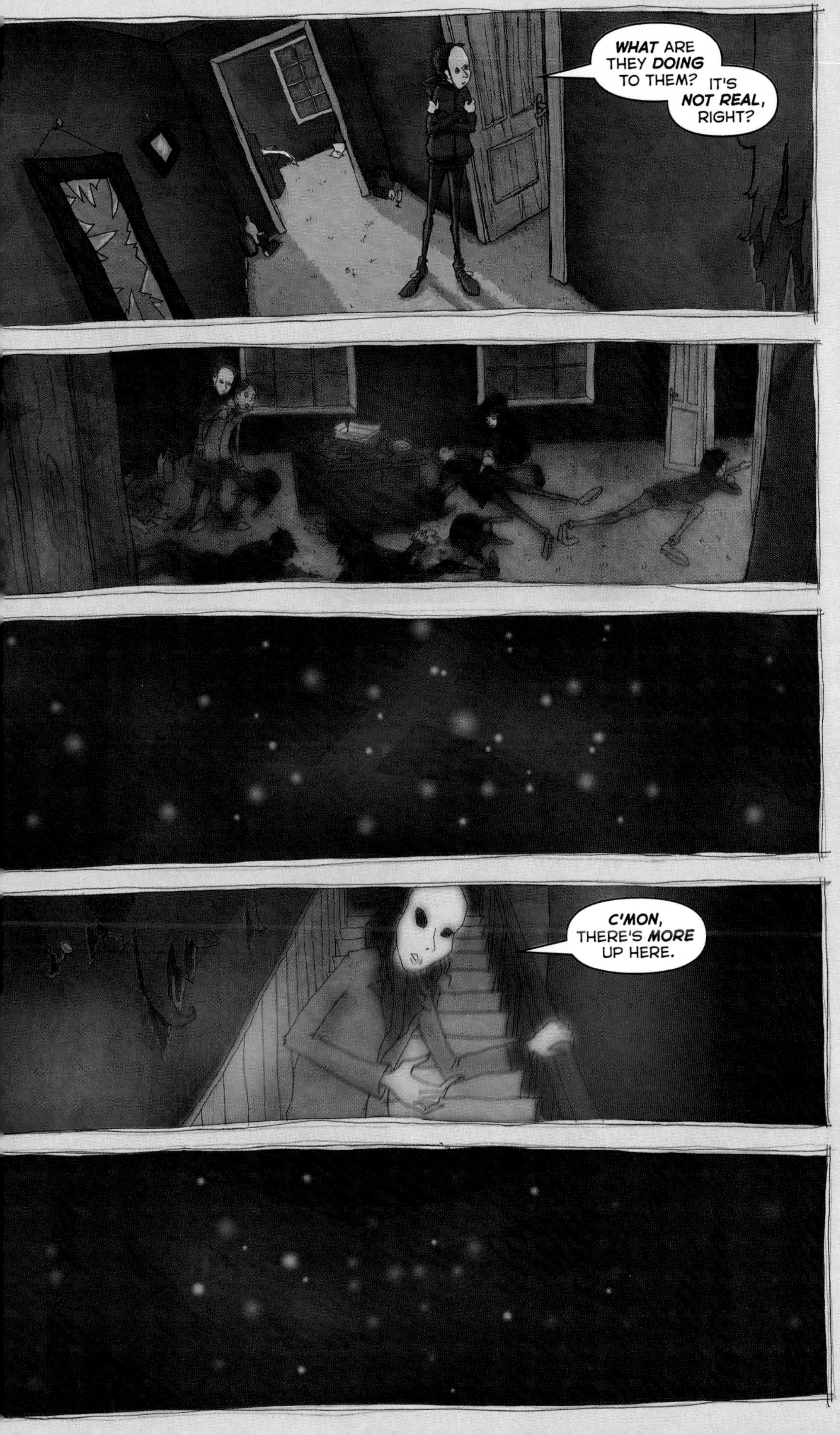
WHAT ARE THEY DOING TO THEM? IT'S NOT REAL, RIGHT?
C'MON, THERE'S MORE UP HERE.

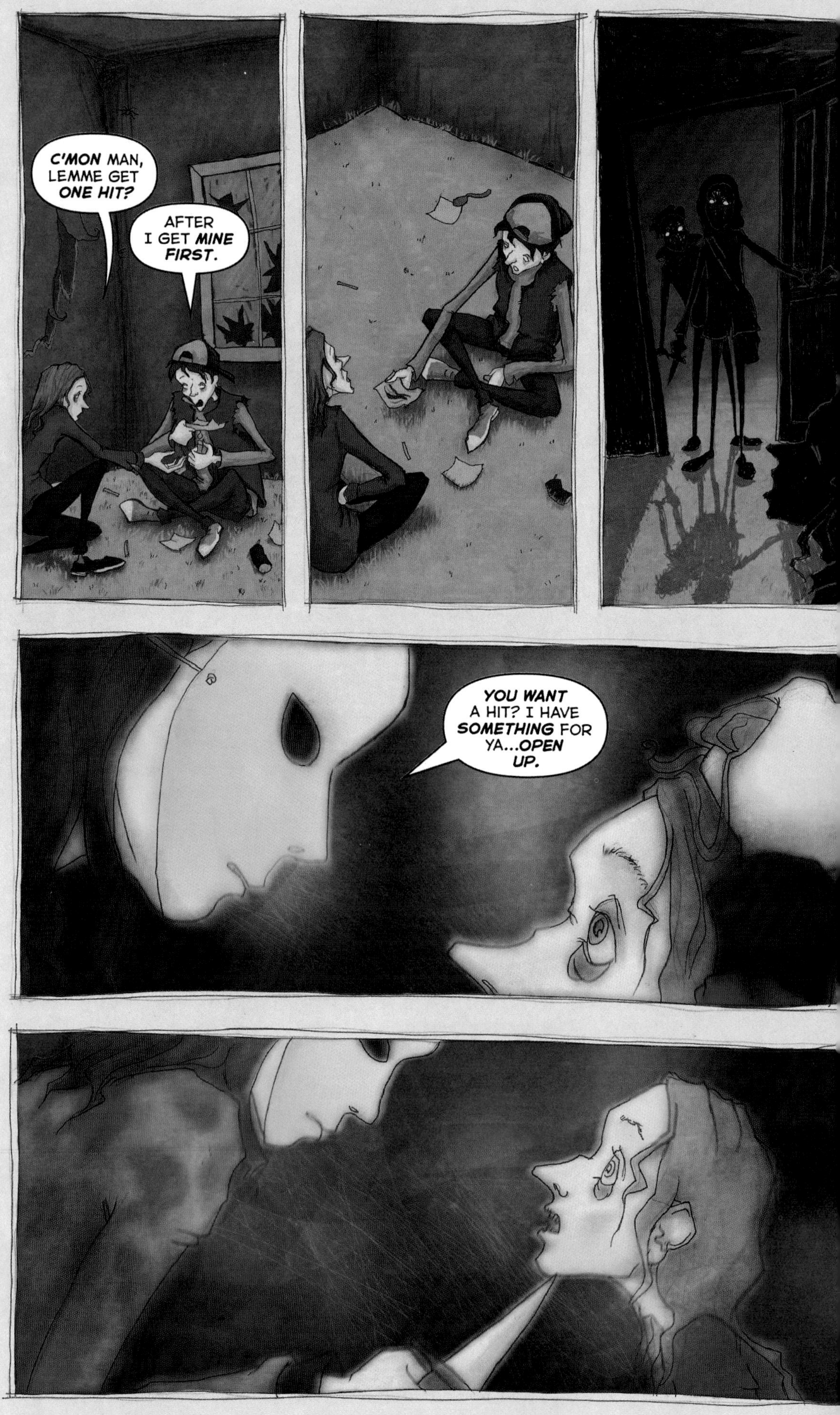
C'MON MAN, LEMME GET ONE HIT?
AFTER I GET MINE FIRST.
YOU WANT A HIT? I HAVE SOMETHING FOR YA...OPEN UP.

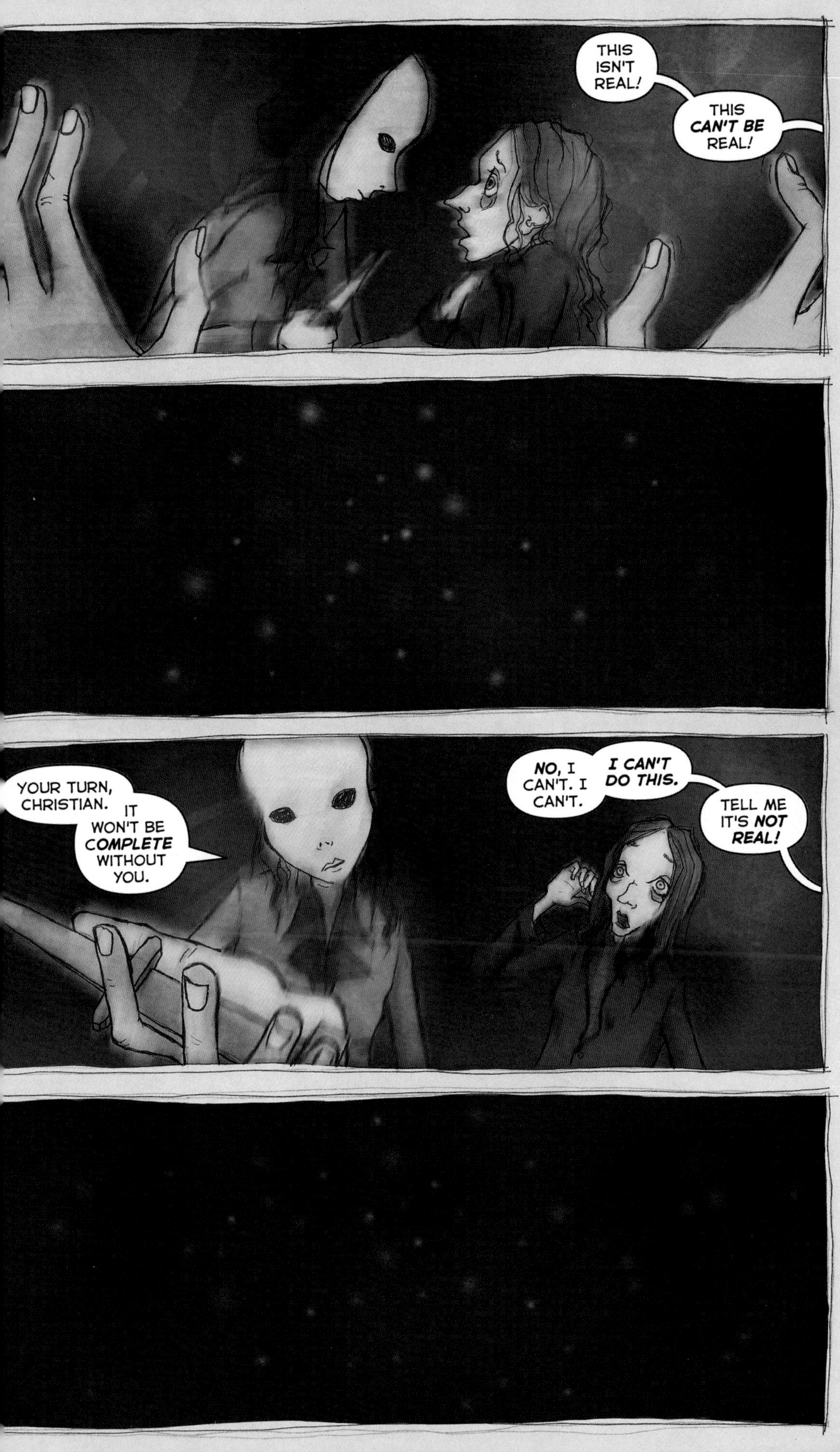
THIS ISN'T REAL!
THIS CAN'T BE REAL!
YOUR TURN, CHRISTIAN.
IT WON'T BE COMPLETE WITHOUT YOU.
NO, I CAN'T. I CAN'T.
I CAN'T DO THIS.
TELL ME IT'S NOT REAL!

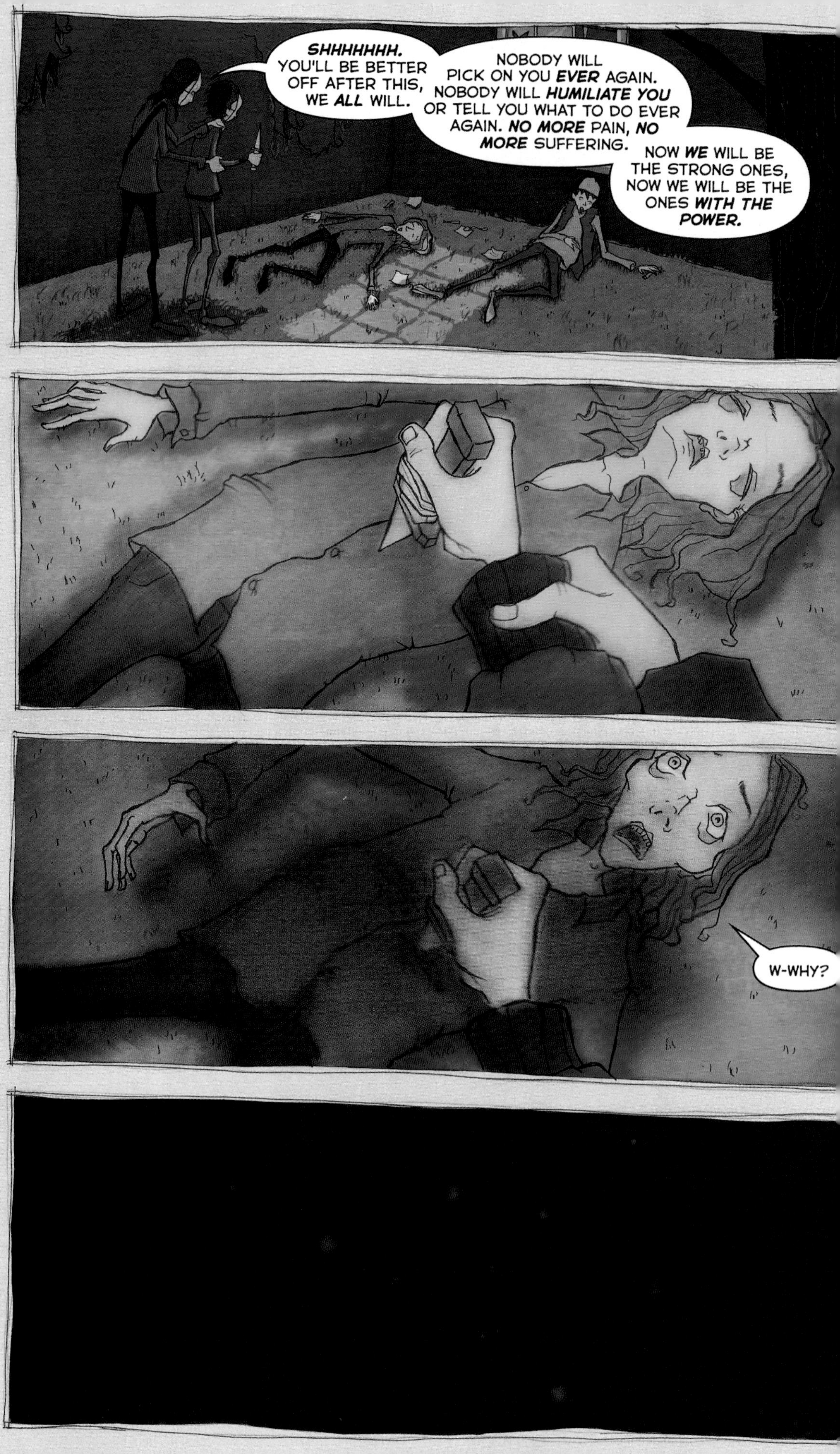
SHHHHHHH. YOU'LL BE BETTER OFF AFTER THIS, WE ALL WILL.
NOBODY WILL PICK ON YOU EVER AGAIN. NOBODY WILL HUMILIATE YOU OR TELL YOU WHAT TO DO EVER AGAIN. NO MORE PAIN, NO MORE SUFFERING.
NOW WE WILL BE THE STRONG ONES, NOW WE WILL BE THE ONES WITH THE POWER.
W-WHY?

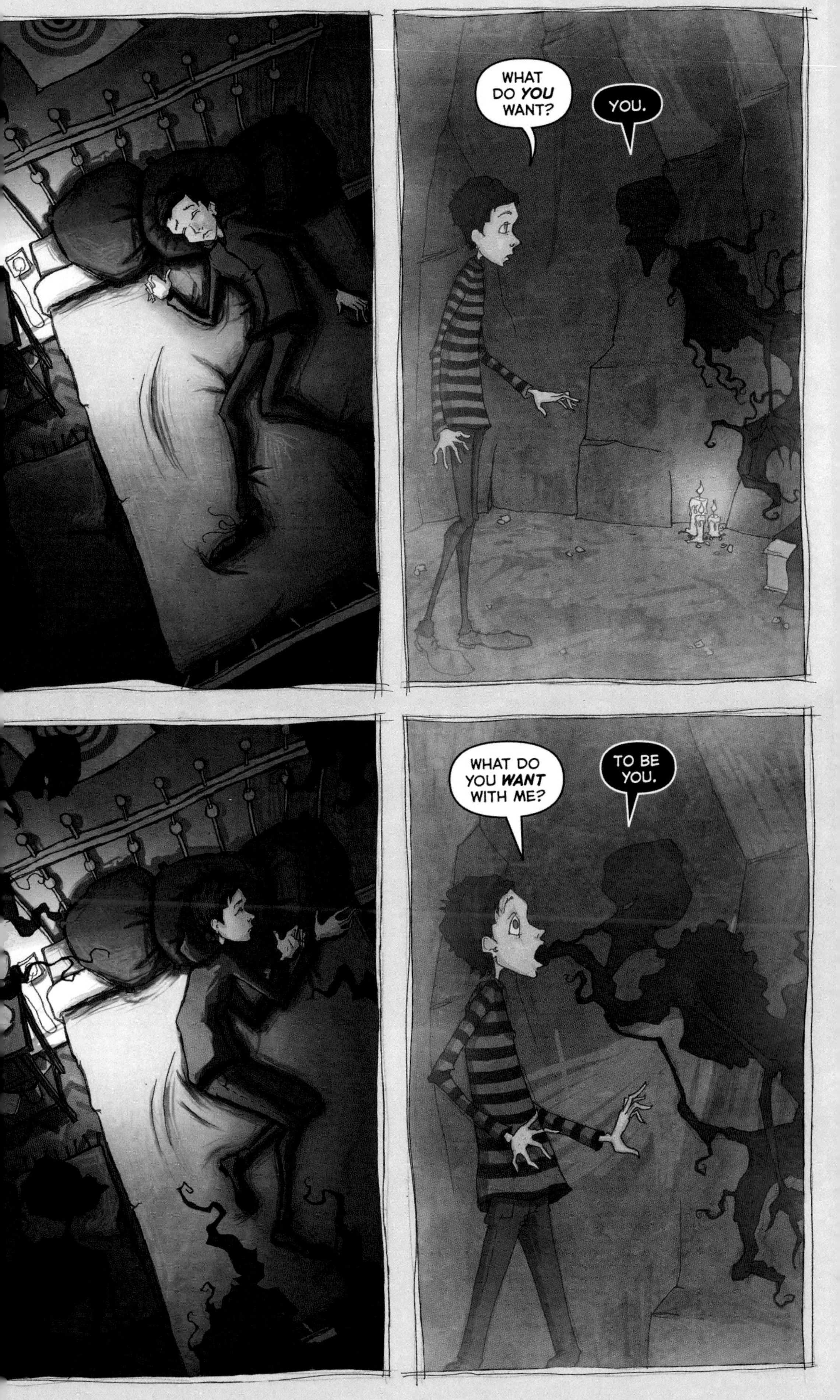
WHAT DO *YOU* WANT?
YOU.
WHAT DO YOU *WANT* WITH ME?
TO BE YOU.

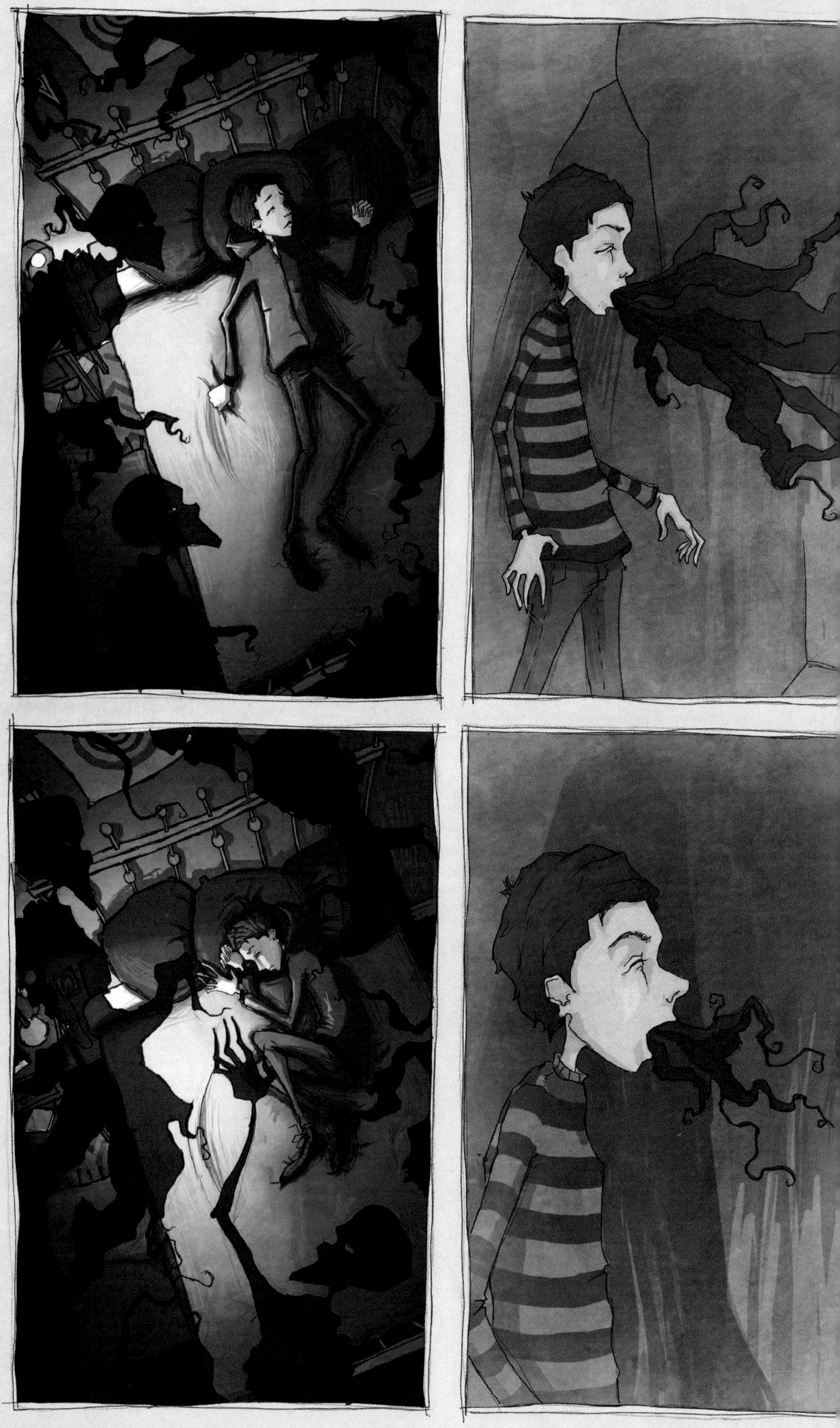

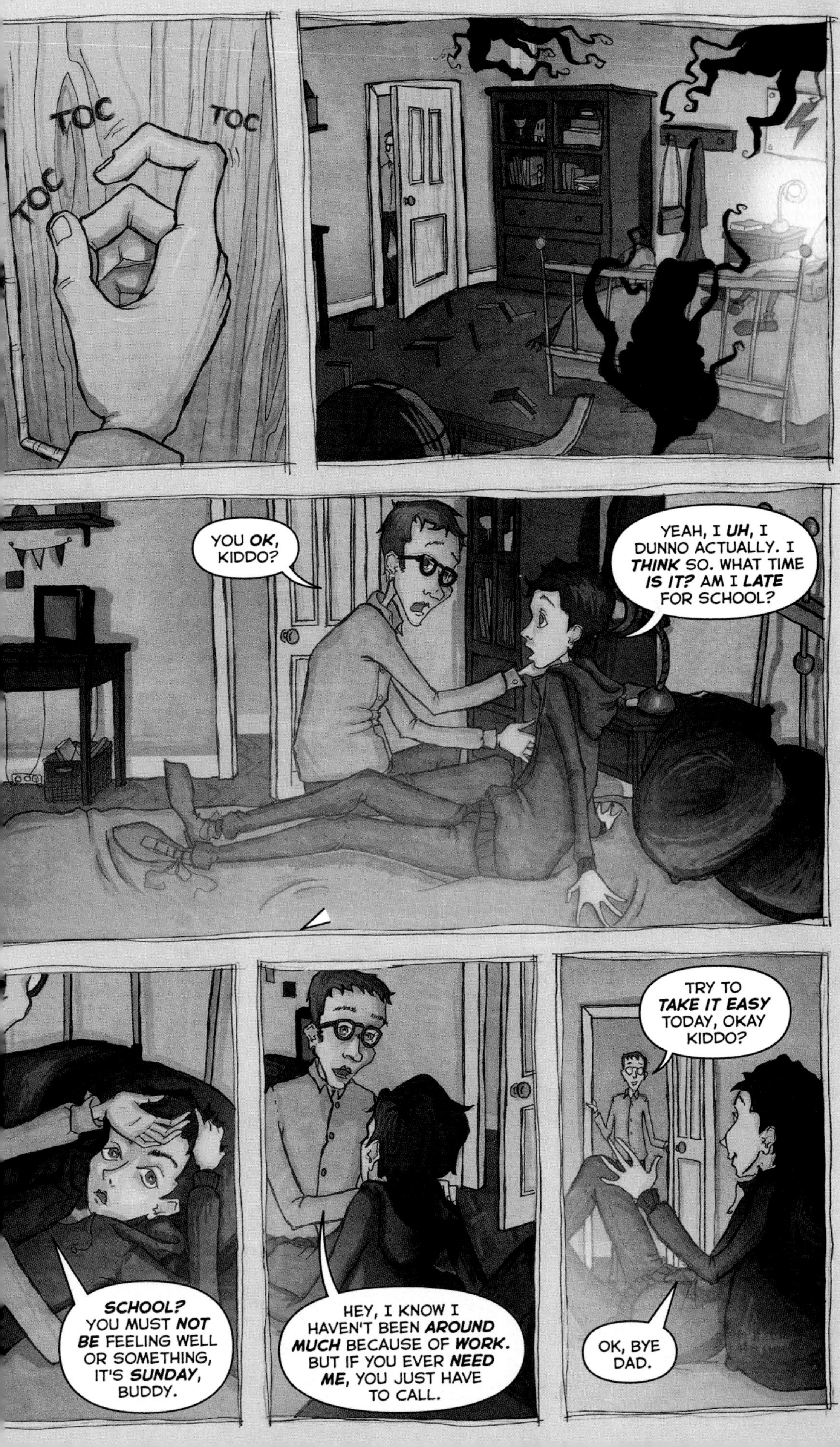
TOC
TOC
TOC
YOU OK, KIDDO?
YEAH, I UH, I DUNNO ACTUALLY. I THINK SO. WHAT TIME IS IT? AM I LATE FOR SCHOOL?
SCHOOL? YOU MUST NOT BE FEELING WELL OR SOMETHING, IT'S SUNDAY, BUDDY.
HEY, I KNOW I HAVEN'T BEEN AROUND MUCH BECAUSE OF WORK. BUT IF YOU EVER NEED ME, YOU JUST HAVE TO CALL.
TRY TO TAKE IT EASY TODAY, OKAY KIDDO?
OK, BYE DAD.

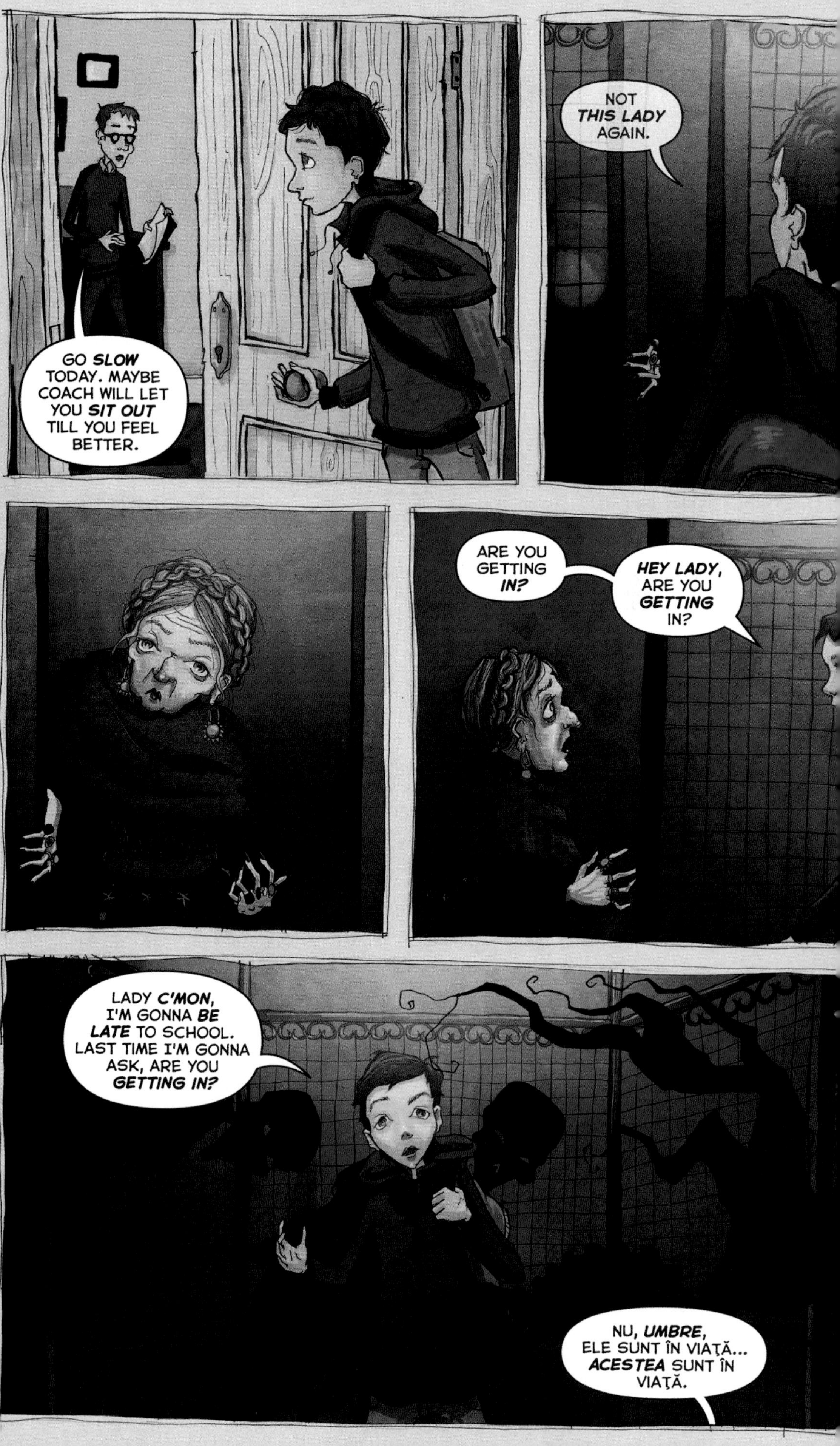
GO **SLOW** TODAY. MAYBE COACH WILL LET YOU **SIT OUT** TILL YOU FEEL BETTER.
NOT **THIS LADY** AGAIN.
ARE YOU GETTING **IN?**
HEY LADY, ARE YOU **GETTING** IN?
LADY **C'MON,** I'M GONNA **BE LATE** TO SCHOOL. LAST TIME I'M GONNA ASK, ARE YOU **GETTING IN?**
NU, **UMBRE,** ELE SUNT ÎN VIAȚĂ... **ACESTEA** SUNT ÎN VIAȚĂ.

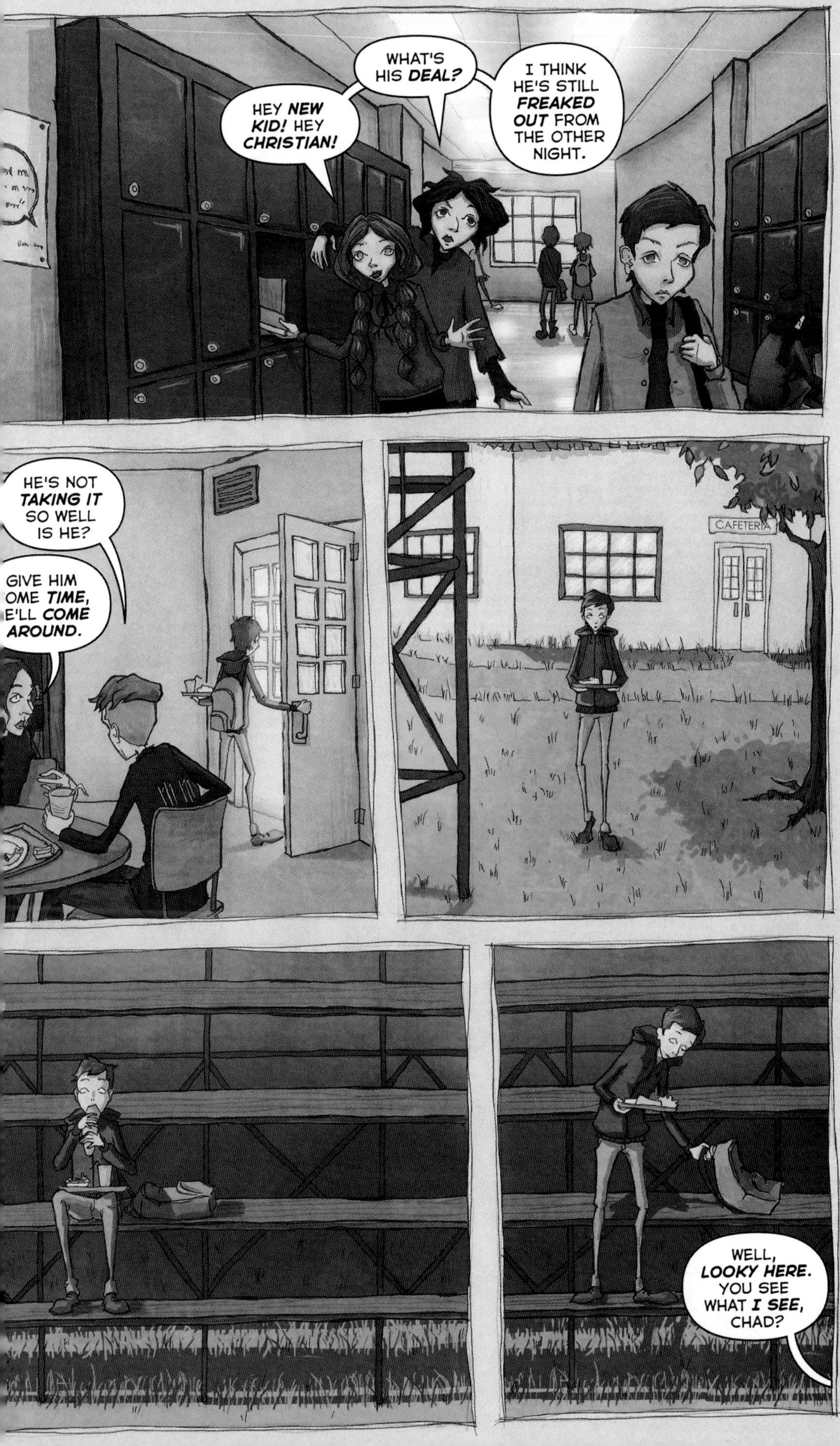
HEY NEW KID! HEY CHRISTIAN!
WHAT'S HIS DEAL?
I THINK HE'S STILL FREAKED OUT FROM THE OTHER NIGHT.
HE'S NOT TAKING IT SO WELL IS HE?
GIVE HIM OME TIME, E'LL COME AROUND.
CAFETERIA
WELL, LOOKY HERE. YOU SEE WHAT I SEE, CHAD?

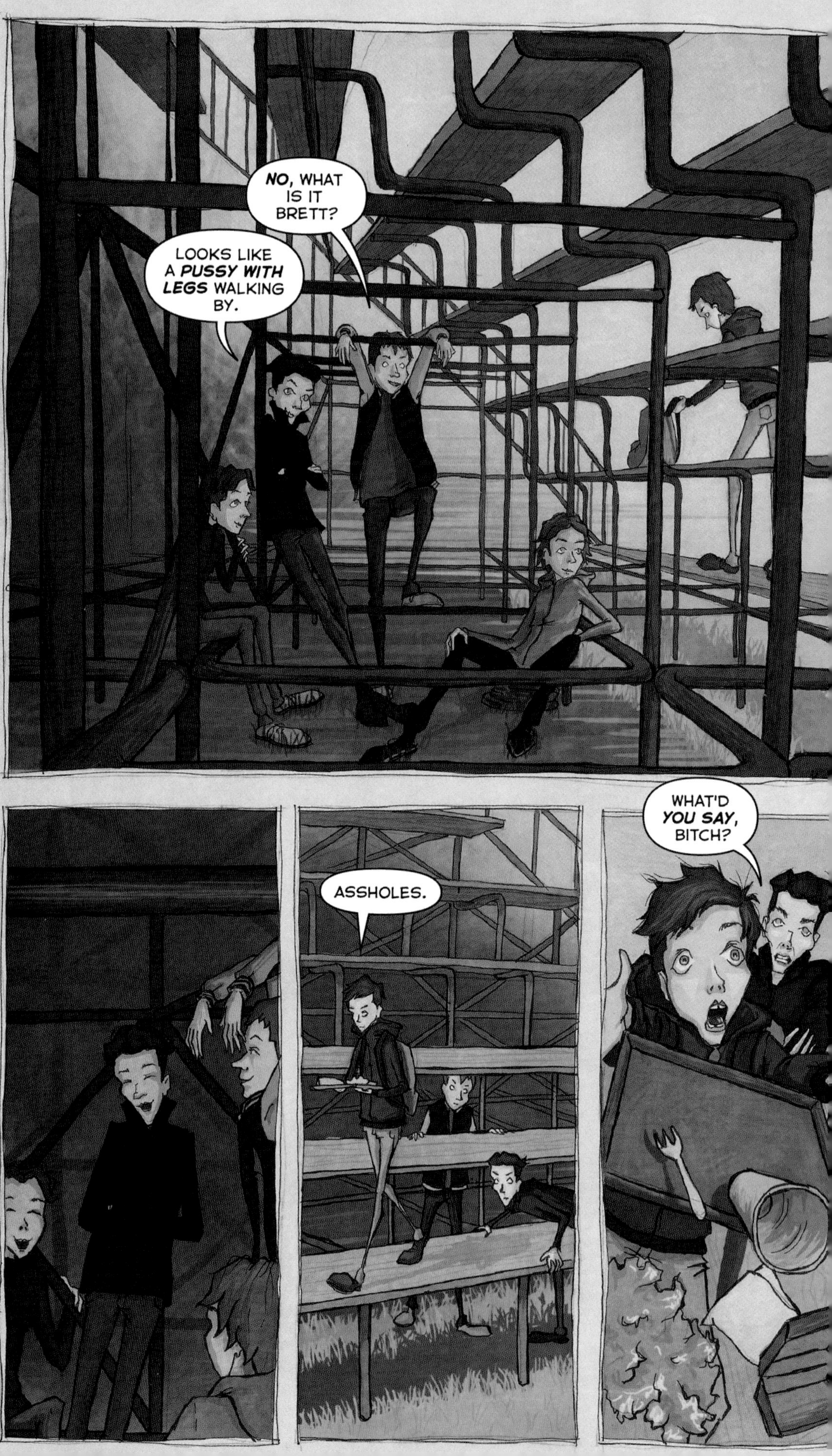
NO, WHAT IS IT BRETT?
LOOKS LIKE A PUSSY WITH LEGS WALKING BY.
ASSHOLES.
WHAT'D YOU SAY, BITCH?

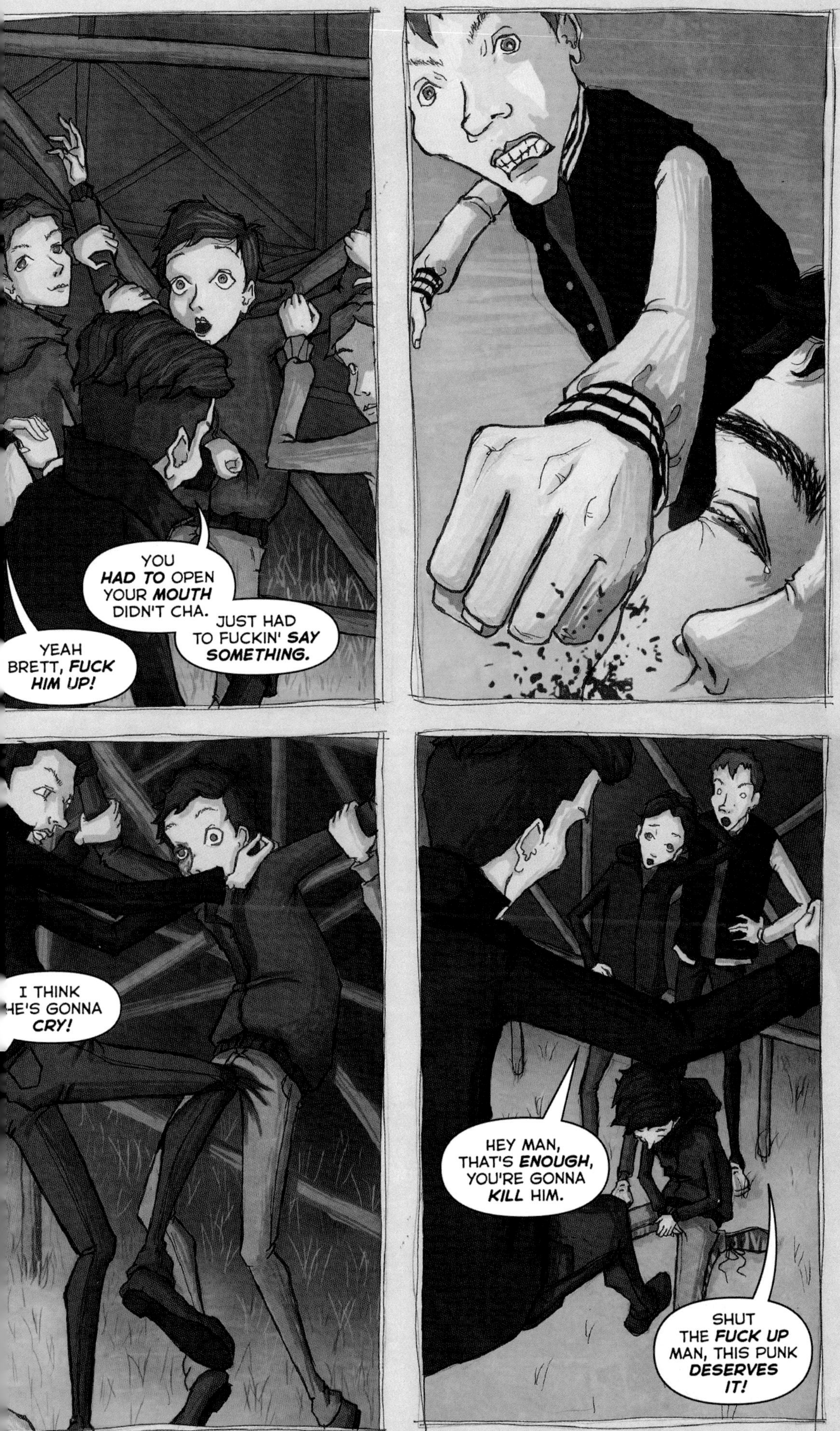
YOU HAD TO OPEN YOUR MOUTH DIDN'T CHA.
JUST HAD TO FUCKIN' SAY SOMETHING.
YEAH BRETT, FUCK HIM UP!
I THINK HE'S GONNA CRY!
HEY MAN, THAT'S ENOUGH, YOU'RE GONNA KILL HIM.
SHUT THE FUCK UP MAN, THIS PUNK DESERVES IT!

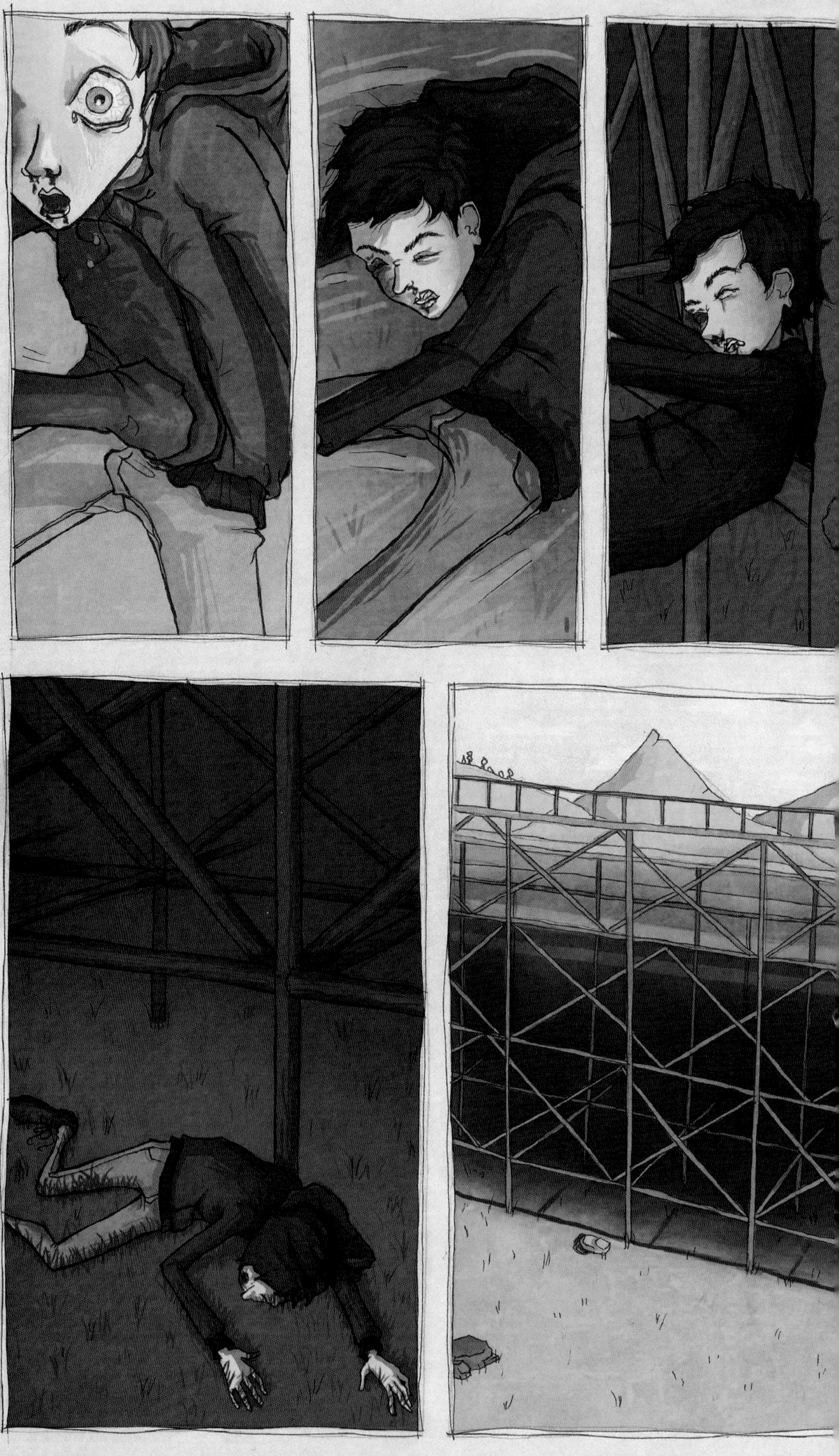

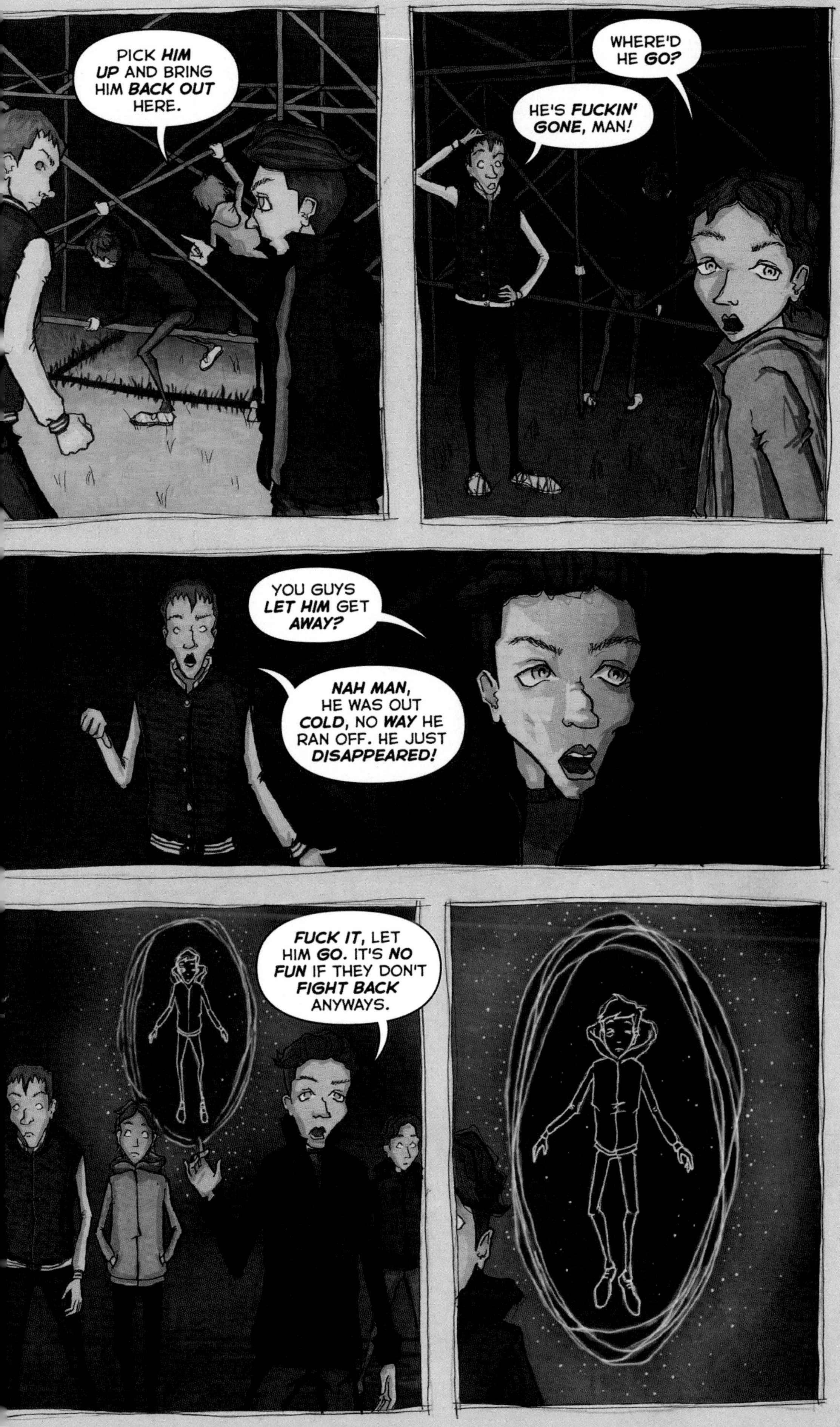
PICK HIM UP AND BRING HIM BACK OUT HERE.
WHERE'D HE GO?
HE'S FUCKIN' GONE, MAN!
YOU GUYS LET HIM GET AWAY?
NAH MAN, HE WAS OUT COLD, NO WAY HE RAN OFF. HE JUST DISAPPEARED!
FUCK IT, LET HIM GO. IT'S NO FUN IF THEY DON'T FIGHT BACK ANYWAYS.

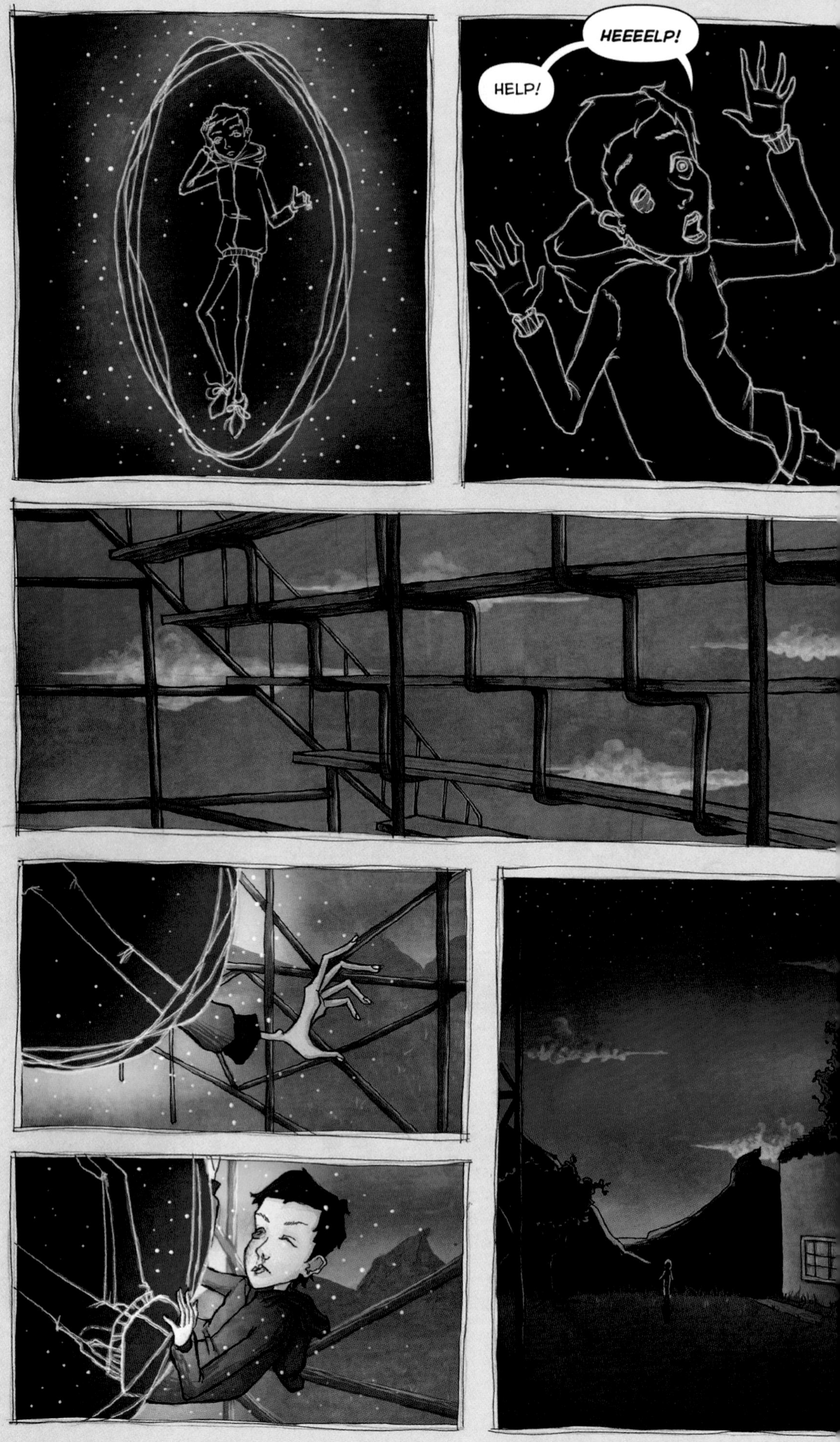
HELP!
HEEEELP!

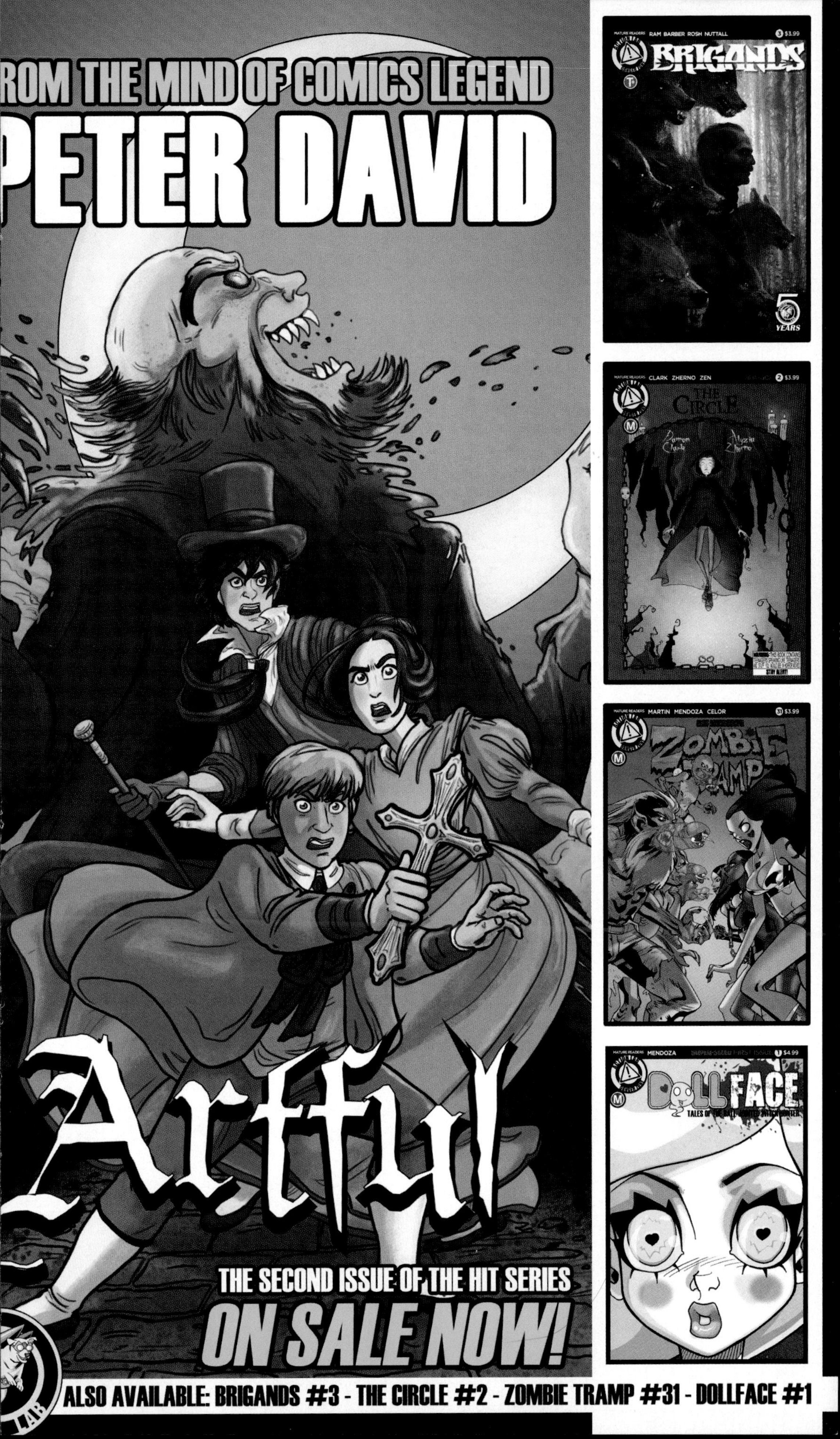

FROM THE MIND OF COMICS LEGEND
PETER DAVID
Artful
THE SECOND ISSUE OF THE HIT SERIES
ON SALE NOW!
MATURE READERS RAM BARBER ROSH NUTTALL 3 $3.99
BRIGANDS
MATURE READERS CLARK ZHERNO ZEN 2 $3.99
THE CIRCLE
MATURE READERS MARTIN MENDOZA CELOR 31 $3.99
ZOMBIE TRAMP
MATURE READERS MENDOZA 1 $4.99
DOLLFACE
ALSO AVAILABLE: BRIGANDS #3 - THE CIRCLE #2 - ZOMBIE TRAMP #31 - DOLLFACE #1

Springing from the pages of Halloween ComicFest comes ZOMBIE TRAMP creator Dan Mendoza & Bryan Seaton's newest hit series!

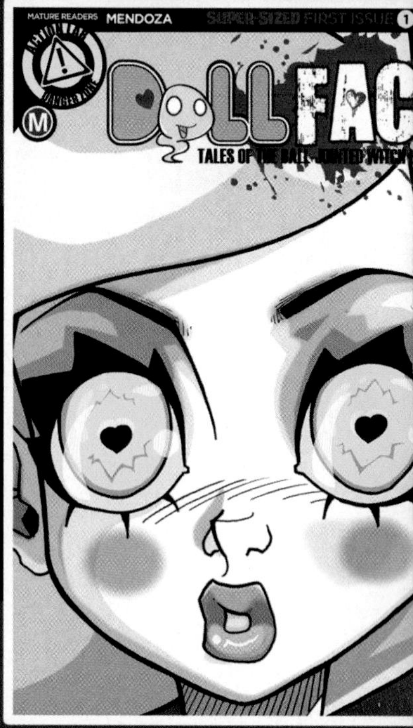
MATURE READERS
MENDOZA
DOLL FACE

In the town of Boston, a witch-hunter lurks among the shadows, but this witch-hunter is like none you've ever seen.

She is Lila, a 17th century soul that has been transported into present time, and into the body of a life size, ball-jointed doll, created by a couple of MIT students trying to use technology and a 3D printer to create the perfect women.

The adventure begins in this DOUBLE-SIZED FIRST ISSUE!

COVER A BY
DAN MENDOZA
NOV161045

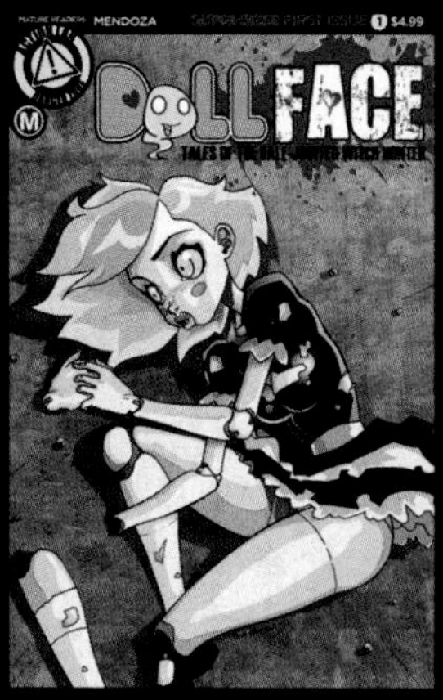
MATURE READERS
MENDOZA
$4.99
DOLL FACE
TALES OF THE BALL-JOINTED WITCH HUNTER

COVER B BY
DAN MENDOZA
NOV161046

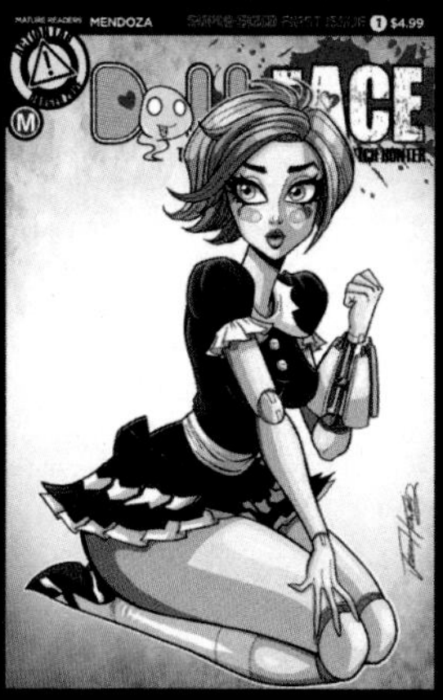
MATURE READERS
MENDOZA
$4.99

COVER C BY
JOSH HOWARD
NOV161047

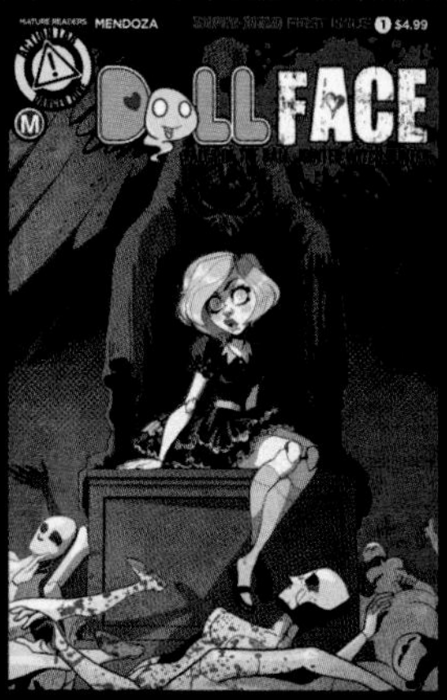
MATURE READERS
MENDOZA
$4.99
DOLL FACE

COVER D BY
VICTORIA HARRIS
NOV161048

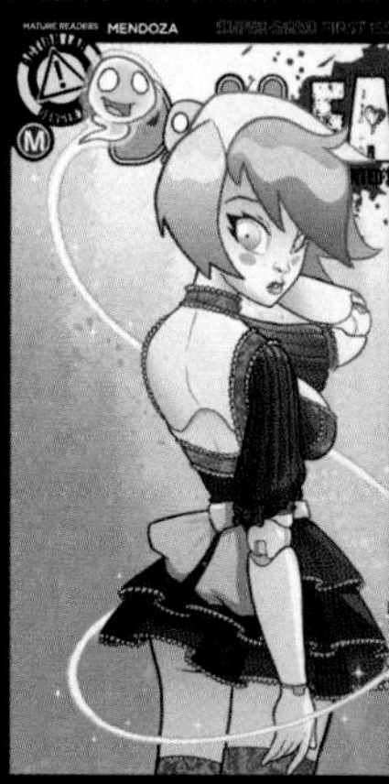
MATURE READERS
MENDOZA

COVER E BY
TONY FLEEC
NOV16104

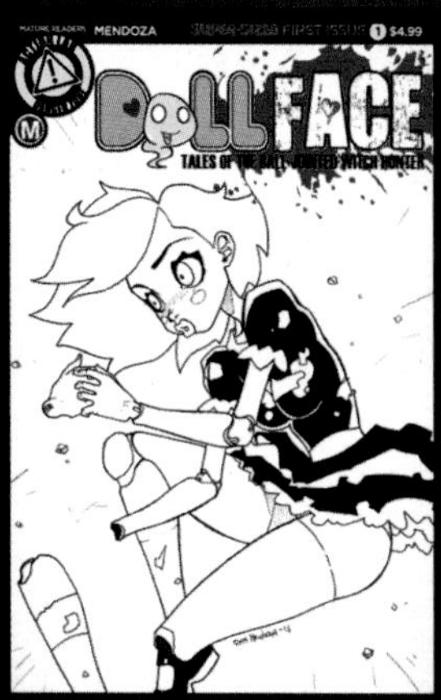
MATURE READERS
MENDOZA
$4.99
DOLL FACE

COVER F BY
MENDOZA SKETCH
NOV161050

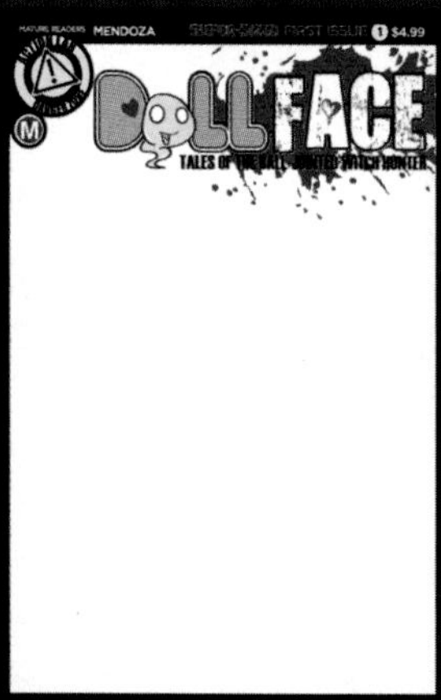
MATURE READERS
MENDOZA
$4.99
DOLL FACE

COVER G BY
BLANK SKETCH
NOV161051

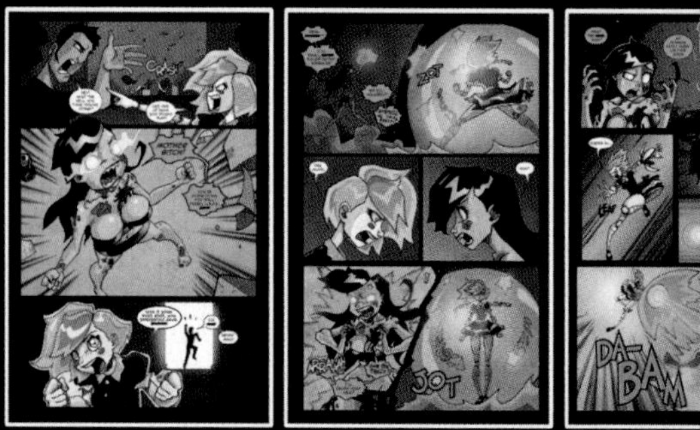
JOT
DA-BAM

LOOK PREVIEW PAGES!

RETAILER EXCLUSIVE COVERS
ALSO AVAILABLE! CONTACT
BSEATON@ACTIONLABCOMICS.COM

PRE-ORDER YOUR COPIES TODAY!

ACTIONLABCOMIC

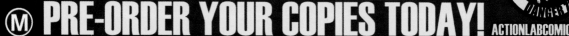

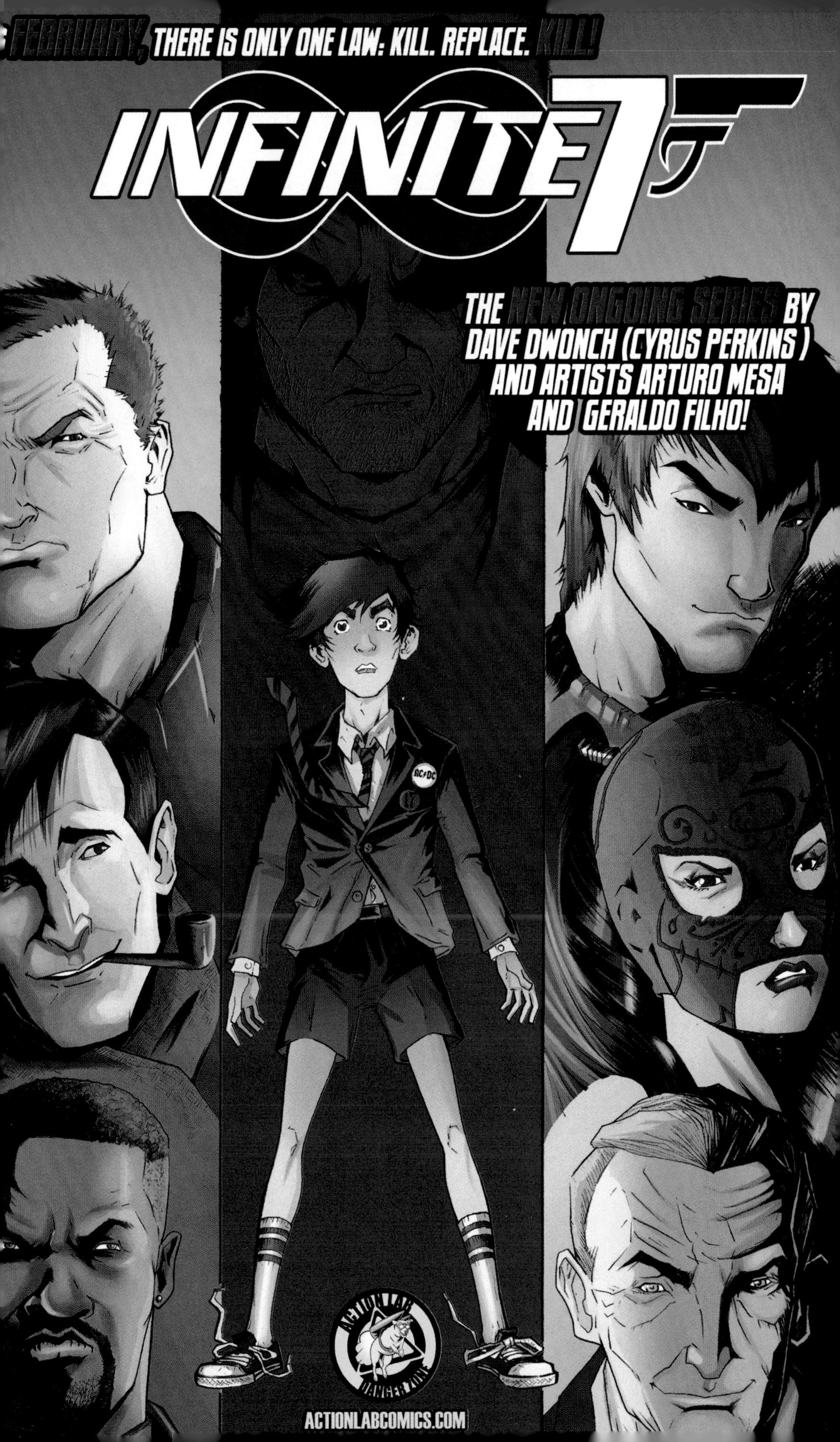

FEBRUARY, THERE IS ONLY ONE LAW: KILL. REPLACE. KILL!
INFINITE 7
THE NEW ONGOING SERIES BY
DAVE DWONCH (CYRUS PERKINS)
AND ARTISTS ARTURO MESA
AND GERALDO FILHO!
AC/DC
ACTION LAB
DANGER ZONE
ACTIONLABCOMICS.COM

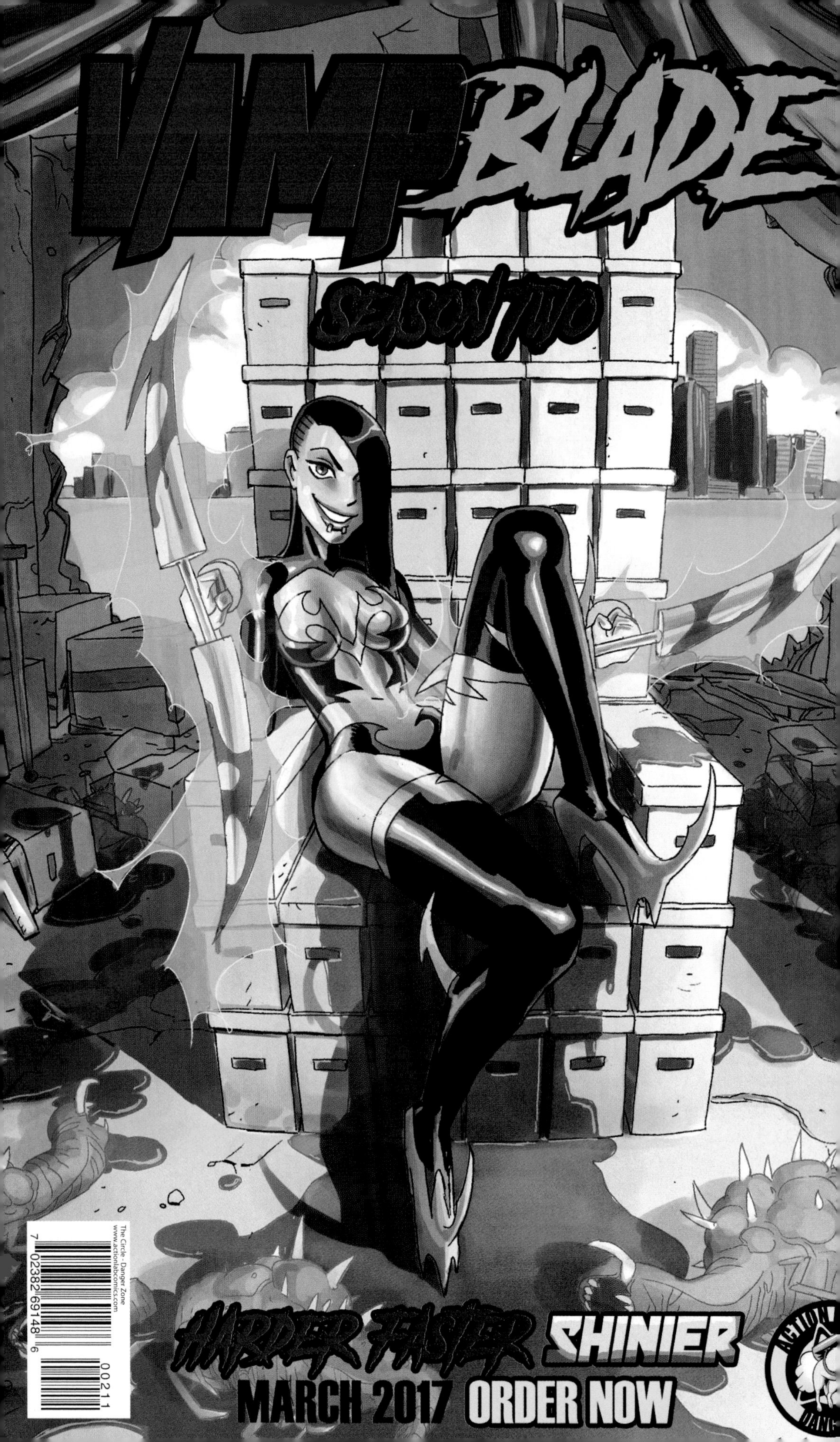

VAMPBLADE
SEASON TWO
HARDER FASTER SHINIER
MARCH 2017 ORDER NOW
The Circle - Danger Zone
www.actionlabcomics.com
7 02382 69148 6 00211

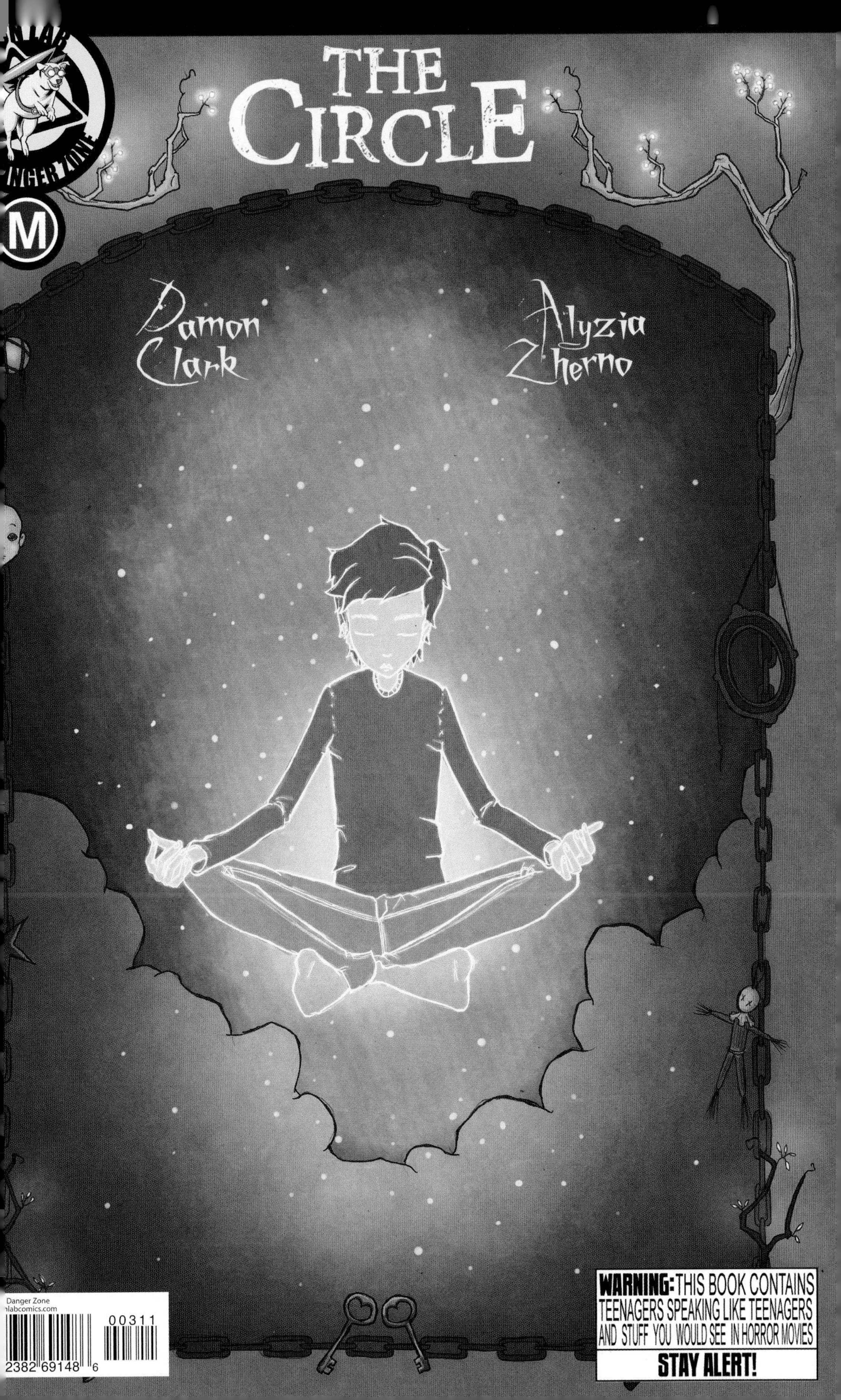
THE CIRCLE
M
Damon Clark
Alyzia Zherno
WARNING: THIS BOOK CONTAINS TEENAGERS SPEAKING LIKE TEENAGERS AND STUFF YOU WOULD SEE IN HORROR MOVIES
STAY ALERT!
Danger Zone
00311

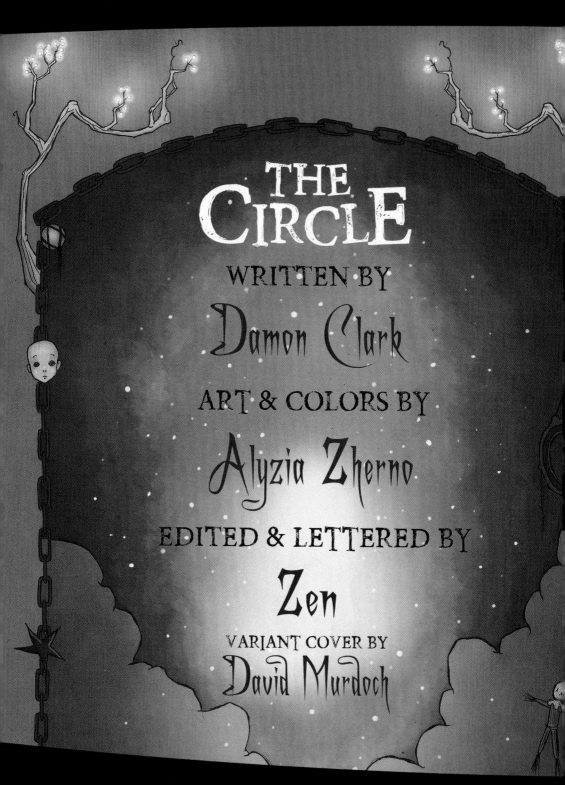

THE CIRCLE

WRITTEN BY

Damon Clark

ART & COLORS BY

Alyzia Zherno

EDITED & LETTERED BY

Zen

VARIANT COVER BY

David Murdoch

JASON MARTIN - PUBLISHER
DAVE DWONCH - PRESIDENT OF MARKETING
SHAWN GABBORIN - EDITOR IN CHIEF
NICOLE D'ANDRIA - MARKETING DIRECTOR/EDITOR
JIM DIETZ - SOCIAL MEDIA MANAGER
SCOTT BRADLEY - CFO
BRYAN SEATON - CEO

THE CIRCLE #3. February 2017.
Copyright Damon Clark and Alyzia Zherno, 2017.
Published by Action Lab Comics.
All rights reserved.

ACTIONLABCOMICS.COM

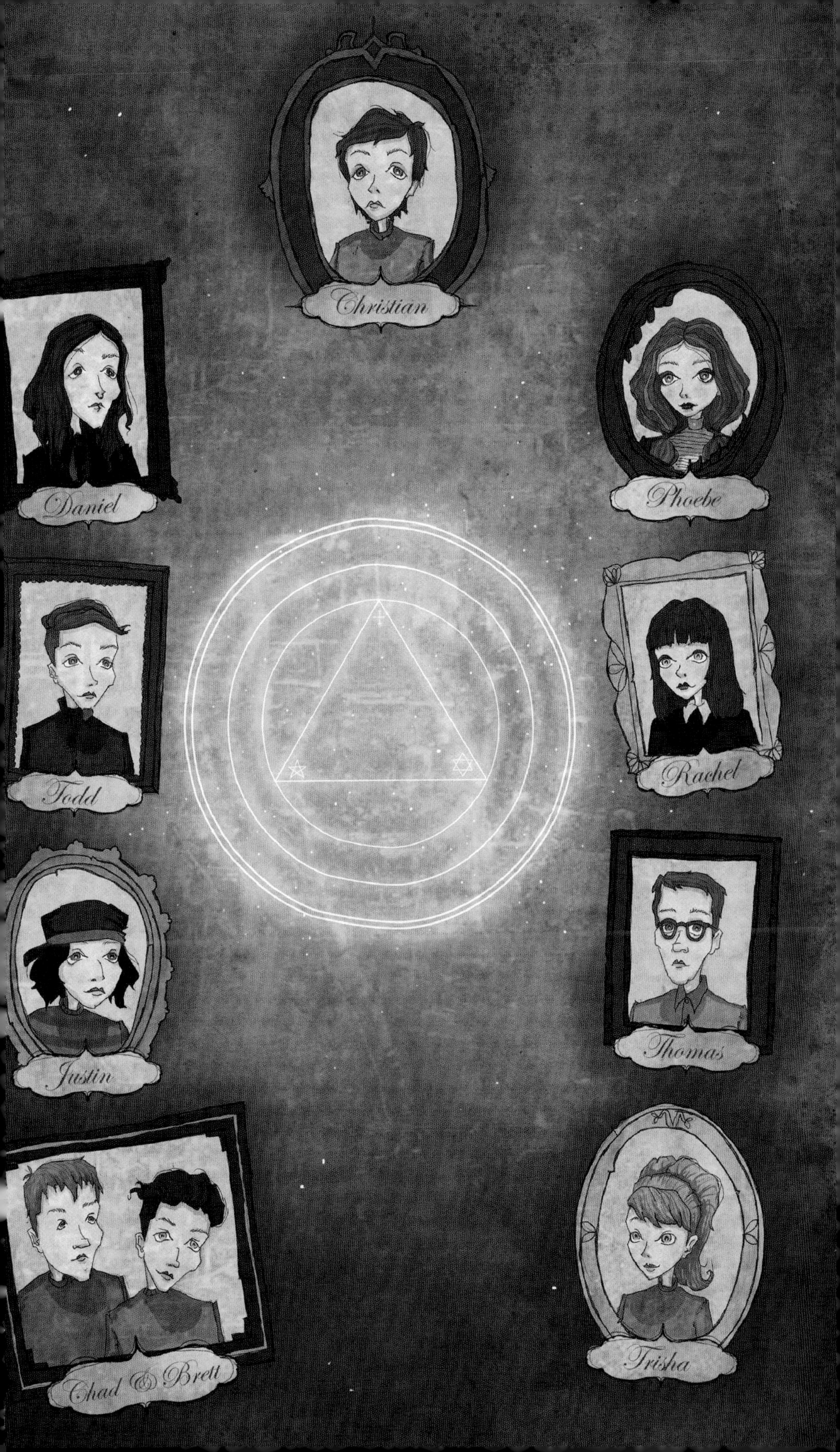
Christian
Daniel
Phoebe
Todd
Rachel
Justin
Thomas
Chad & Brett
Trisha

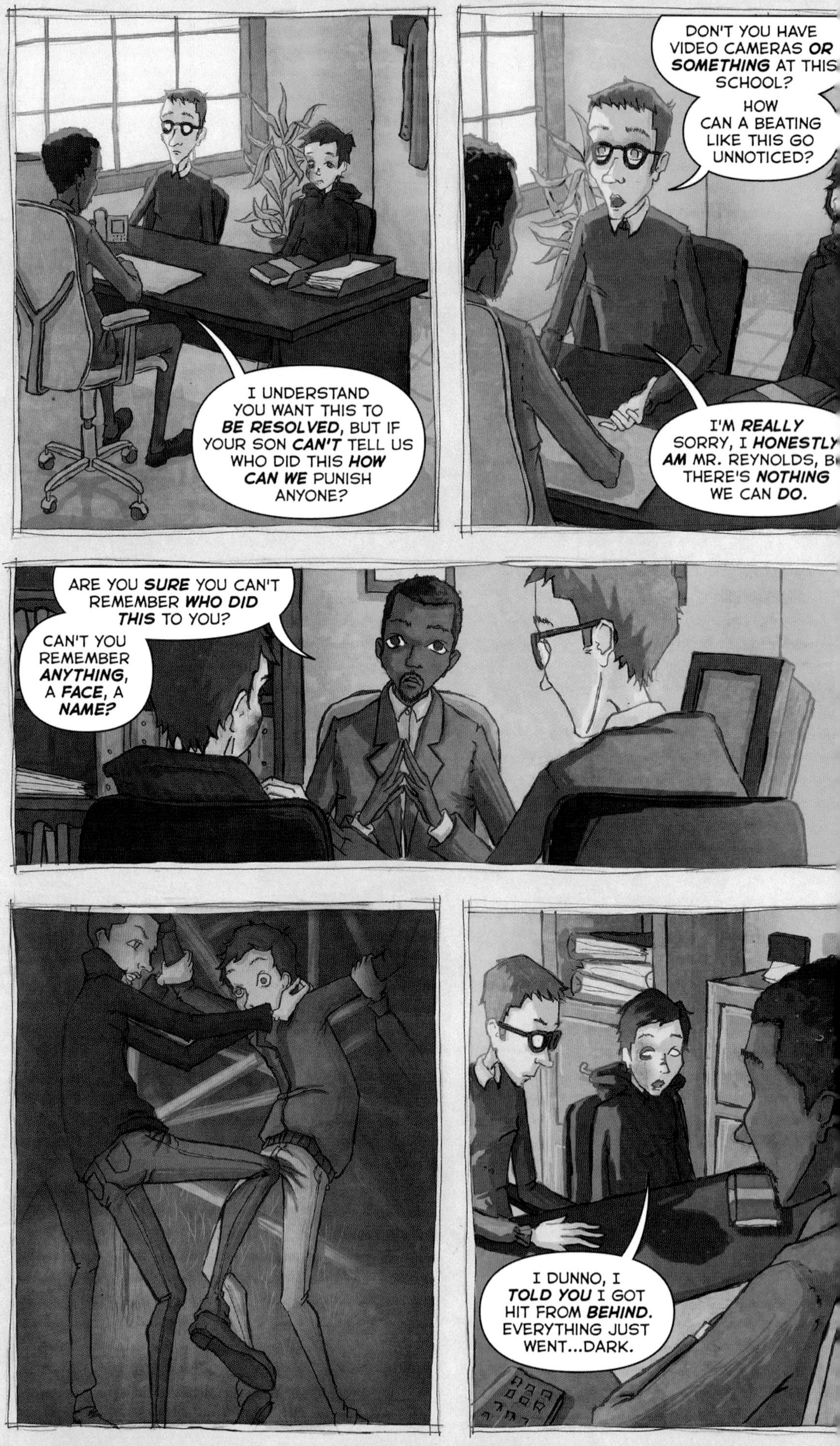
I UNDERSTAND YOU WANT THIS TO BE RESOLVED, BUT IF YOUR SON CAN'T TELL US WHO DID THIS HOW CAN WE PUNISH ANYONE?
DON'T YOU HAVE VIDEO CAMERAS OR SOMETHING AT THIS SCHOOL?
HOW CAN A BEATING LIKE THIS GO UNNOTICED?
I'M REALLY SORRY, I HONESTLY AM MR. REYNOLDS, B THERE'S NOTHING WE CAN DO.
ARE YOU SURE YOU CAN'T REMEMBER WHO DID THIS TO YOU?
CAN'T YOU REMEMBER ANYTHING, A FACE, A NAME?
I DUNNO, I TOLD YOU I GOT HIT FROM BEHIND. EVERYTHING JUST WENT...DARK.

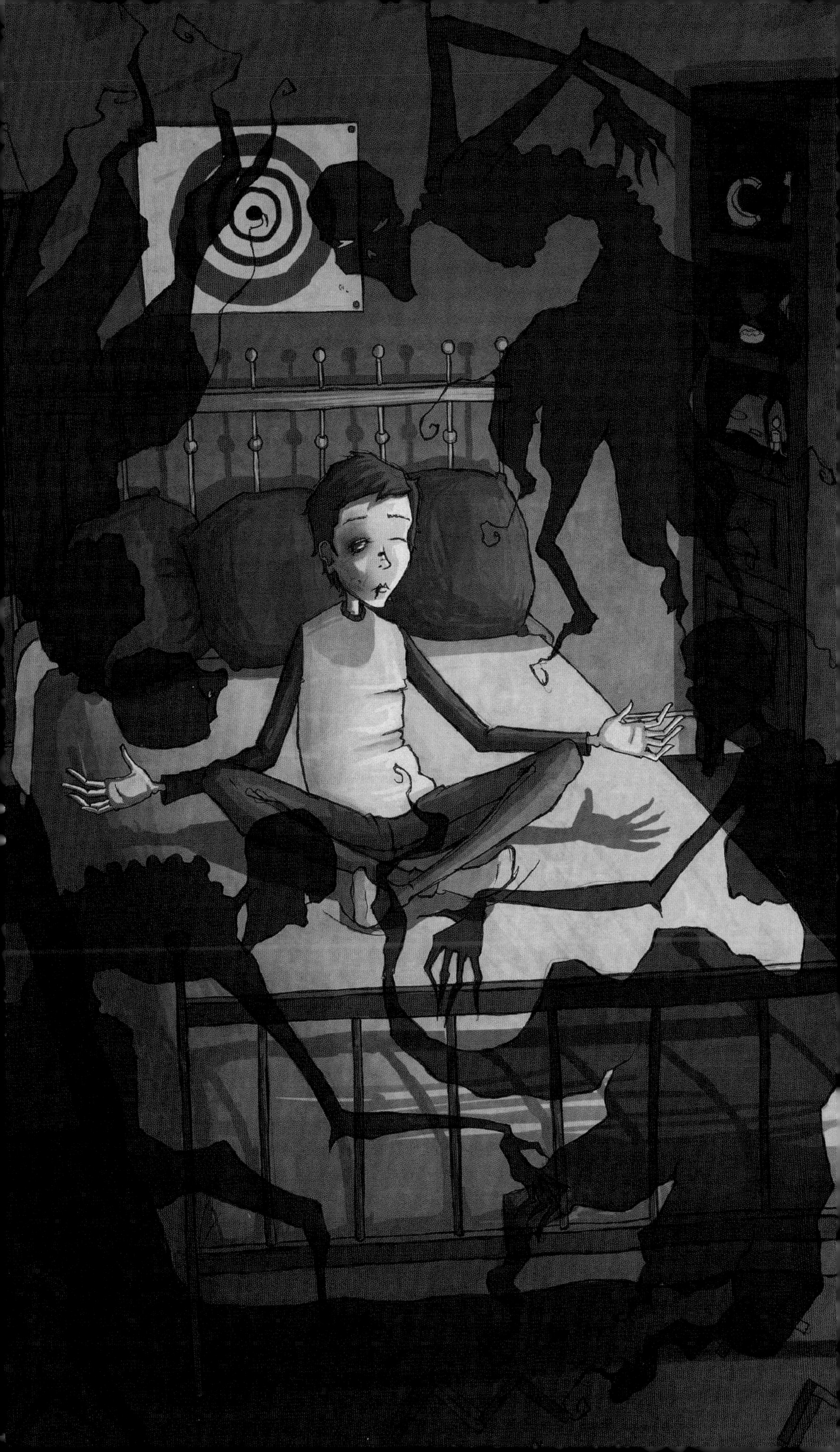

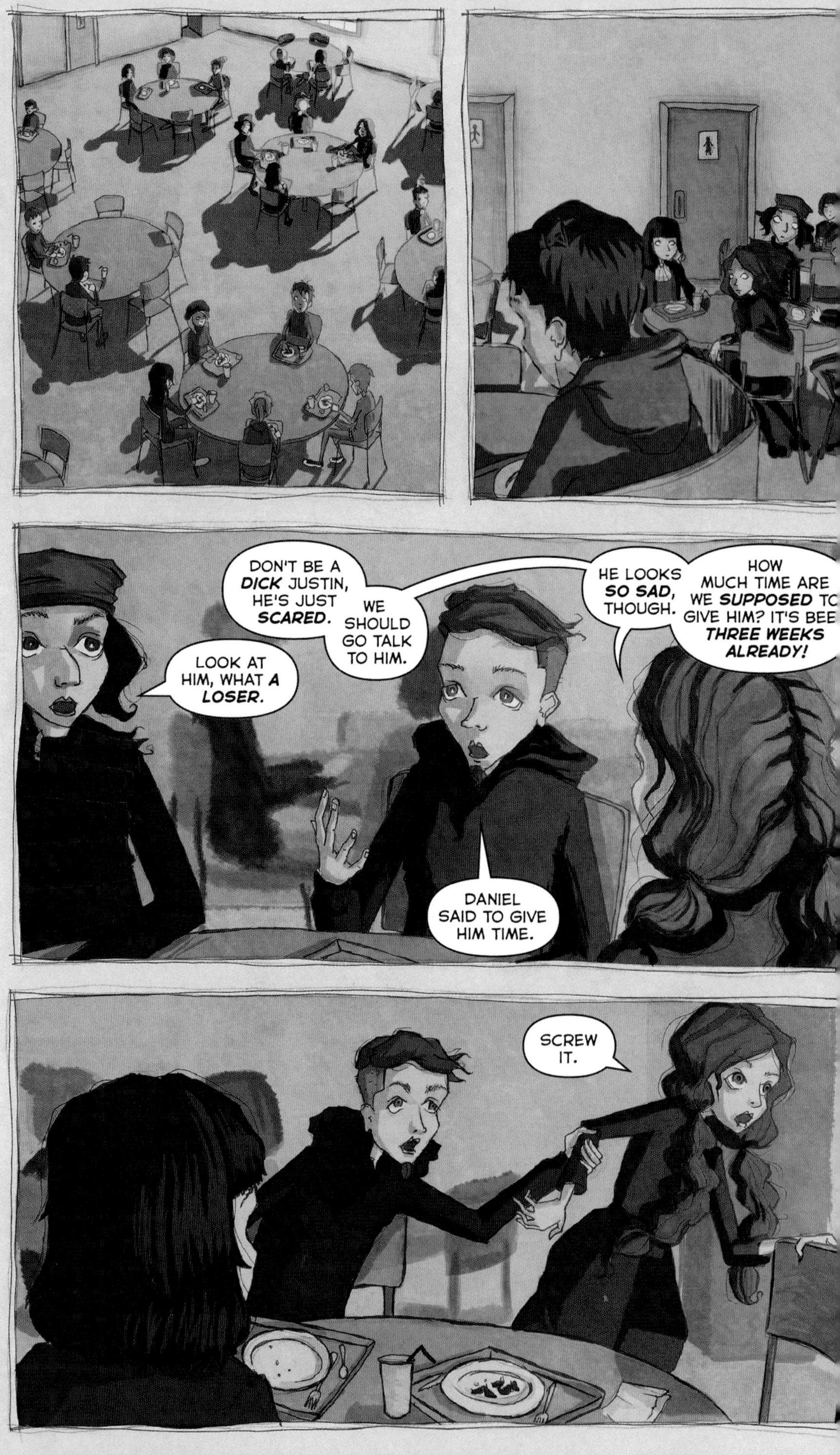
LOOK AT HIM, WHAT A LOSER.
DON'T BE A DICK JUSTIN, HE'S JUST SCARED.
WE SHOULD GO TALK TO HIM.
HE LOOKS SO SAD, THOUGH.
HOW MUCH TIME ARE WE SUPPOSED TO GIVE HIM? IT'S BEE THREE WEEKS ALREADY!
DANIEL SAID TO GIVE HIM TIME.
SCREW IT.

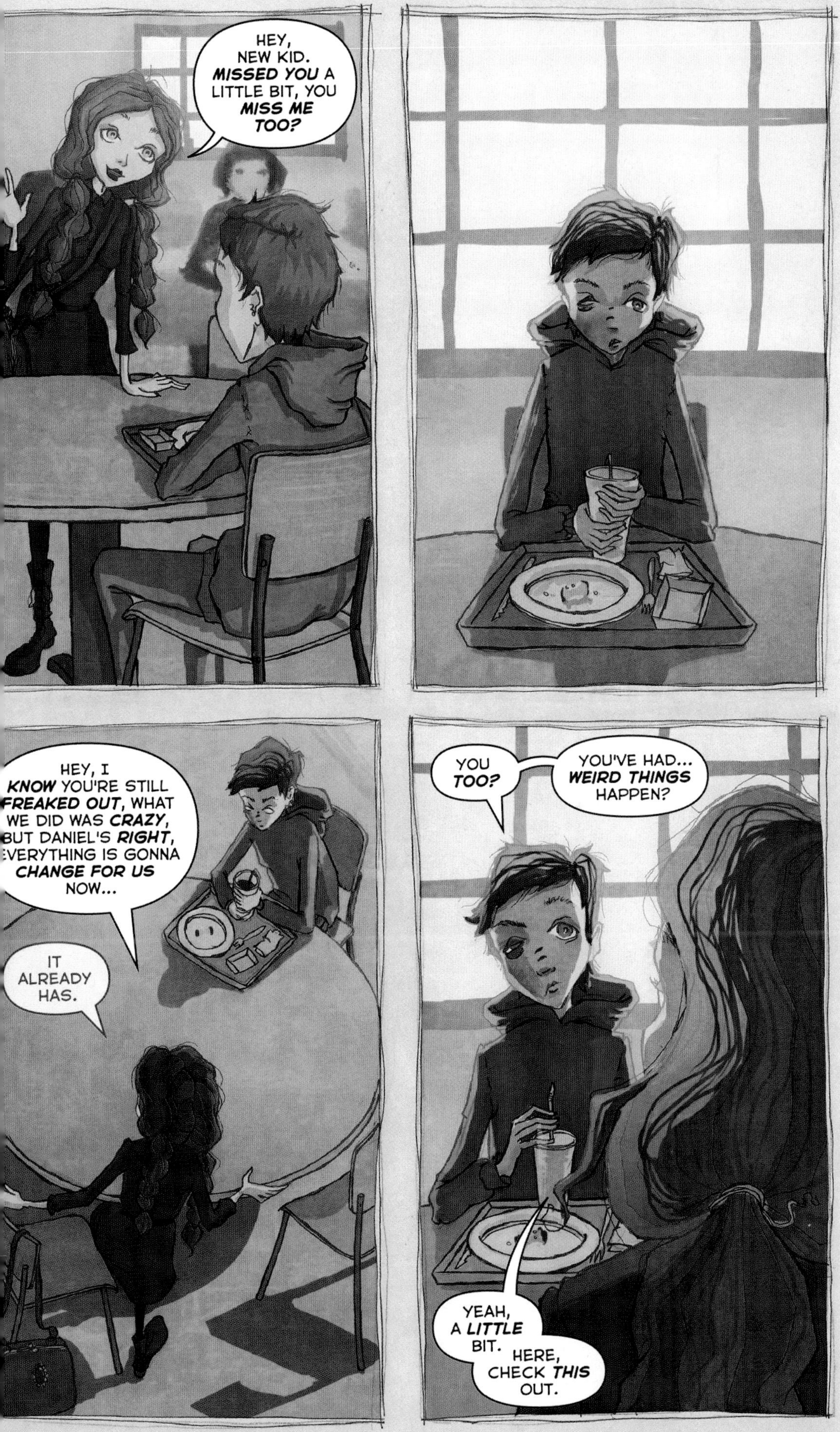
HEY, NEW KID. MISSED YOU A LITTLE BIT, YOU MISS ME TOO?
HEY, I KNOW YOU'RE STILL FREAKED OUT, WHAT WE DID WAS CRAZY, BUT DANIEL'S RIGHT, EVERYTHING IS GONNA CHANGE FOR US NOW...
IT ALREADY HAS.
YOU'VE HAD... WEIRD THINGS HAPPEN?
YOU TOO?
YEAH, A LITTLE BIT.
HERE, CHECK THIS OUT.

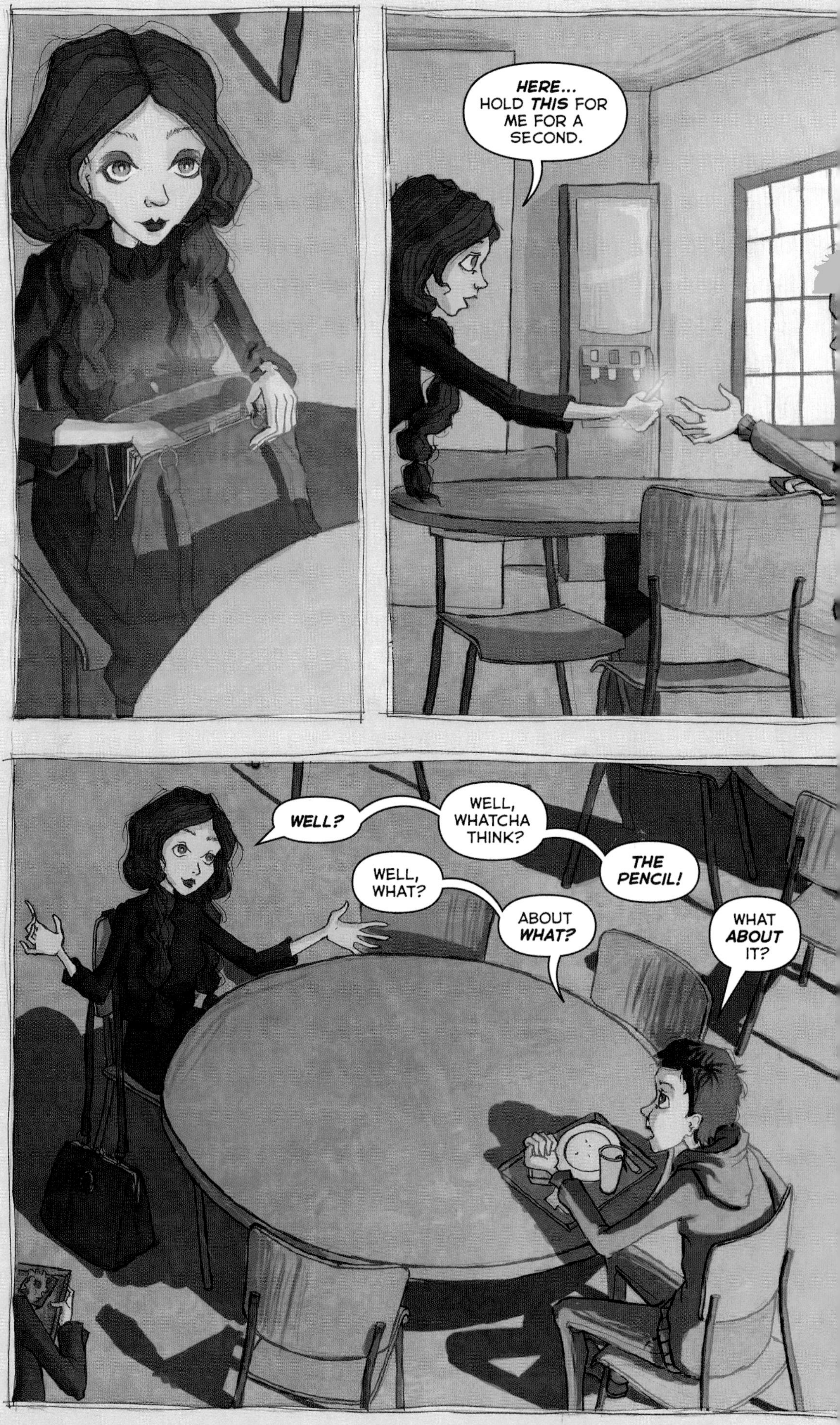
HERE... HOLD THIS FOR ME FOR A SECOND.
WELL?
WELL, WHAT?
WELL, WHATCHA THINK?
ABOUT WHAT?
THE PENCIL!
WHAT ABOUT IT?

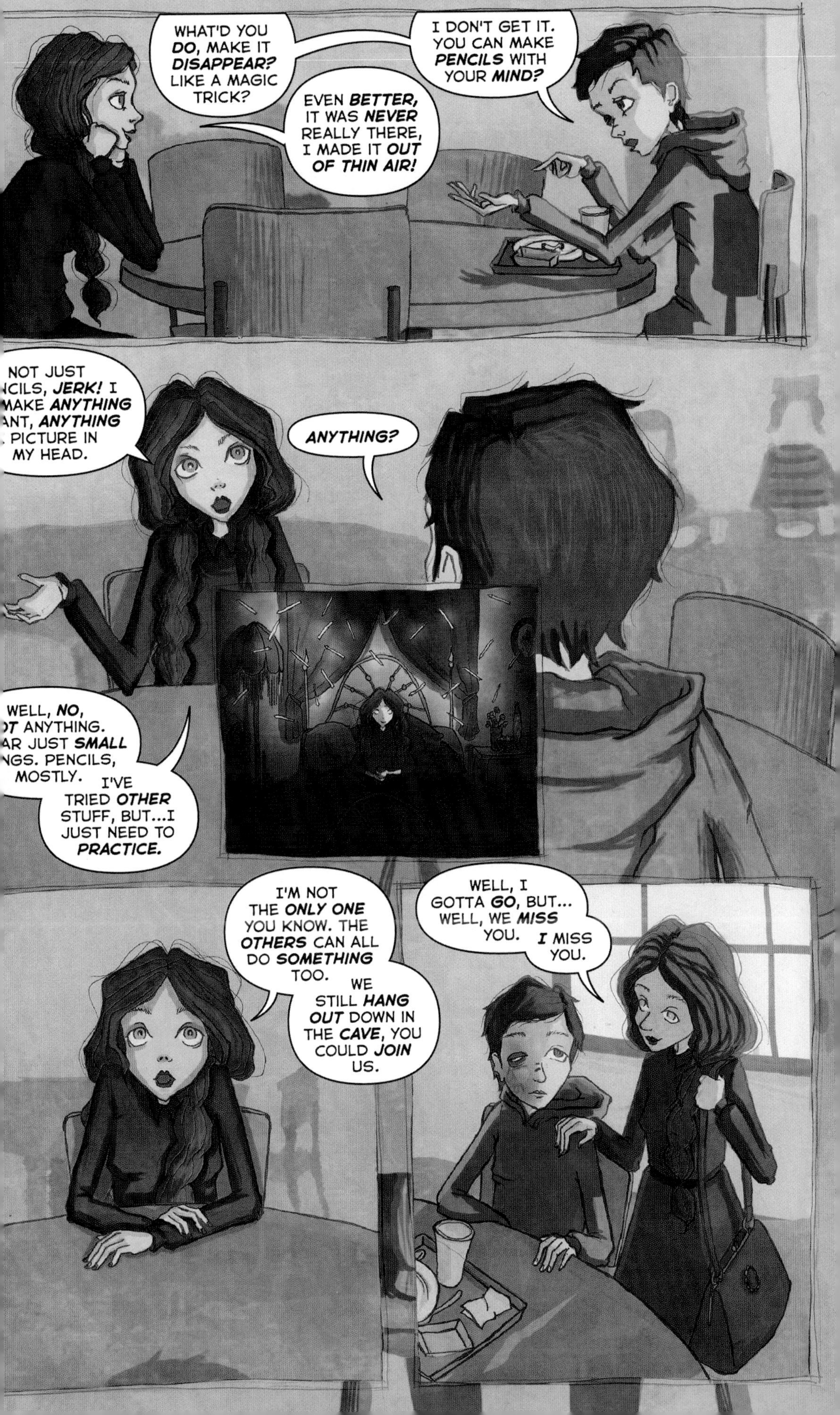
I DON'T GET IT. YOU CAN MAKE PENCILS WITH YOUR MIND?
WHAT'D YOU DO, MAKE IT DISAPPEAR? LIKE A MAGIC TRICK?
EVEN BETTER, IT WAS NEVER REALLY THERE, I MADE IT OUT OF THIN AIR!
NOT JUST
NCILS, JERK! I
MAKE ANYTHING
ANT, ANYTHING
PICTURE IN
MY HEAD.
ANYTHING?
WELL, NO,
OT ANYTHING.
AR JUST SMALL
NGS. PENCILS,
MOSTLY.
I'VE TRIED OTHER STUFF, BUT...I JUST NEED TO PRACTICE.
I'M NOT THE ONLY ONE YOU KNOW. THE OTHERS CAN ALL DO SOMETHING TOO.
WE STILL HANG OUT DOWN IN THE CAVE, YOU COULD JOIN US.
WELL, I GOTTA GO, BUT... WELL, WE MISS YOU.
I MISS YOU.

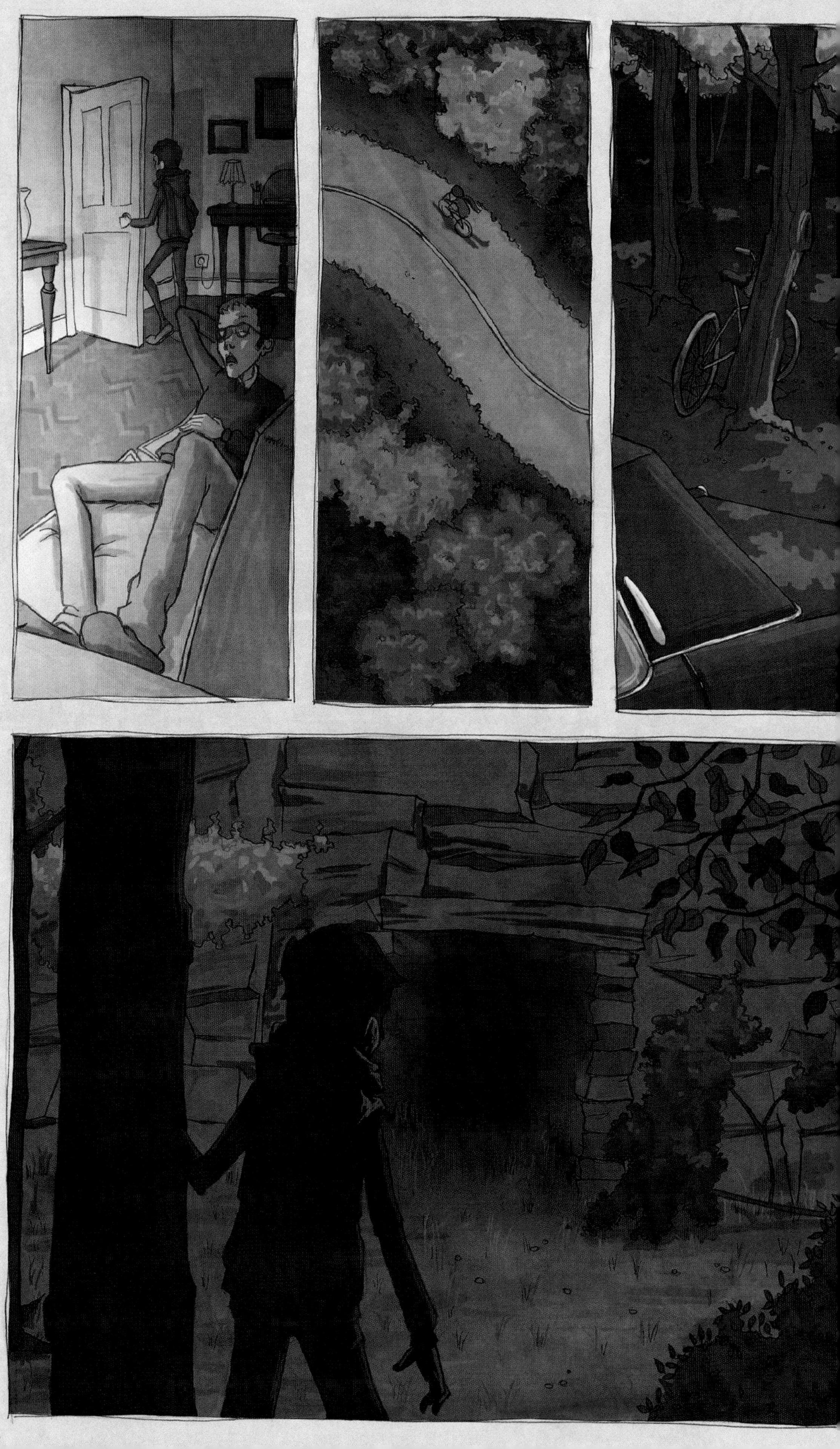

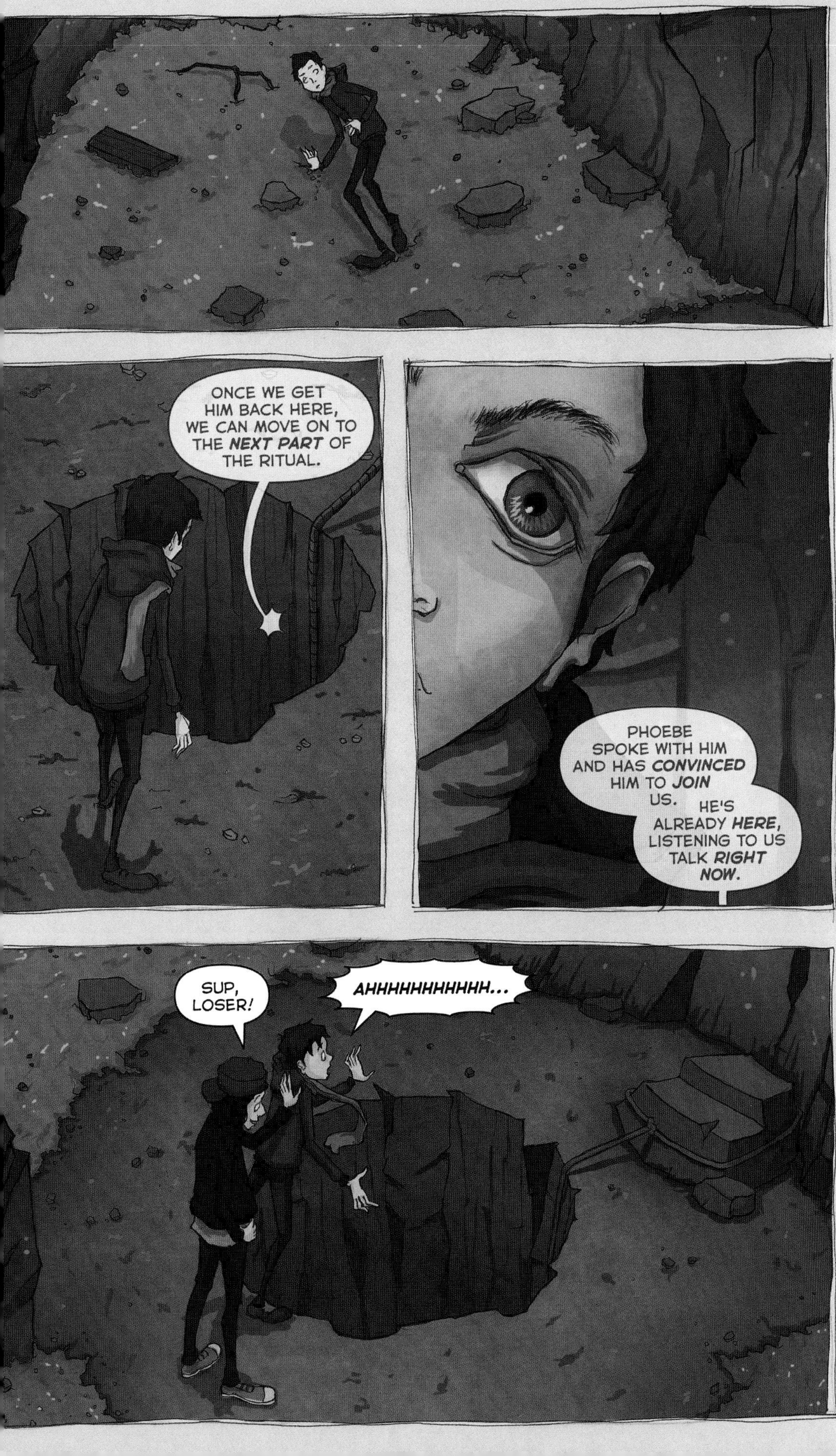
ONCE WE GET HIM BACK HERE, WE CAN MOVE ON TO THE NEXT PART OF THE RITUAL.
PHOEBE SPOKE WITH HIM AND HAS CONVINCED HIM TO JOIN US.
HE'S ALREADY HERE, LISTENING TO US TALK RIGHT NOW.
SUP, LOSER!
AHHHHHHHHHHH...

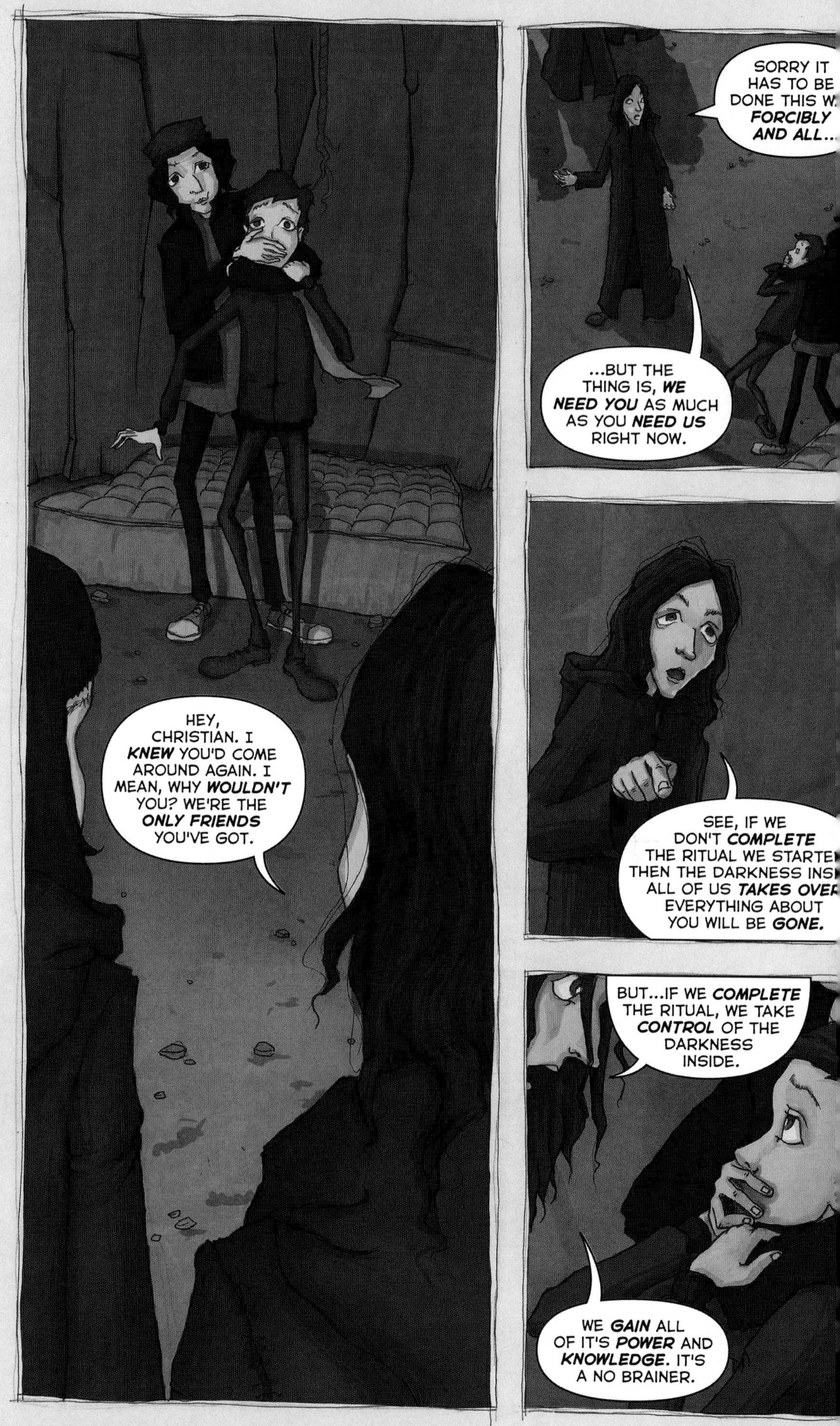
HEY, CHRISTIAN. I **KNEW** YOU'D COME AROUND AGAIN. I MEAN, WHY **WOULDN'T** YOU? WE'RE THE **ONLY FRIENDS** YOU'VE GOT.
SORRY IT HAS TO BE DONE THIS W **FORCIBLY AND ALL...**
...BUT THE THING IS, **WE NEED YOU** AS MUCH AS YOU **NEED US** RIGHT NOW.
SEE, IF WE DON'T **COMPLETE** THE RITUAL WE STARTE THEN THE DARKNESS INS ALL OF US **TAKES OVE** EVERYTHING ABOUT YOU WILL BE **GONE.**
BUT...IF WE **COMPLETE** THE RITUAL, WE TAKE **CONTROL** OF THE DARKNESS INSIDE.
WE **GAIN** ALL OF IT'S **POWER** AND **KNOWLEDGE.** IT'S A NO BRAINER.

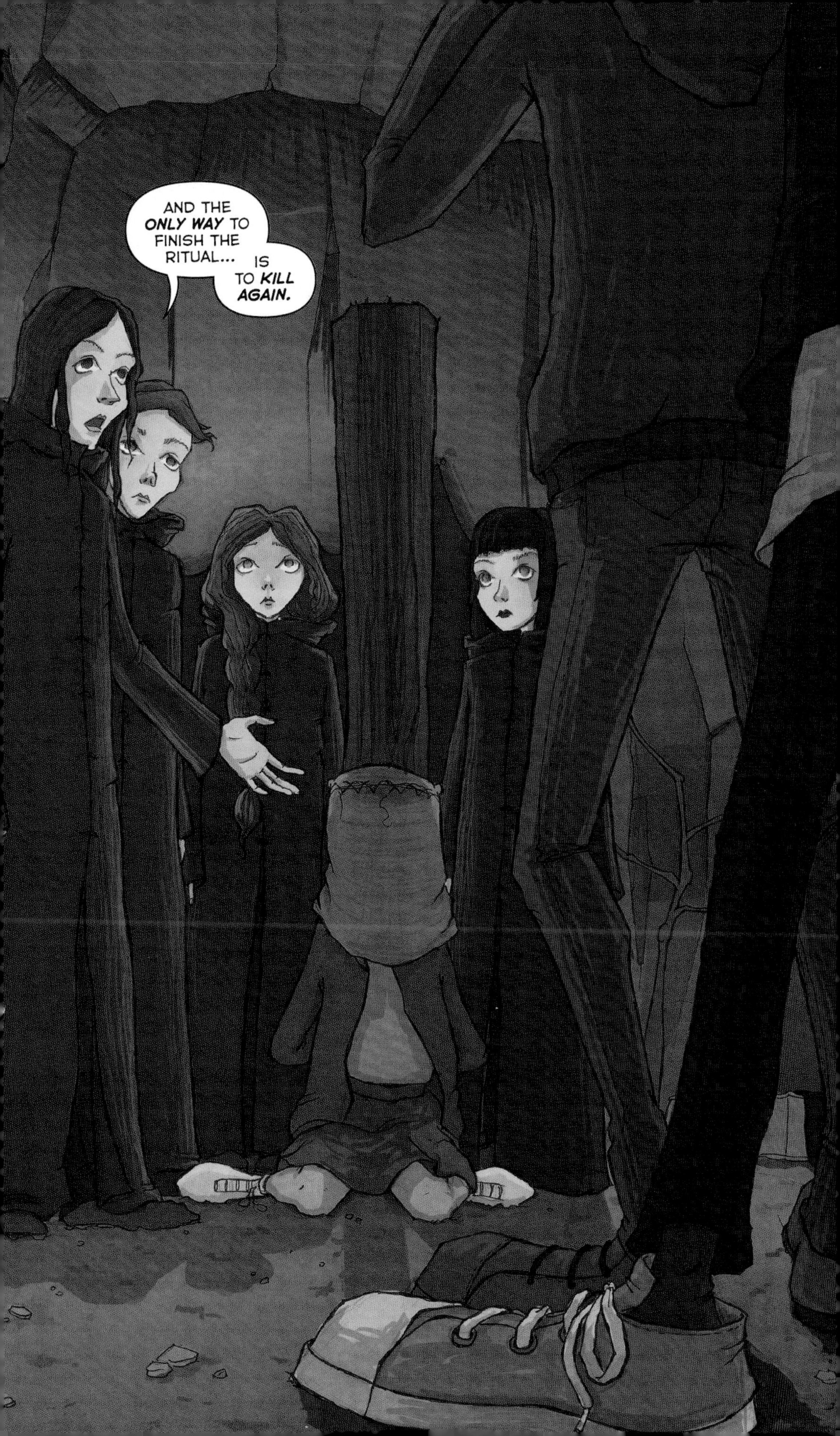
AND THE ONLY WAY TO FINISH THE RITUAL...
IS TO KILL AGAIN.

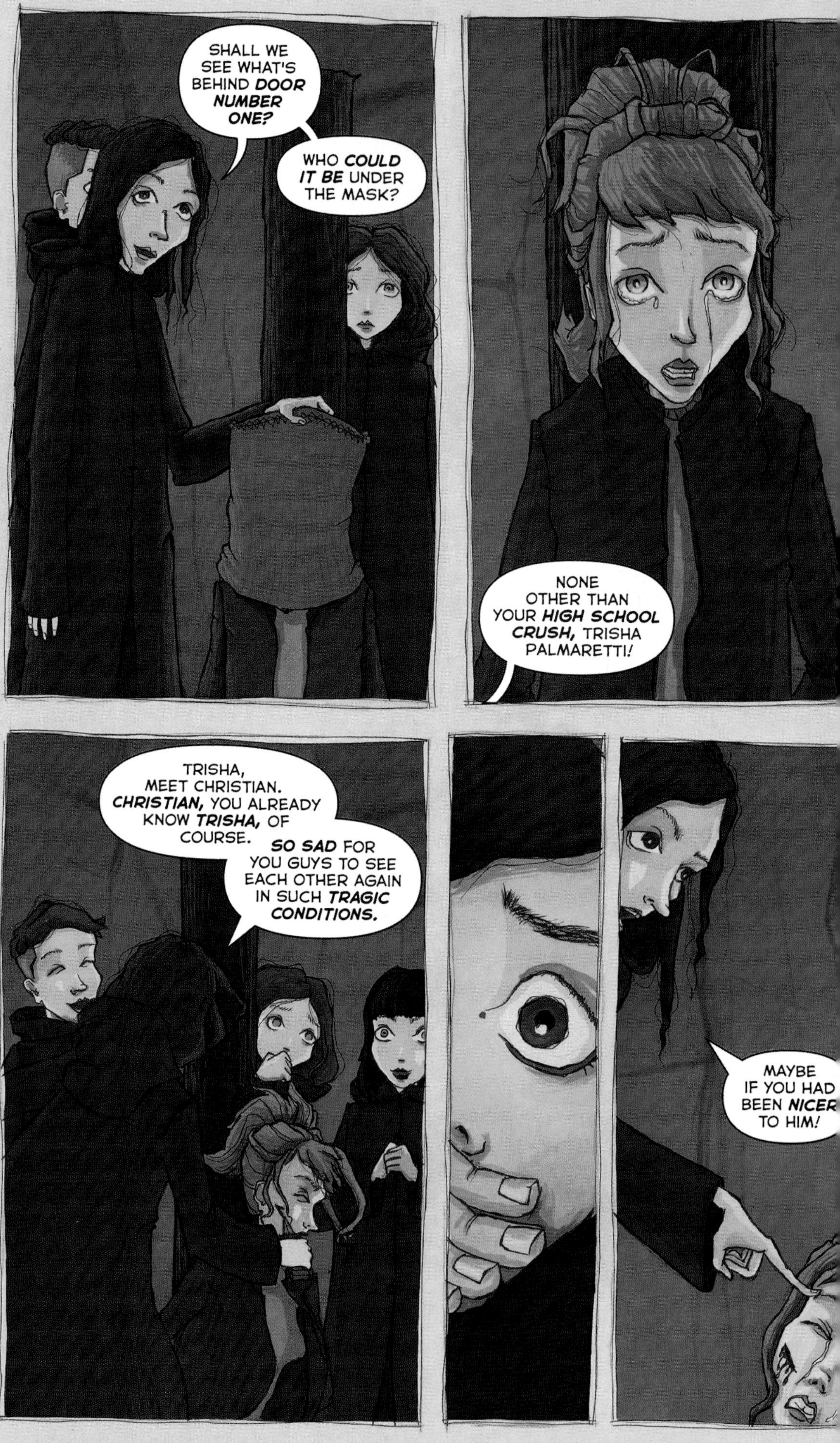
SHALL WE SEE WHAT'S BEHIND DOOR NUMBER ONE?
WHO COULD IT BE UNDER THE MASK?
NONE OTHER THAN YOUR HIGH SCHOOL CRUSH, TRISHA PALMARETTI!
TRISHA, MEET CHRISTIAN. CHRISTIAN, YOU ALREADY KNOW TRISHA, OF COURSE.
SO SAD FOR YOU GUYS TO SEE EACH OTHER AGAIN IN SUCH TRAGIC CONDITIONS.
MAYBE IF YOU HAD BEEN NICER TO HIM!

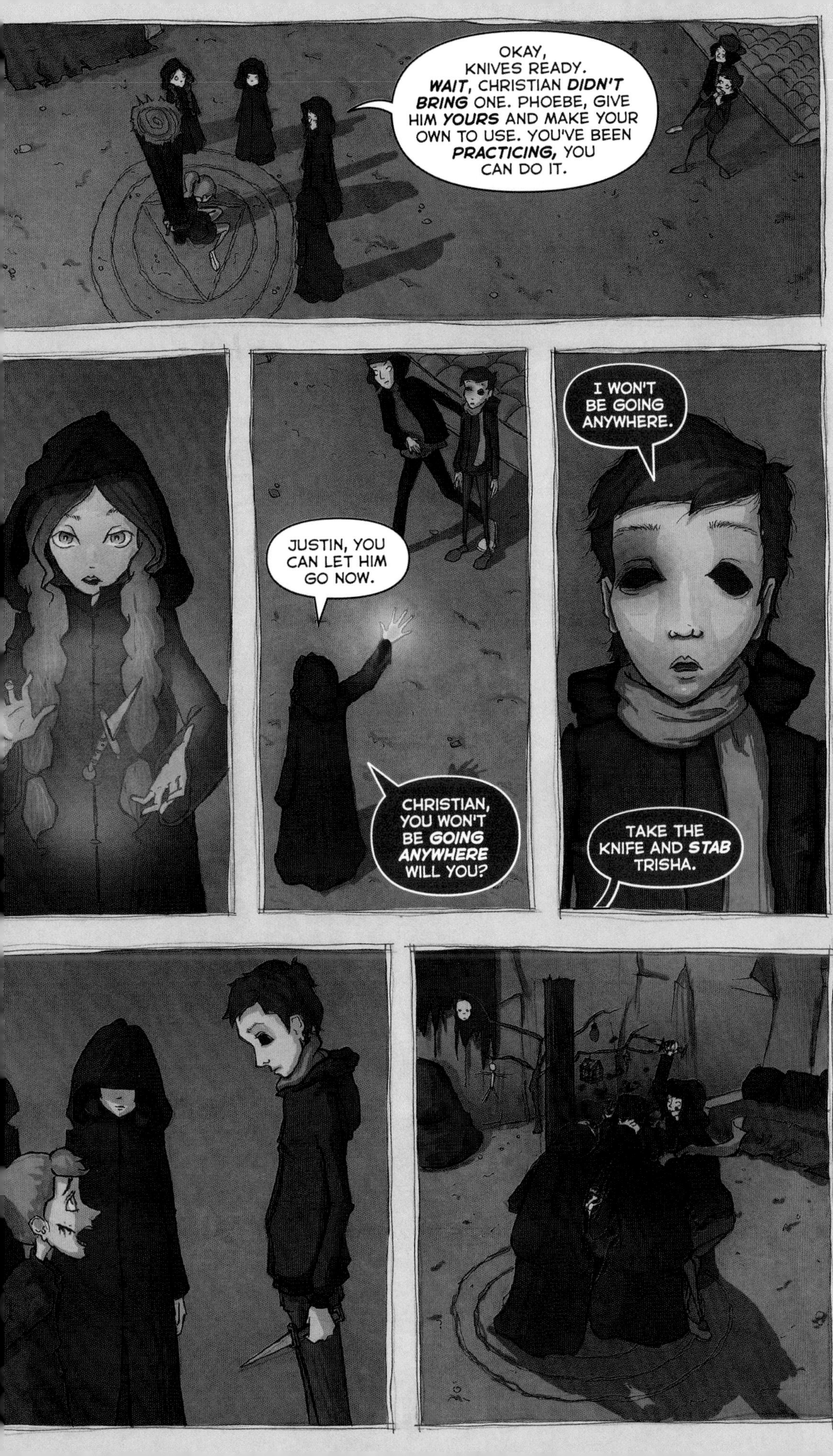
OKAY, KNIVES READY. WAIT, CHRISTIAN DIDN'T BRING ONE. PHOEBE, GIVE HIM YOURS AND MAKE YOUR OWN TO USE. YOU'VE BEEN PRACTICING, YOU CAN DO IT.
JUSTIN, YOU CAN LET HIM GO NOW.
CHRISTIAN, YOU WON'T BE GOING ANYWHERE WILL YOU?
I WON'T BE GOING ANYWHERE.
TAKE THE KNIFE AND STAB TRISHA.

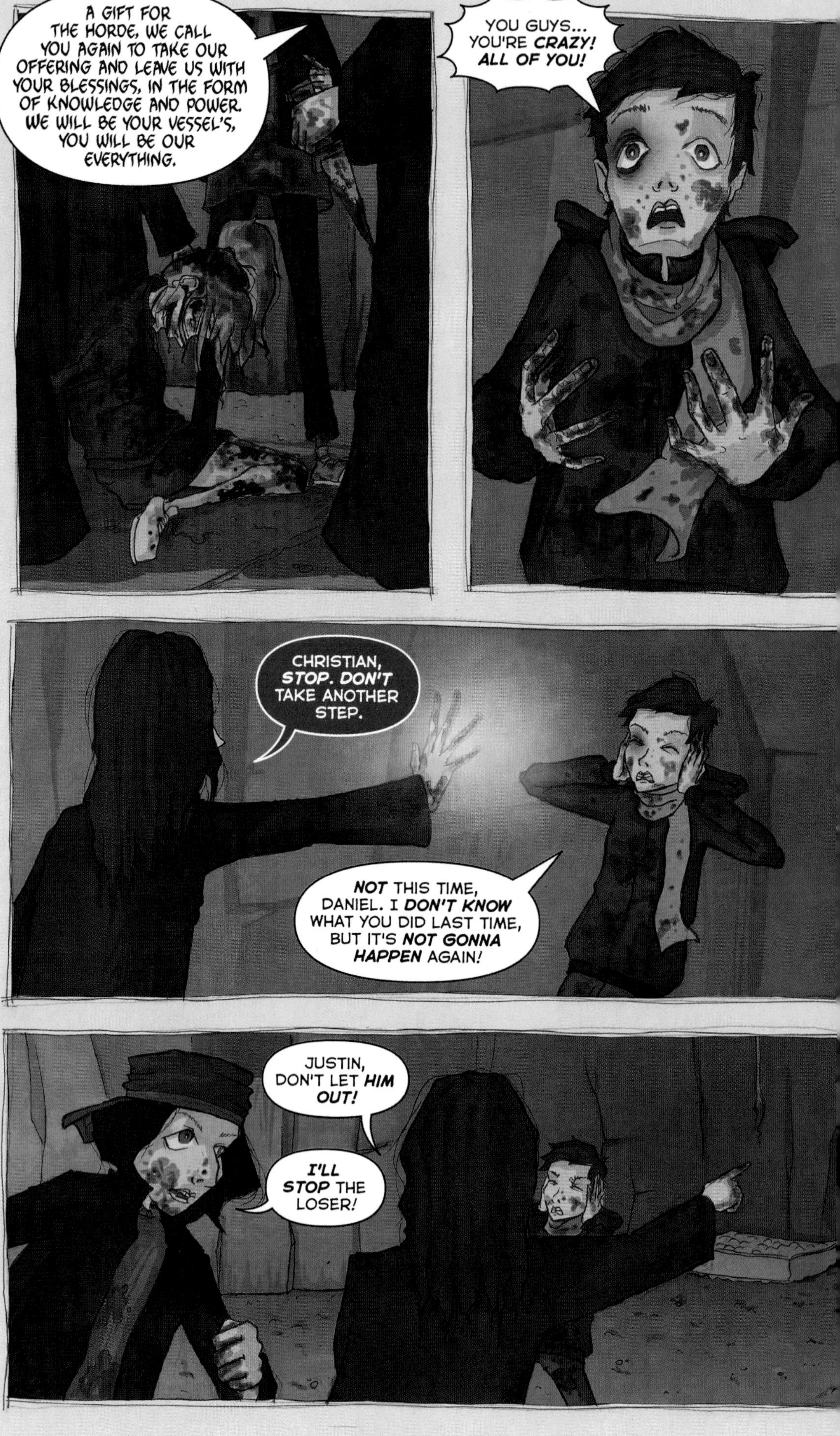
A GIFT FOR THE HORDE, WE CALL YOU AGAIN TO TAKE OUR OFFERING AND LEAVE US WITH YOUR BLESSINGS, IN THE FORM OF KNOWLEDGE AND POWER. WE WILL BE YOUR VESSEL'S, YOU WILL BE OUR EVERYTHING.
YOU GUYS... YOU'RE CRAZY! ALL OF YOU!
CHRISTIAN, STOP. DON'T TAKE ANOTHER STEP.
NOT THIS TIME, DANIEL. I DON'T KNOW WHAT YOU DID LAST TIME, BUT IT'S NOT GONNA HAPPEN AGAIN!
JUSTIN, DON'T LET HIM OUT!
I'LL STOP THE LOSER!

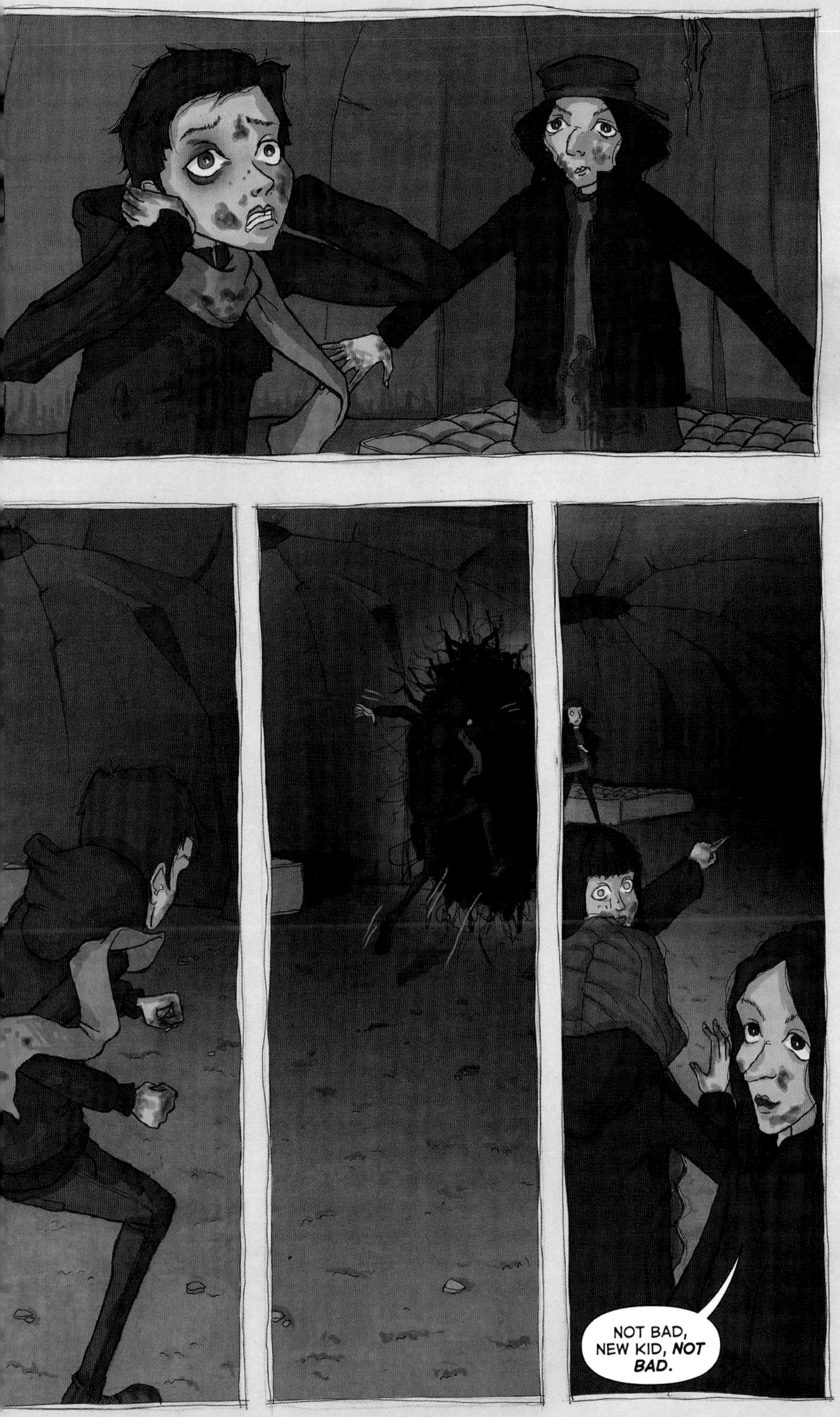
NOT BAD, NEW KID, NOT BAD.

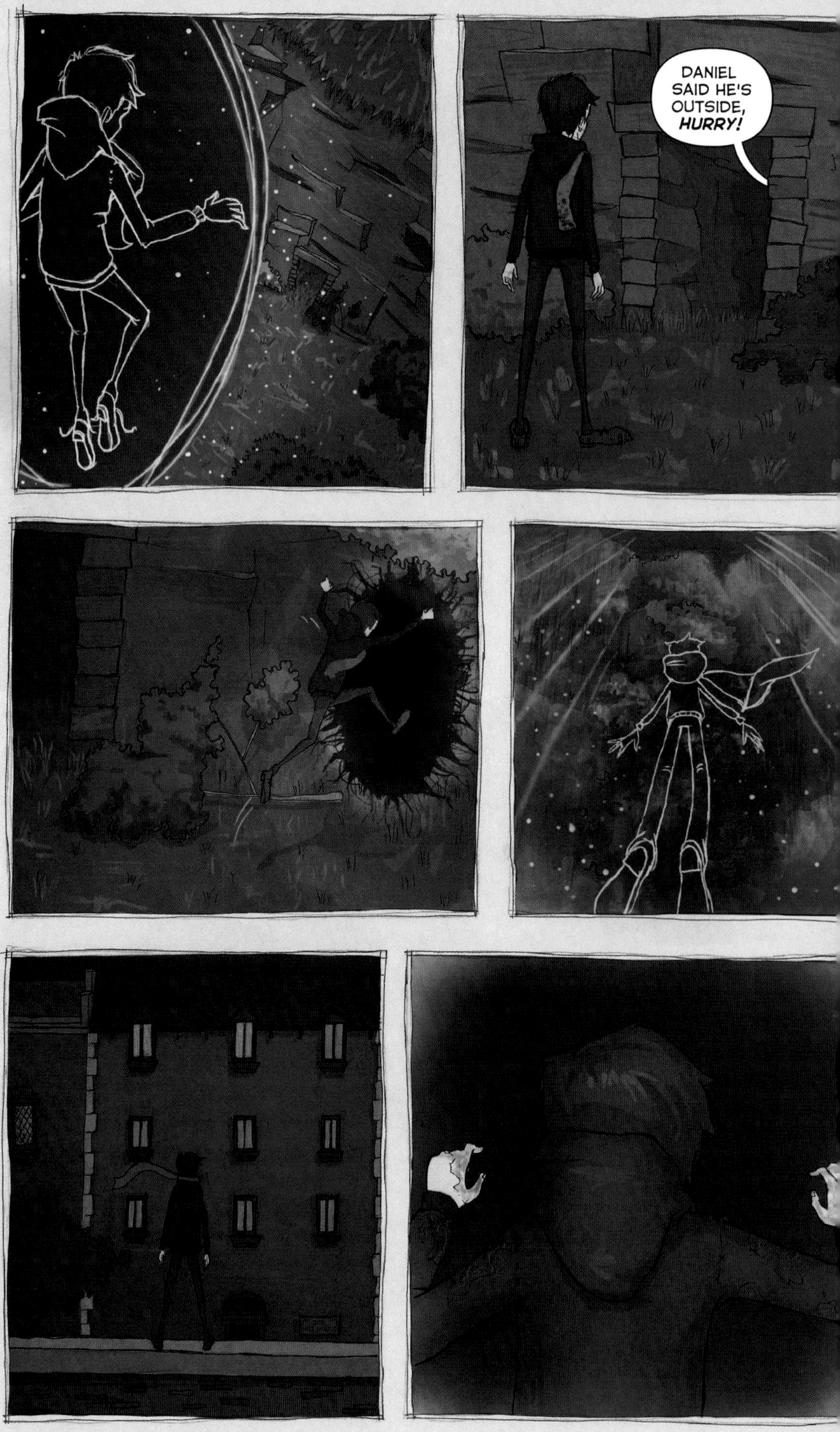
DANIEL SAID HE'S OUTSIDE, ***HURRY!***

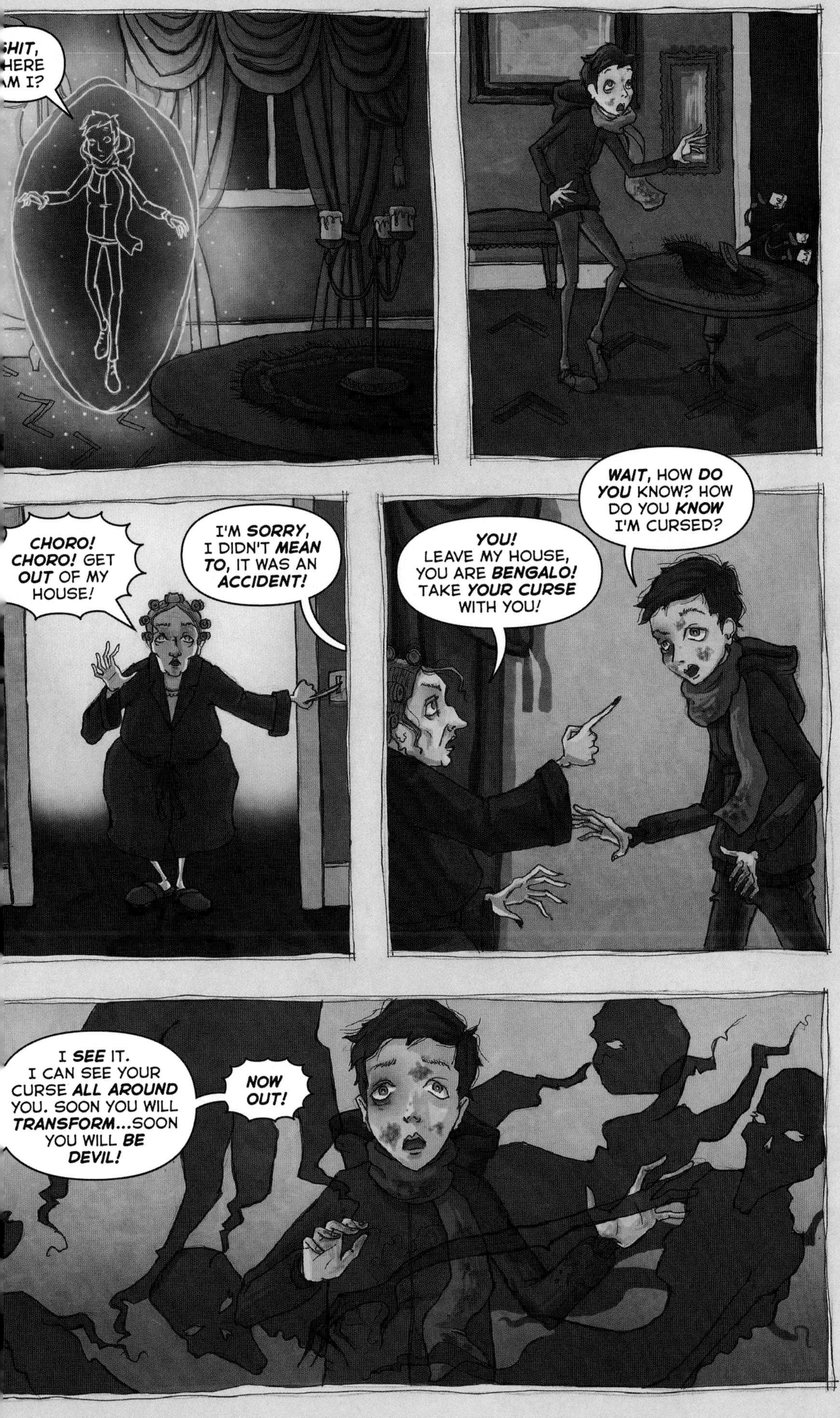
SHIT, HERE AM I?
CHORO! CHORO! GET OUT OF MY HOUSE!
I'M SORRY, I DIDN'T MEAN TO, IT WAS AN ACCIDENT!
YOU! LEAVE MY HOUSE, YOU ARE BENGALO! TAKE YOUR CURSE WITH YOU!
WAIT, HOW DO YOU KNOW? HOW DO YOU KNOW I'M CURSED?
I SEE IT. I CAN SEE YOUR CURSE ALL AROUND YOU. SOON YOU WILL TRANSFORM...SOON YOU WILL BE DEVIL!
NOW OUT!

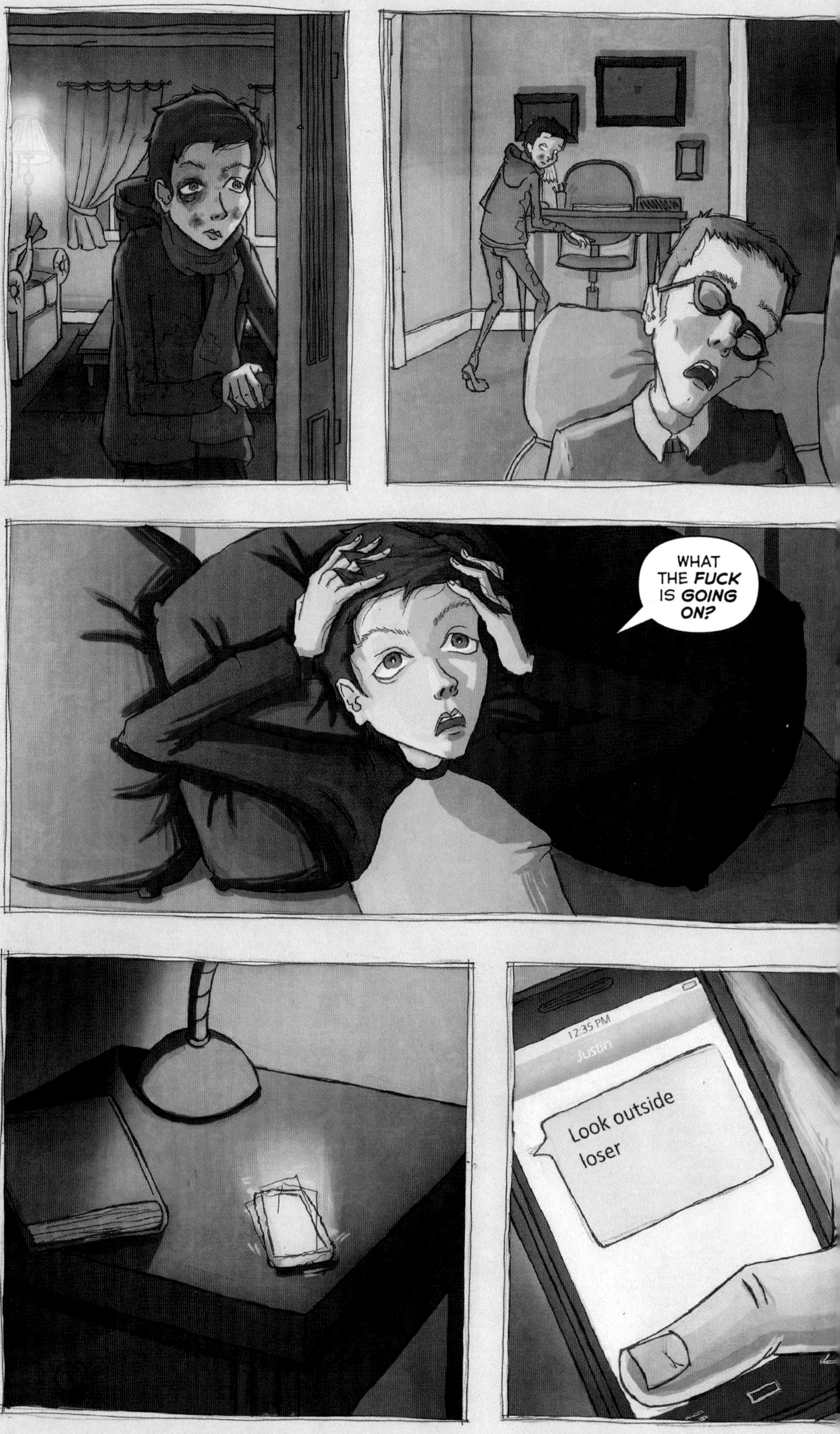
WHAT THE FUCK IS GOING ON?
12:35 PM
Justin
Look outside loser

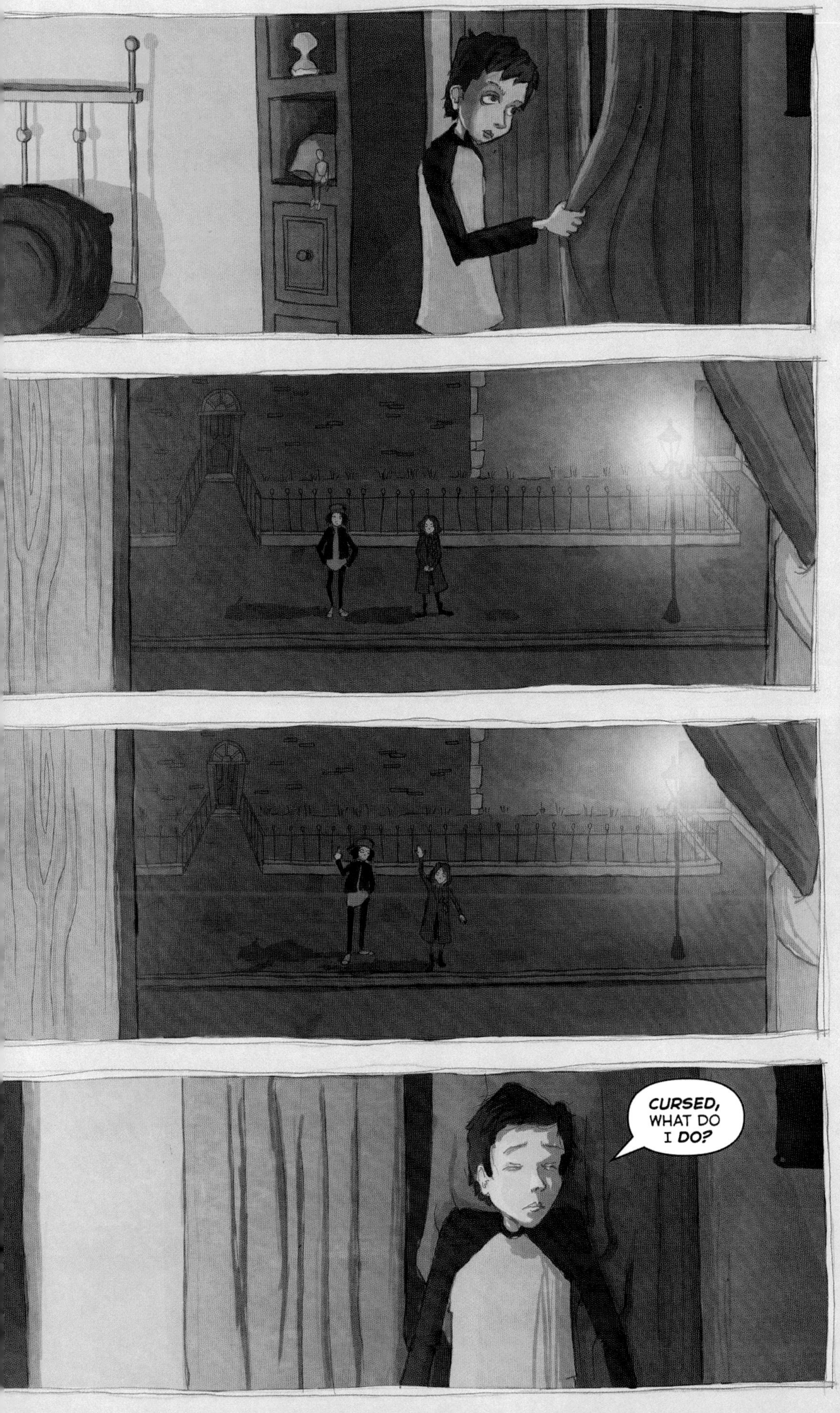
CURSED, WHAT DO I DO?

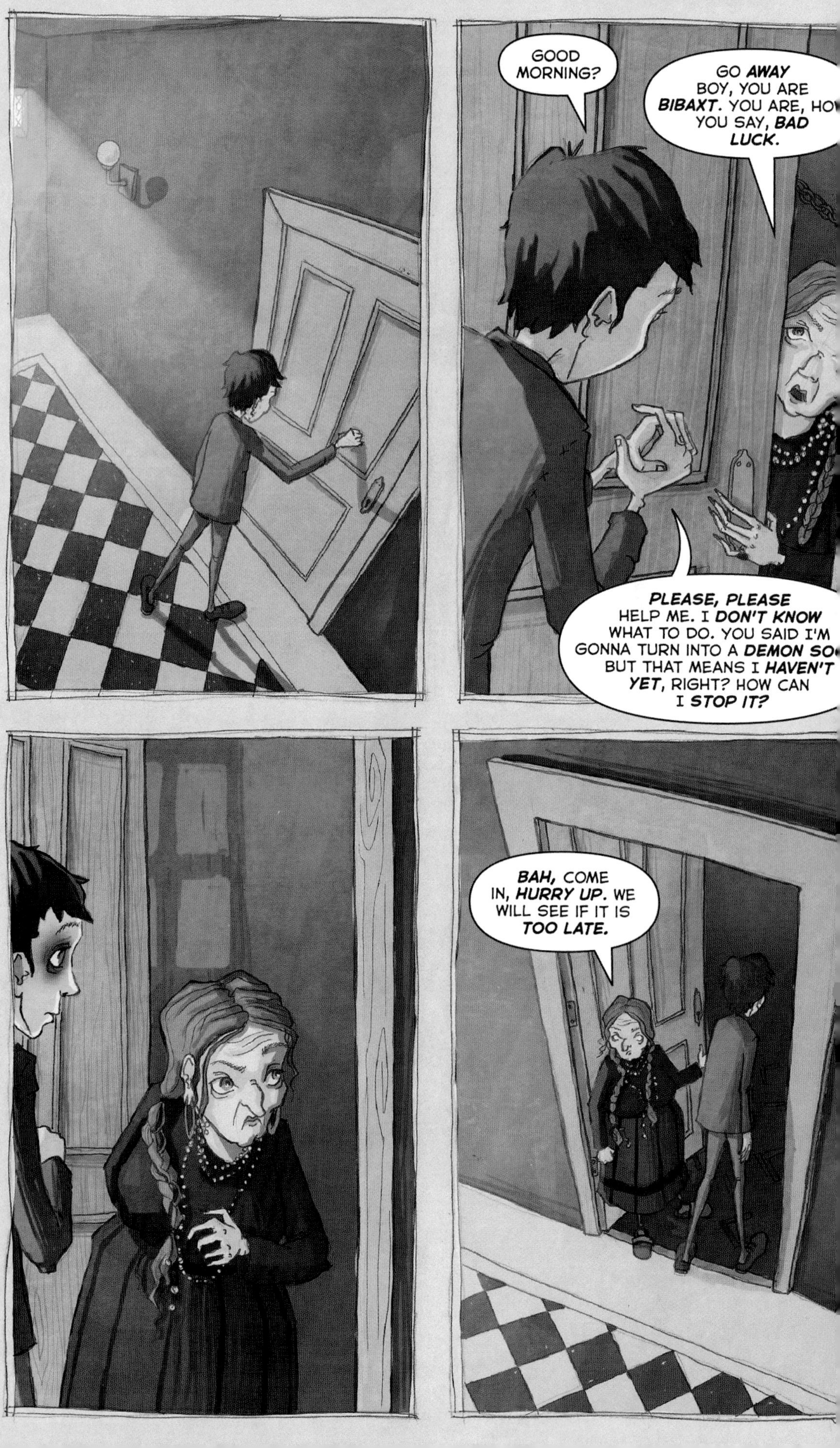
GOOD MORNING?
GO AWAY BOY, YOU ARE BIBAXT. YOU ARE, HO YOU SAY, BAD LUCK.
PLEASE, PLEASE HELP ME. I DON'T KNOW WHAT TO DO. YOU SAID I'M GONNA TURN INTO A DEMON SO BUT THAT MEANS I HAVEN'T YET, RIGHT? HOW CAN I STOP IT?
BAH, COME IN, HURRY UP. WE WILL SEE IF IT IS TOO LATE.

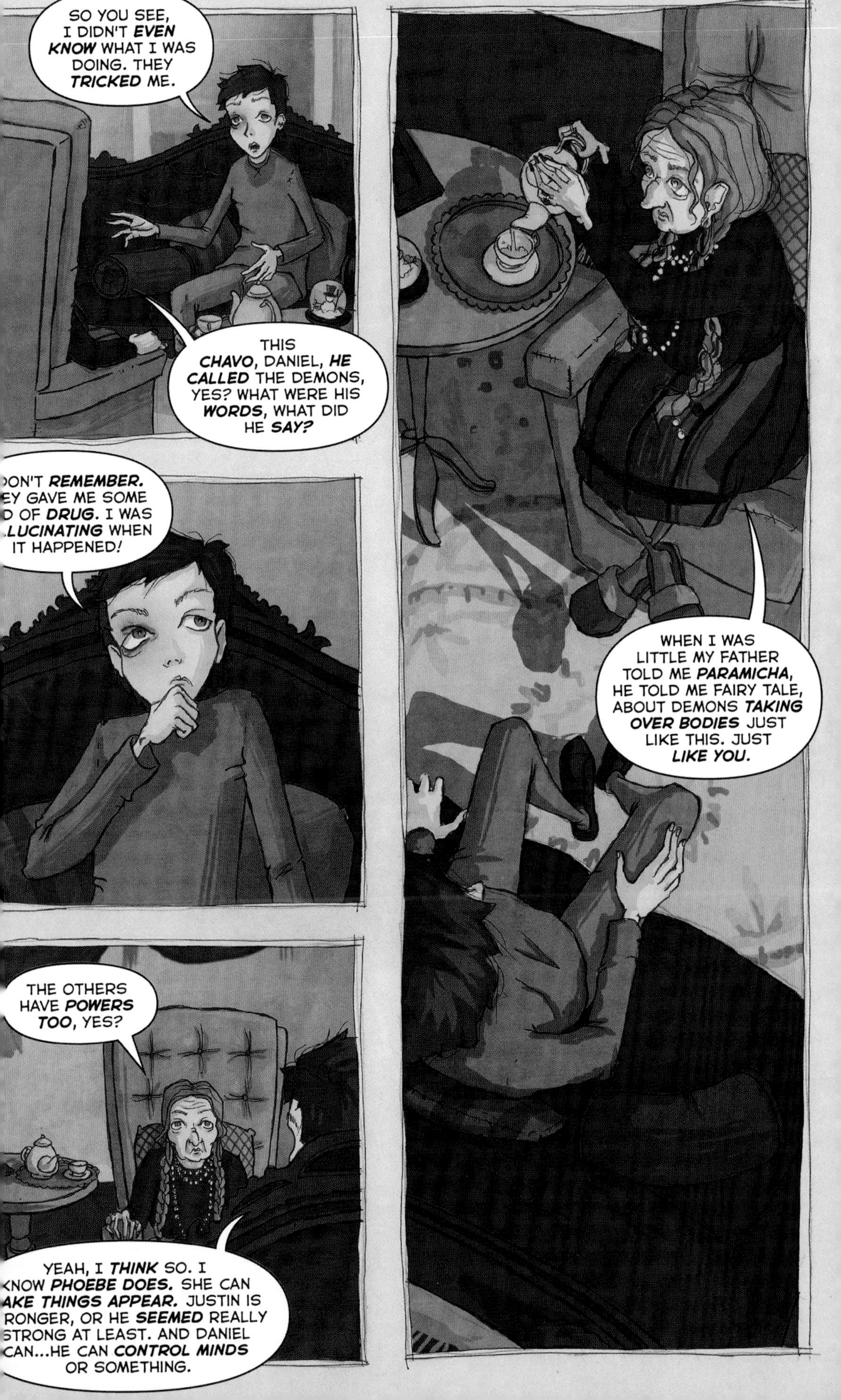
SO YOU SEE, I DIDN'T ***EVEN KNOW*** WHAT I WAS DOING. THEY ***TRICKED*** ME.
THIS ***CHAVO***, DANIEL, ***HE CALLED*** THE DEMONS, YES? WHAT WERE HIS ***WORDS***, WHAT DID HE ***SAY?***
ON'T ***REMEMBER.*** EY GAVE ME SOME D OF ***DRUG.*** I WAS LUCINATING WHEN IT HAPPENED!
WHEN I WAS LITTLE MY FATHER TOLD ME ***PARAMICHA***, HE TOLD ME FAIRY TALE, ABOUT DEMONS ***TAKING OVER BODIES*** JUST LIKE THIS. JUST ***LIKE YOU.***
THE OTHERS HAVE ***POWERS TOO***, YES?
YEAH, I ***THINK*** SO. I NOW ***PHOEBE DOES.*** SHE CAN AKE ***THINGS APPEAR.*** JUSTIN IS RONGER, OR HE ***SEEMED*** REALLY STRONG AT LEAST. AND DANIEL CAN...HE CAN ***CONTROL MINDS*** OR SOMETHING.

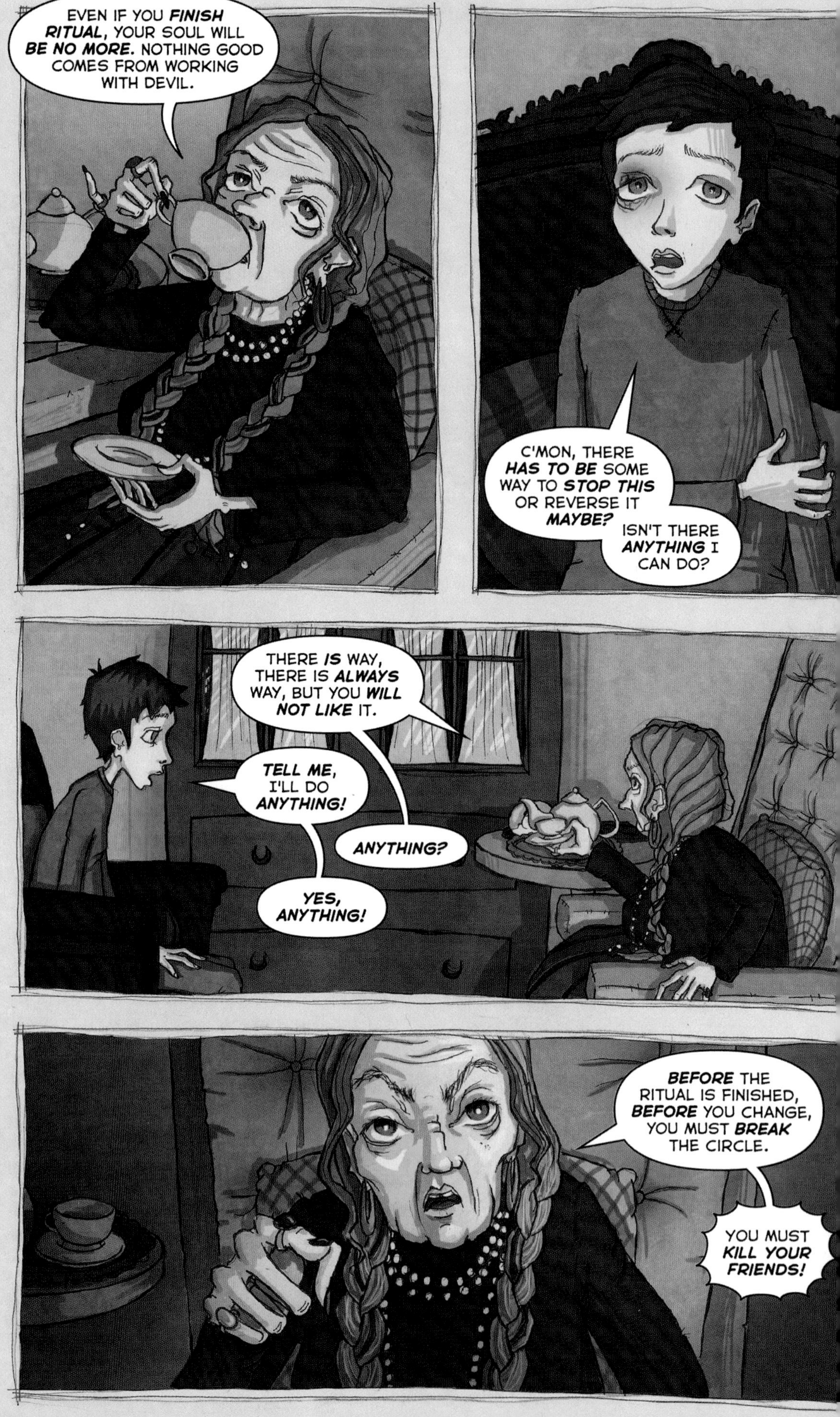
EVEN IF YOU FINISH RITUAL, YOUR SOUL WILL BE NO MORE. NOTHING GOOD COMES FROM WORKING WITH DEVIL.
C'MON, THERE HAS TO BE SOME WAY TO STOP THIS OR REVERSE IT MAYBE?
ISN'T THERE ANYTHING I CAN DO?
THERE IS WAY, THERE IS ALWAYS WAY, BUT YOU WILL NOT LIKE IT.
TELL ME, I'LL DO ANYTHING!
ANYTHING?
YES, ANYTHING!
BEFORE THE RITUAL IS FINISHED, BEFORE YOU CHANGE, YOU MUST BREAK THE CIRCLE.
YOU MUST KILL YOUR FRIENDS!

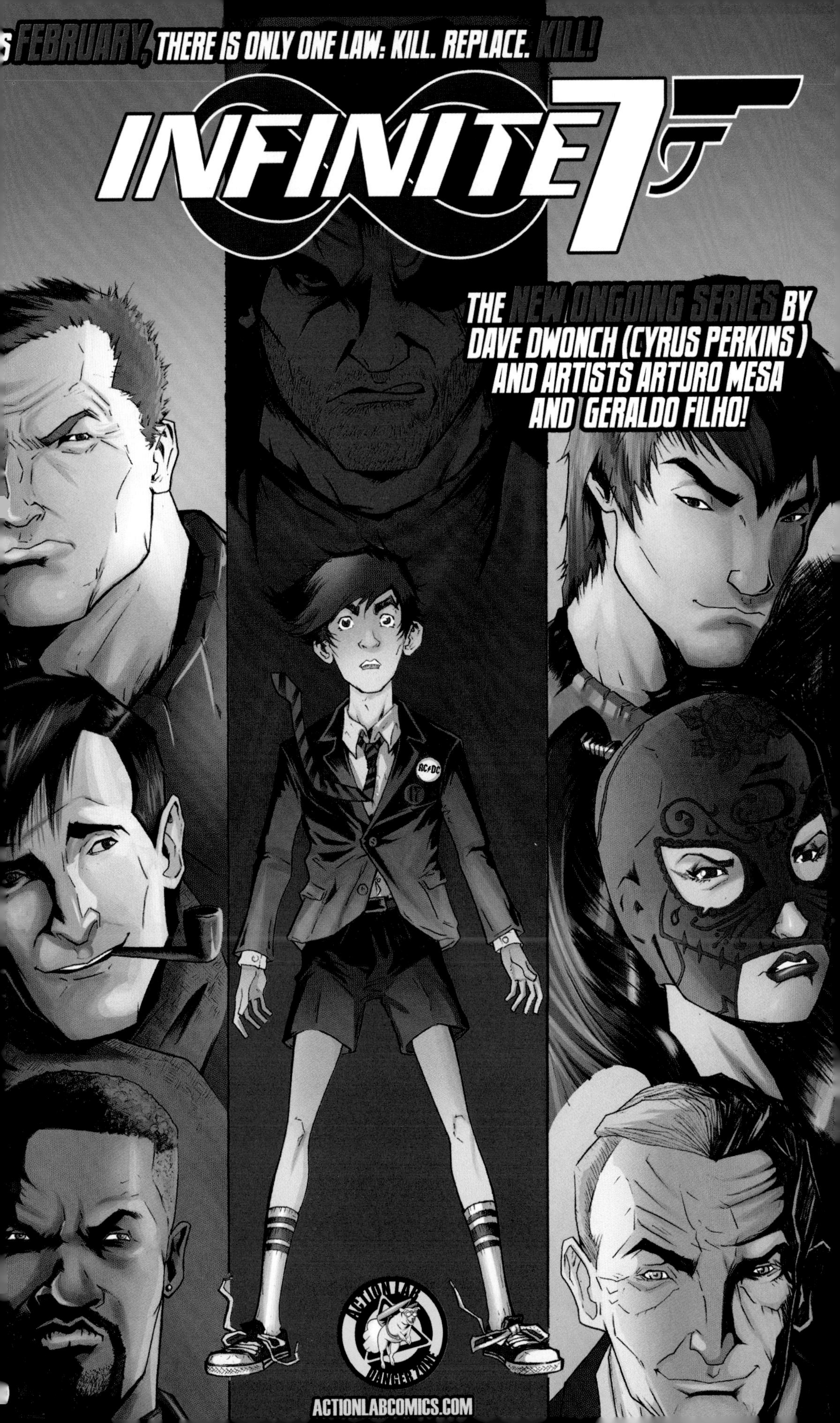

S FEBRUARY, THERE IS ONLY ONE LAW: KILL. REPLACE. KILL!
INFINITE 7
THE NEW ONGOING SERIES BY
DAVE DWONCH (CYRUS PERKINS)
AND ARTISTS ARTURO MESA
AND GERALDO FILHO!
AC/DC
ACTION LAB
DANGER ZONE
ACTIONLABCOMICS.COM

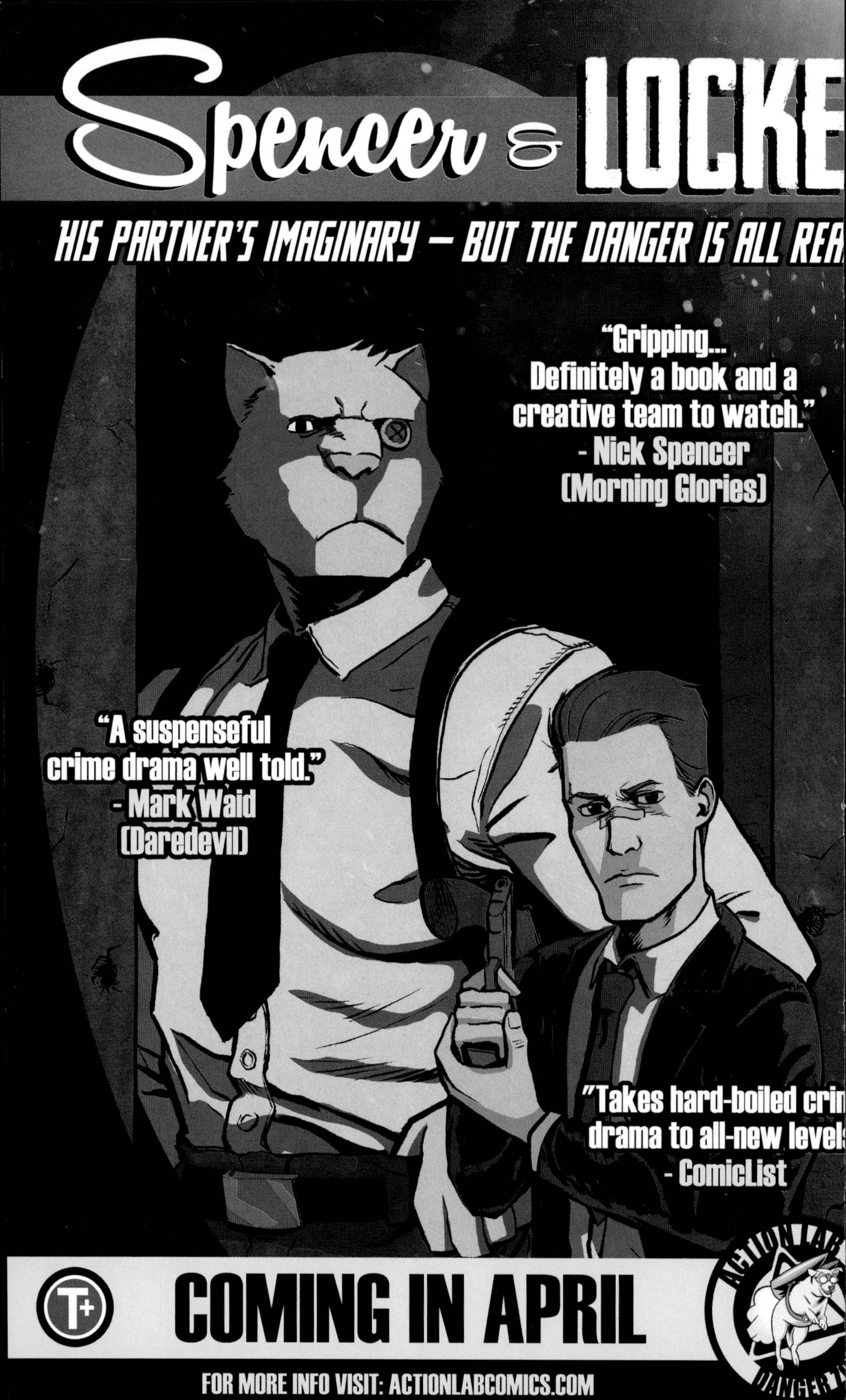

Spencer & LOCKE
HIS PARTNER'S IMAGINARY — BUT THE DANGER IS ALL REA
"Gripping... Definitely a book and a creative team to watch." - Nick Spencer (Morning Glories)
"A suspenseful crime drama well told." - Mark Waid (Daredevil)
"Takes hard-boiled crin drama to all-new levels - ComicList
T+
COMING IN APRIL
FOR MORE INFO VISIT: ACTIONLABCOMICS.COM

RAMBO.
JOHN MCCLANE.
SNAKE PLISSKEN.
RALPH MACCHIO.

NOW ACTION HAS A NEW NAME.
SAM KICKWELL IS

MARCH 2017

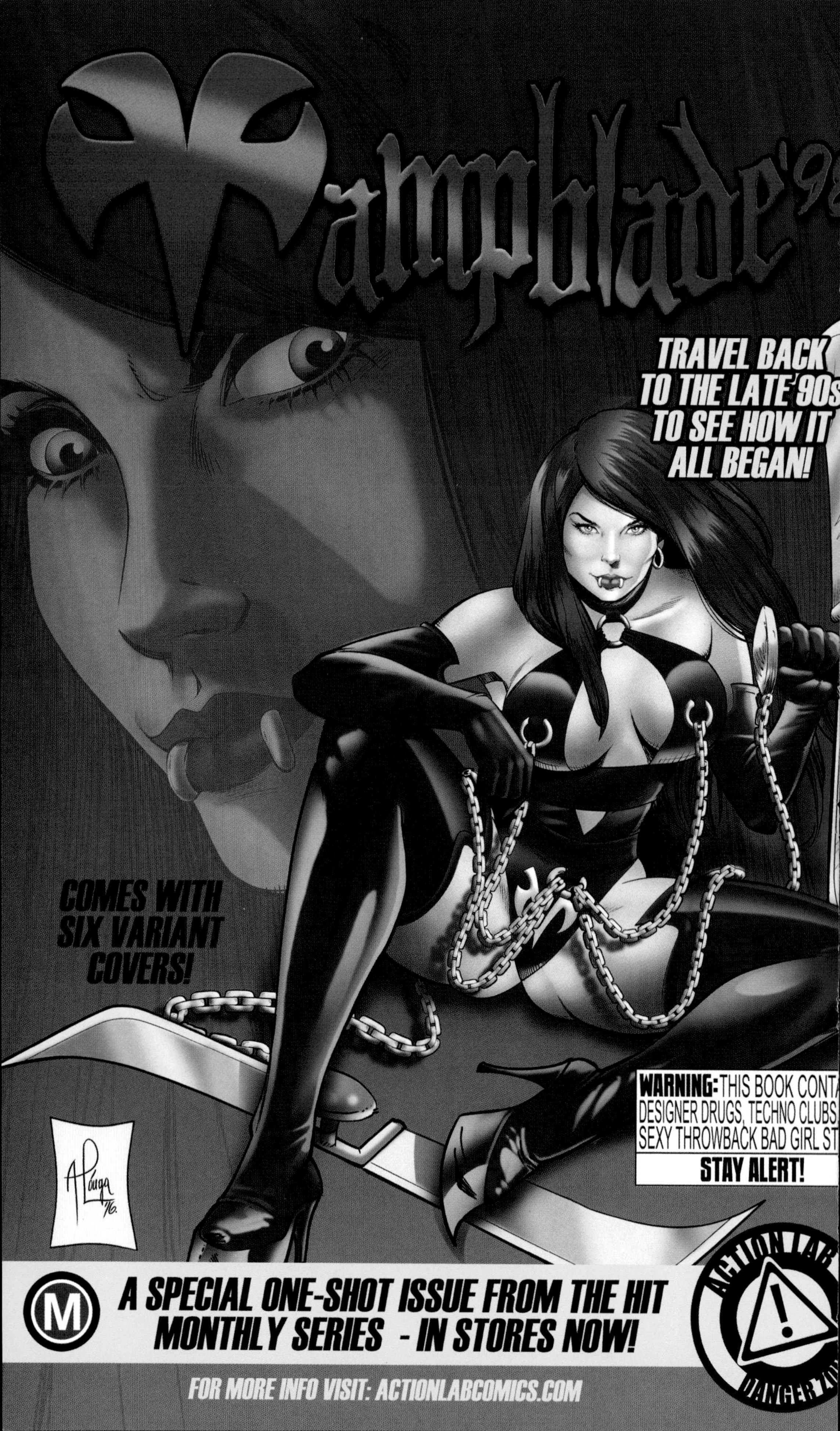

TRAVEL BACK TO THE LATE '90s TO SEE HOW IT ALL BEGAN!
COMES WITH SIX VARIANT COVERS!
WARNING: THIS BOOK CONTA
DESIGNER DRUGS, TECHNO CLUBS
SEXY THROWBACK BAD GIRL ST
STAY ALERT!
M
A SPECIAL ONE-SHOT ISSUE FROM THE HIT MONTHLY SERIES - IN STORES NOW!
ACTION LAB
DANGER ZO
FOR MORE INFO VISIT: ACTIONLABCOMICS.COM

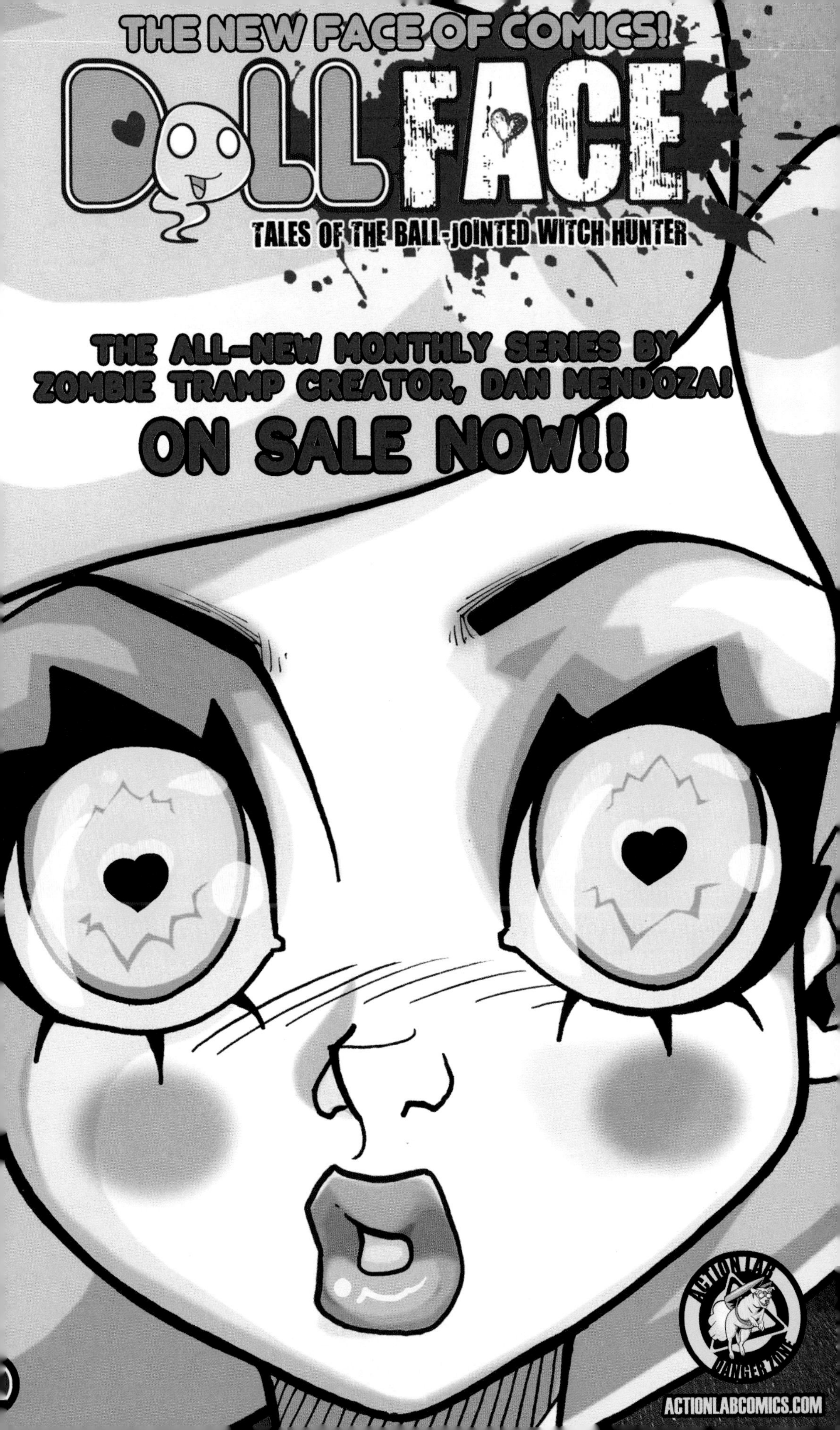

THE NEW FACE OF COMICS!
DOLL FACE
TALES OF THE BALL-JOINTED WITCH HUNTER
THE ALL-NEW MONTHLY SERIES BY
ZOMBIE TRAMP CREATOR, DAN MENDOZA!
ON SALE NOW!!
ACTION LAB
DANGER ZONE
ACTIONLABCOMICS.COM

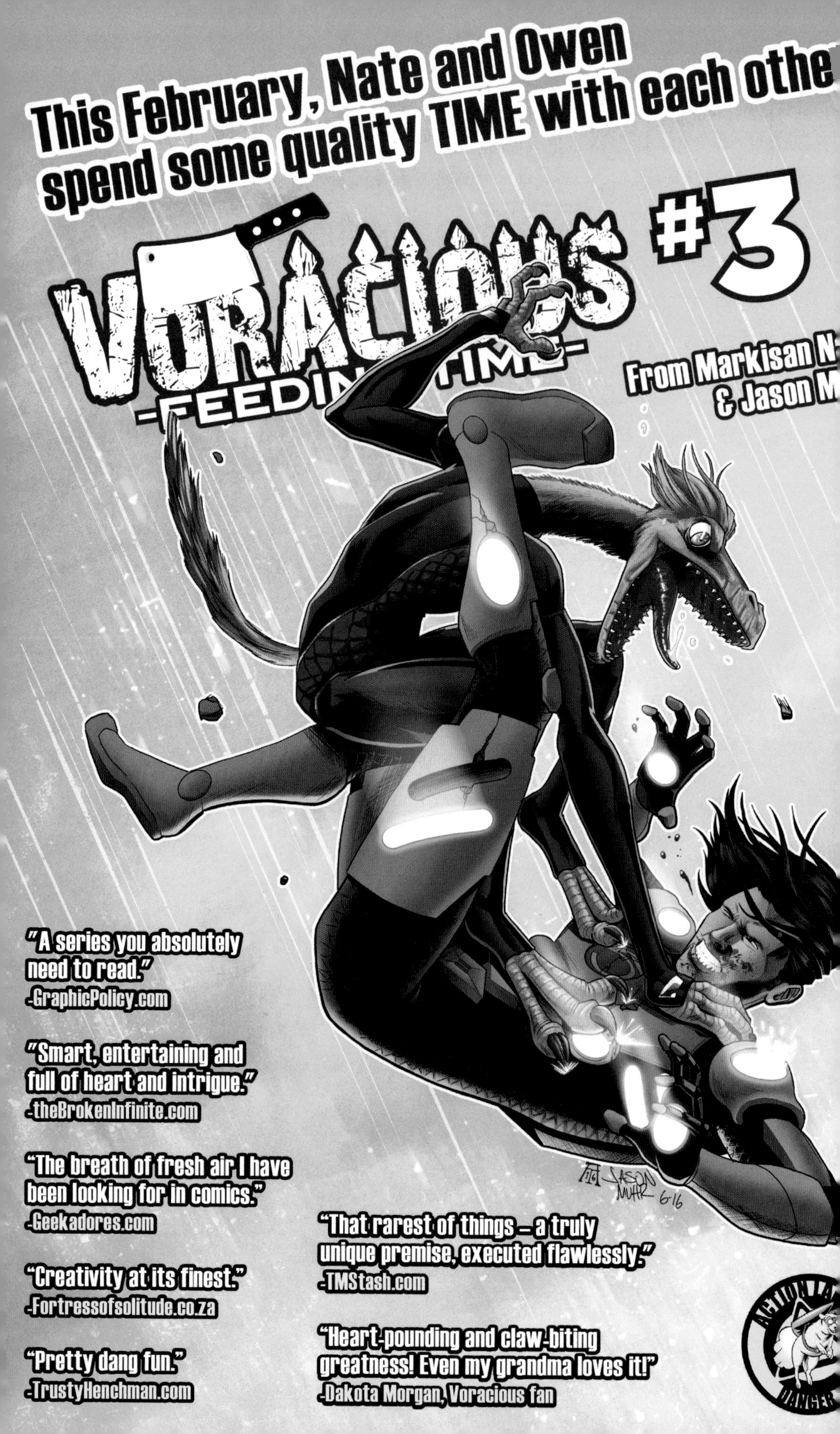

This February, Nate and Owen spend some quality TIME with each othe
VORACIOUS #3
-FEEDIN TIME-
From Markisan N
& Jason M
"A series you absolutely need to read."
-GraphicPolicy.com
"Smart, entertaining and full of heart and intrigue."
-theBrokenInfinite.com
"The breath of fresh air I have been looking for in comics."
-Geekadores.com
"Creativity at its finest."
-Fortressofsolitude.co.za
"Pretty dang fun."
-TrustyHenchman.com
"That rarest of things – a truly unique premise, executed flawlessly."
-TMStash.com
"Heart-pounding and claw-biting greatness! Even my grandma loves it!"
-Dakota Morgan, Voracious fan
JASON MUHR 6·16

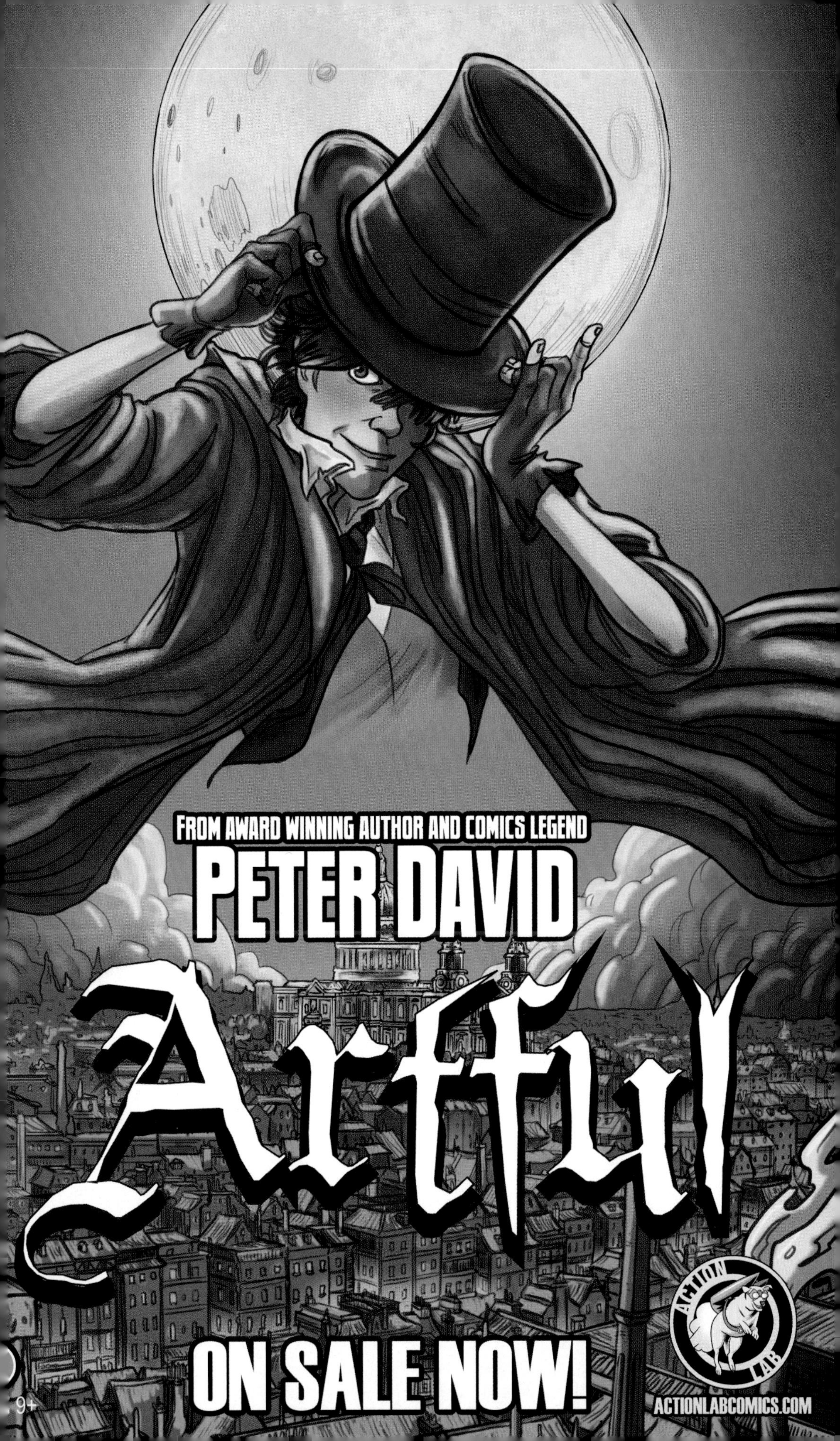

FROM AWARD WINNING AUTHOR AND COMICS LEGEND
PETER DAVID
Artful
ON SALE NOW!
ACTIONLABCOMICS.COM
9+

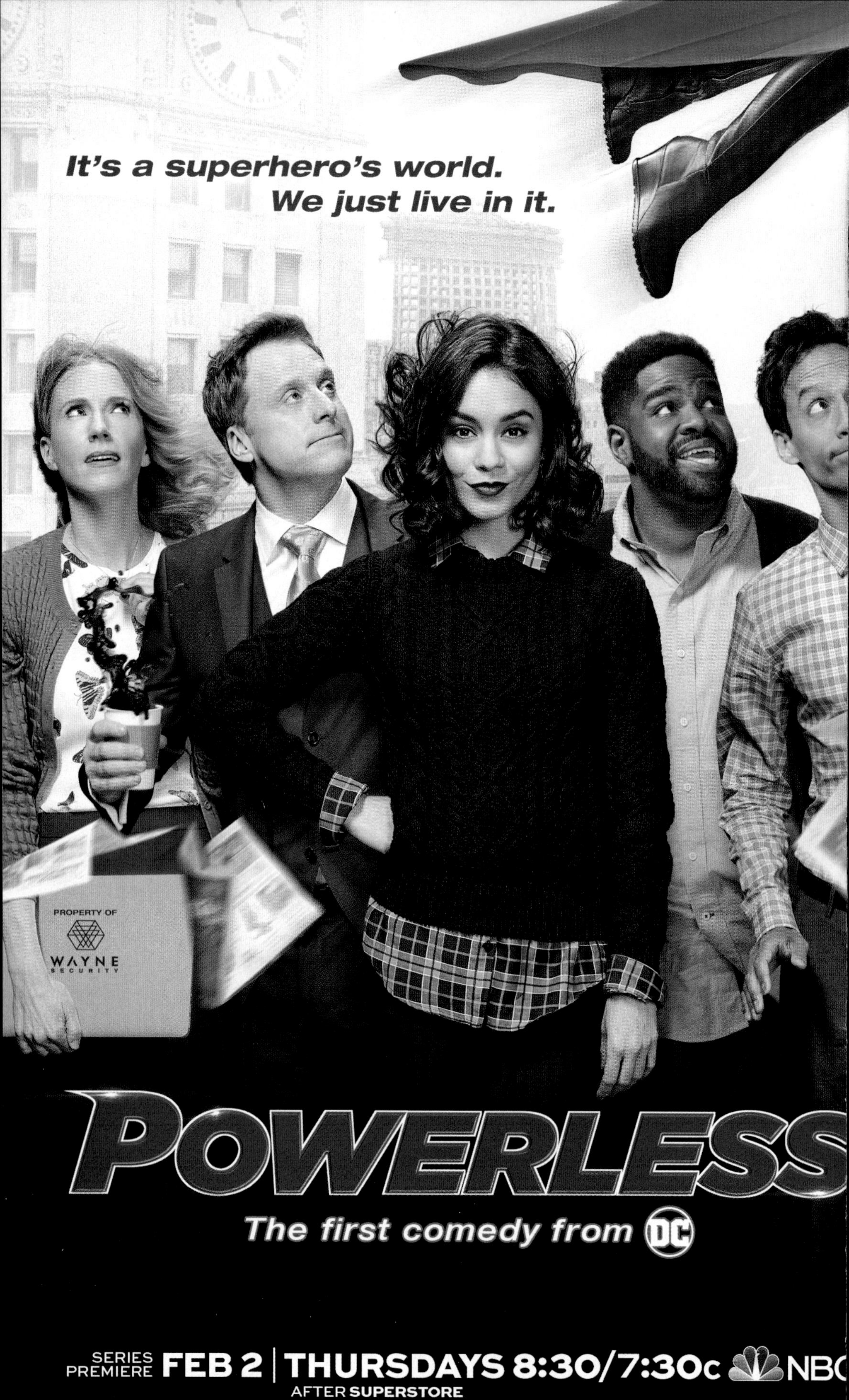

It's a superhero's world.
We just live in it.
PROPERTY OF
WAYNE
SECURITY
POWERLESS
The first comedy from DC
SERIES PREMIERE FEB 2 | THURSDAYS 8:30/7:30c NBC
AFTER SUPERSTORE

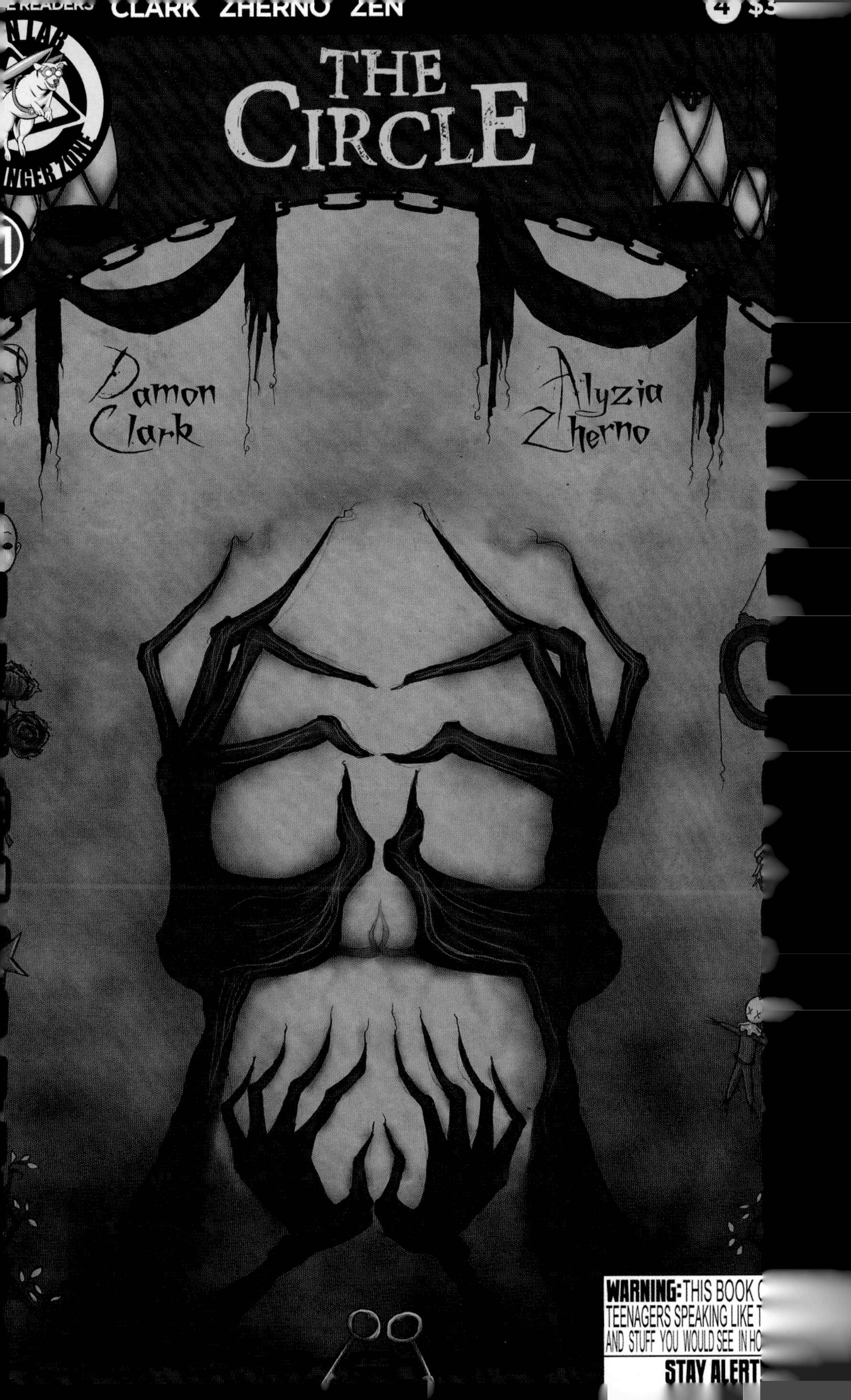
CLARK ZHERNO ZEN
THE CIRCLE
Damon Clark
Alyzia Zherno
WARNING: THIS BOOK
TEENAGERS SPEAKING LIKE
AND STUFF YOU WOULD SEE IN
STAY ALERT

ACTION LAB: DANGER ZONE PRESENTS

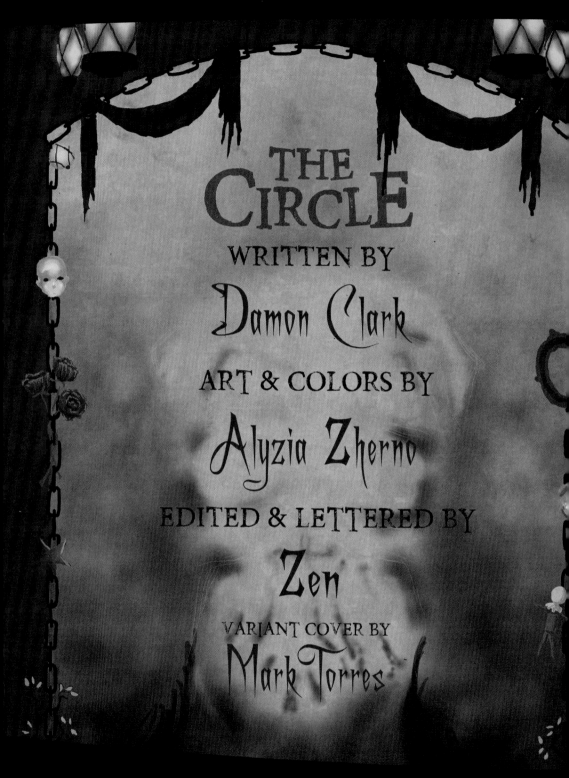

THE CIRCLE

WRITTEN BY

Damon Clark

ART & COLORS BY

Alyzia Zherno

EDITED & LETTERED BY

Zen

VARIANT COVER BY

Mark Torres

JASON MARTIN - PUBLISHER
DAVE DWONCH - PRESIDENT OF MARKETING
SHAWN GABBORIN - EDITOR IN CHIEF
NICOLE D'ANDRIA - MARKETING DIRECTOR/EDITOR
JIM DIETZ - SOCIAL MEDIA MANAGER
SCOTT BRADLEY - CFO
BRYAN SEATON - CEO

THE CIRCLE #4. March 2017.

Published by Action Lab Comics.

Printed in Canada.
First printing.

ACTIONLABCOMICS.COM

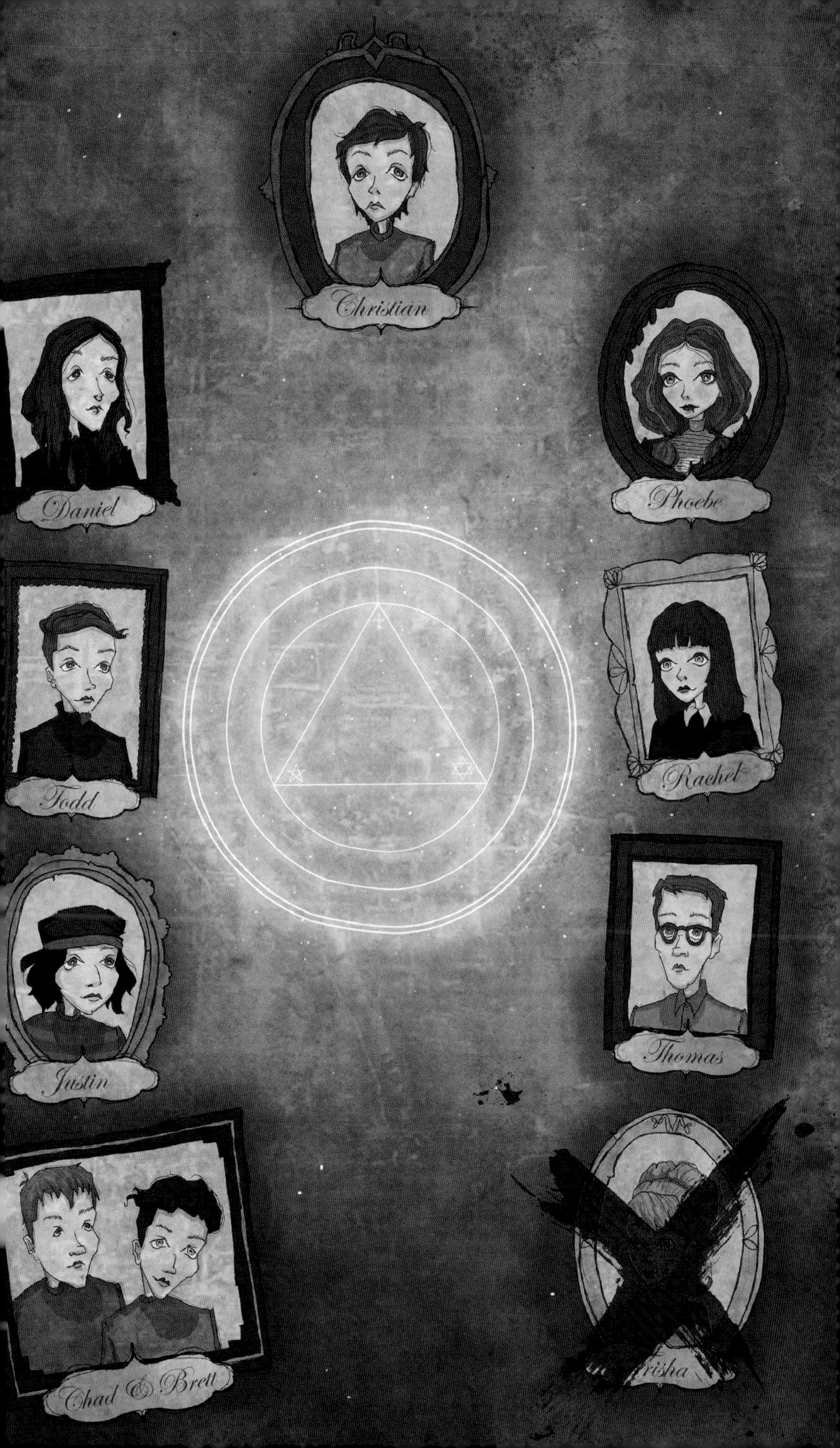
Christian
Daniel
Phoebe
Todd
Rachel
Justin
Thomas
Chad & Brett
risha

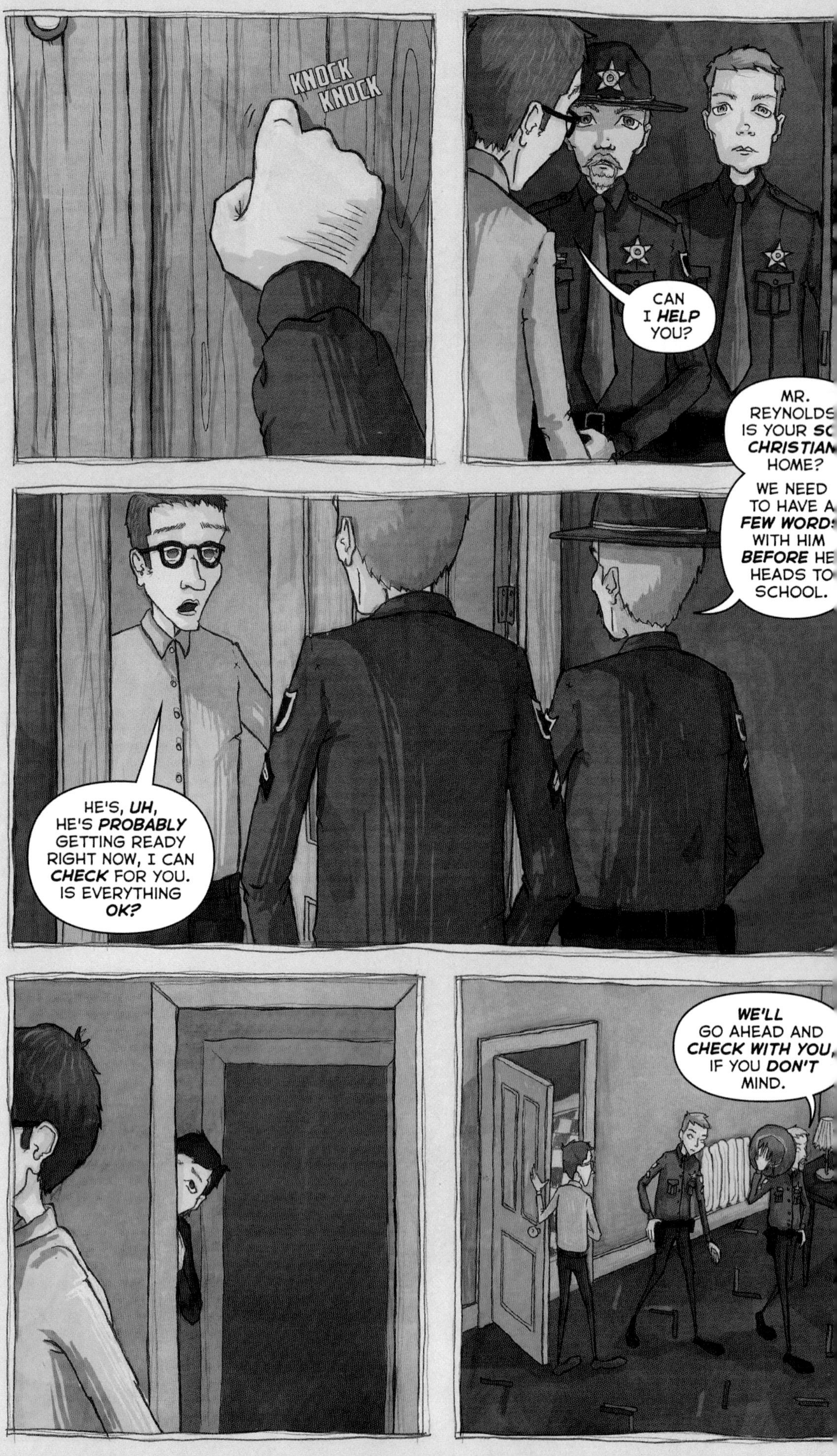
KNOCK KNOCK
CAN I HELP YOU?
MR. REYNOLDS IS YOUR SC CHRISTIAN HOME?
WE NEED TO HAVE A FEW WORDS WITH HIM BEFORE HE HEADS TO SCHOOL.
HE'S, UH, HE'S PROBABLY GETTING READY RIGHT NOW, I CAN CHECK FOR YOU. IS EVERYTHING OK?
WE'LL GO AHEAD AND CHECK WITH YOU, IF YOU DON'T MIND.

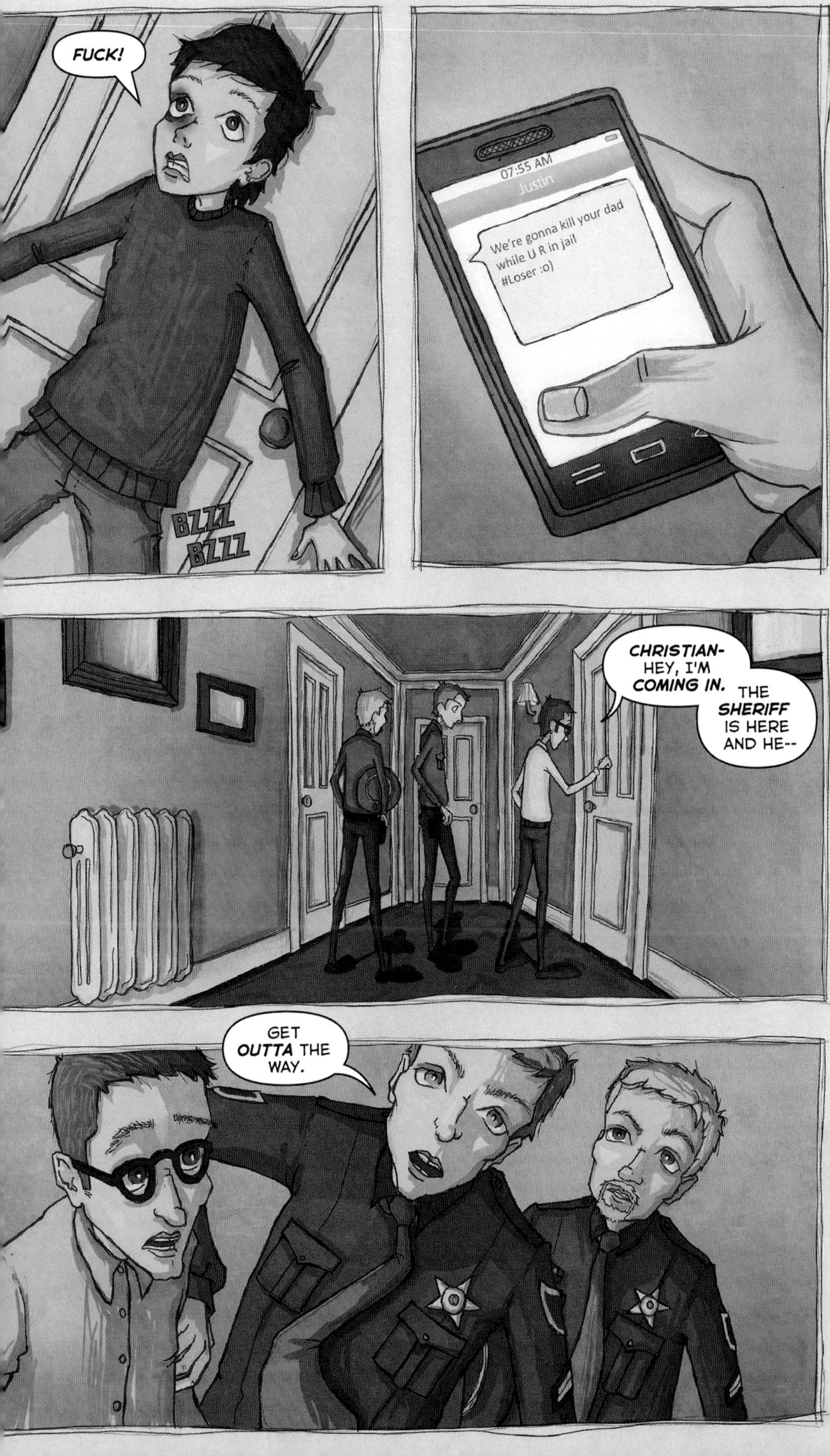
FUCK!
BZZZ BZZZ
07:55 AM
Justin
We're gonna kill your dad while U R in jail #Loser :o)
CHRISTIAN- HEY, I'M COMING IN.
THE SHERIFF IS HERE AND HE--
GET OUTTA THE WAY.

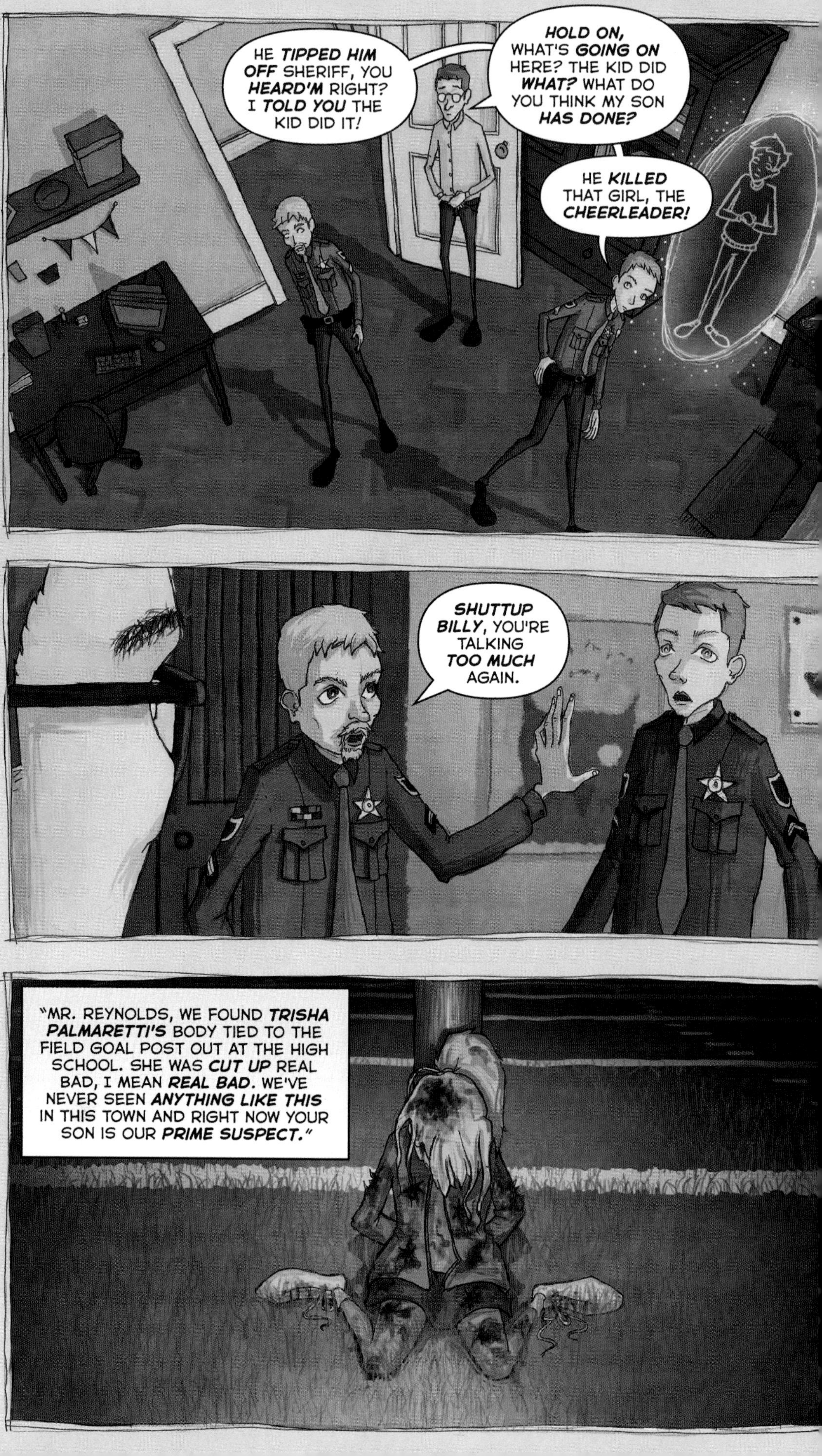
HE TIPPED HIM OFF SHERIFF, YOU HEARD'M RIGHT? I TOLD YOU THE KID DID IT!
HOLD ON, WHAT'S GOING ON HERE? THE KID DID WHAT? WHAT DO YOU THINK MY SON HAS DONE?
HE KILLED THAT GIRL, THE CHEERLEADER!
SHUTTUP BILLY, YOU'RE TALKING TOO MUCH AGAIN.
"MR. REYNOLDS, WE FOUND TRISHA PALMARETTI'S BODY TIED TO THE FIELD GOAL POST OUT AT THE HIGH SCHOOL. SHE WAS CUT UP REAL BAD, I MEAN REAL BAD. WE'VE NEVER SEEN ANYTHING LIKE THIS IN THIS TOWN AND RIGHT NOW YOUR SON IS OUR PRIME SUSPECT."

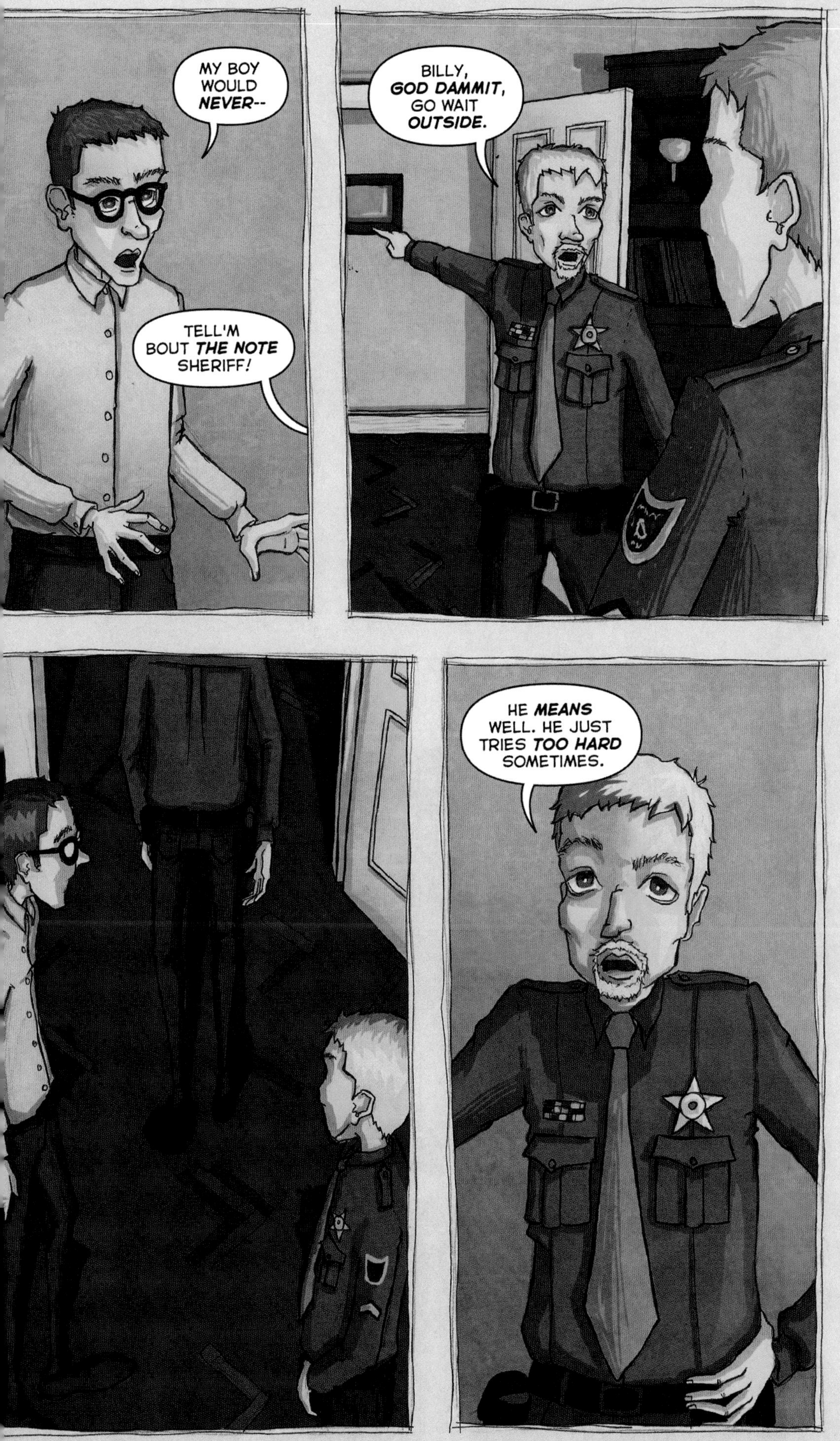
MY BOY WOULD NEVER--
TELL'M BOUT THE NOTE SHERIFF!
BILLY, GOD DAMMIT, GO WAIT OUTSIDE.
HE MEANS WELL. HE JUST TRIES TOO HARD SOMETIMES.

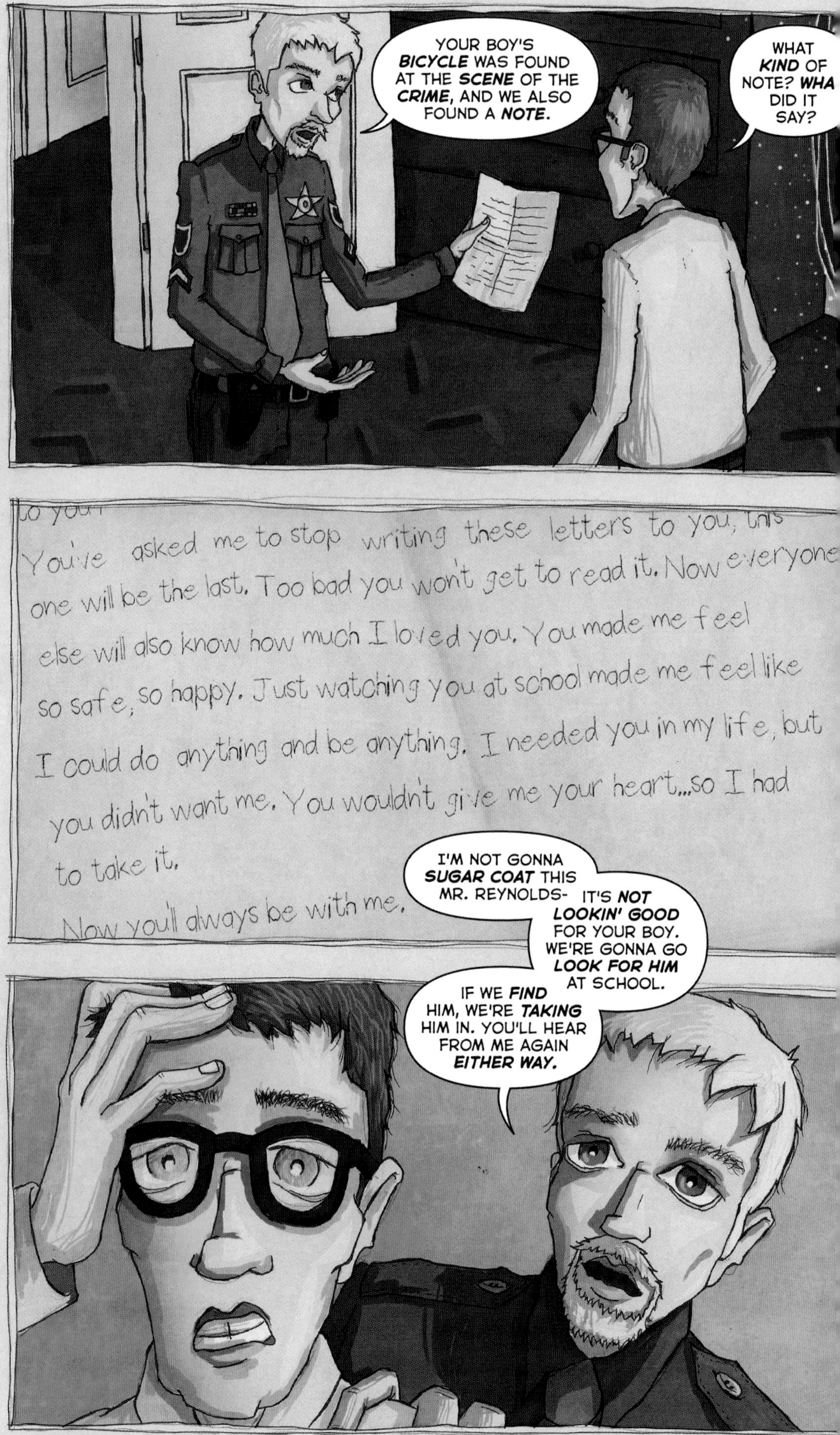
YOUR BOY'S *BICYCLE* WAS FOUND AT THE *SCENE* OF THE *CRIME*, AND WE ALSO FOUND A *NOTE*.
WHAT *KIND* OF NOTE? *WHA* DID IT SAY?
You've asked me to stop writing these letters to you, this one will be the last. Too bad you won't get to read it. Now everyone else will also know how much I loved you. You made me feel so safe, so happy. Just watching you at school made me feel like I could do anything and be anything. I needed you in my life, but you didn't want me. You wouldn't give me your heart...so I had to take it.
Now you'll always be with me.
I'M NOT GONNA *SUGAR COAT* THIS MR. REYNOLDS-
IT'S *NOT LOOKIN' GOOD* FOR YOUR BOY. WE'RE GONNA GO *LOOK FOR HIM* AT SCHOOL.
IF WE *FIND* HIM, WE'RE *TAKING* HIM IN. YOU'LL HEAR FROM ME AGAIN *EITHER WAY.*

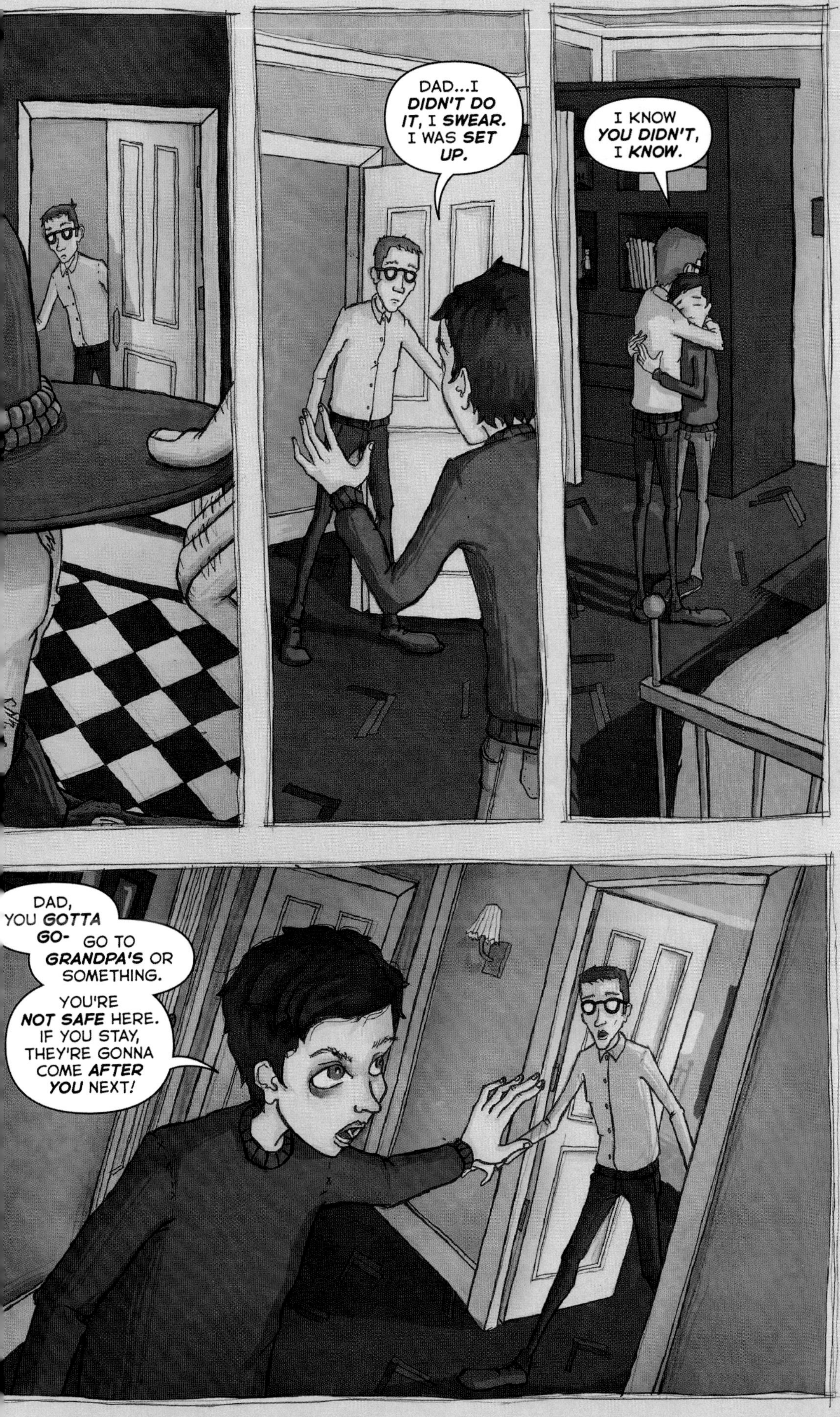
DAD...I **DIDN'T DO IT**, I **SWEAR.** I WAS **SET UP.**
I KNOW **YOU DIDN'T**, I **KNOW.**
DAD, YOU **GOTTA GO-** GO TO **GRANDPA'S** OR SOMETHING.
YOU'RE **NOT SAFE** HERE. IF YOU STAY, THEY'RE GONNA COME **AFTER YOU** NEXT!

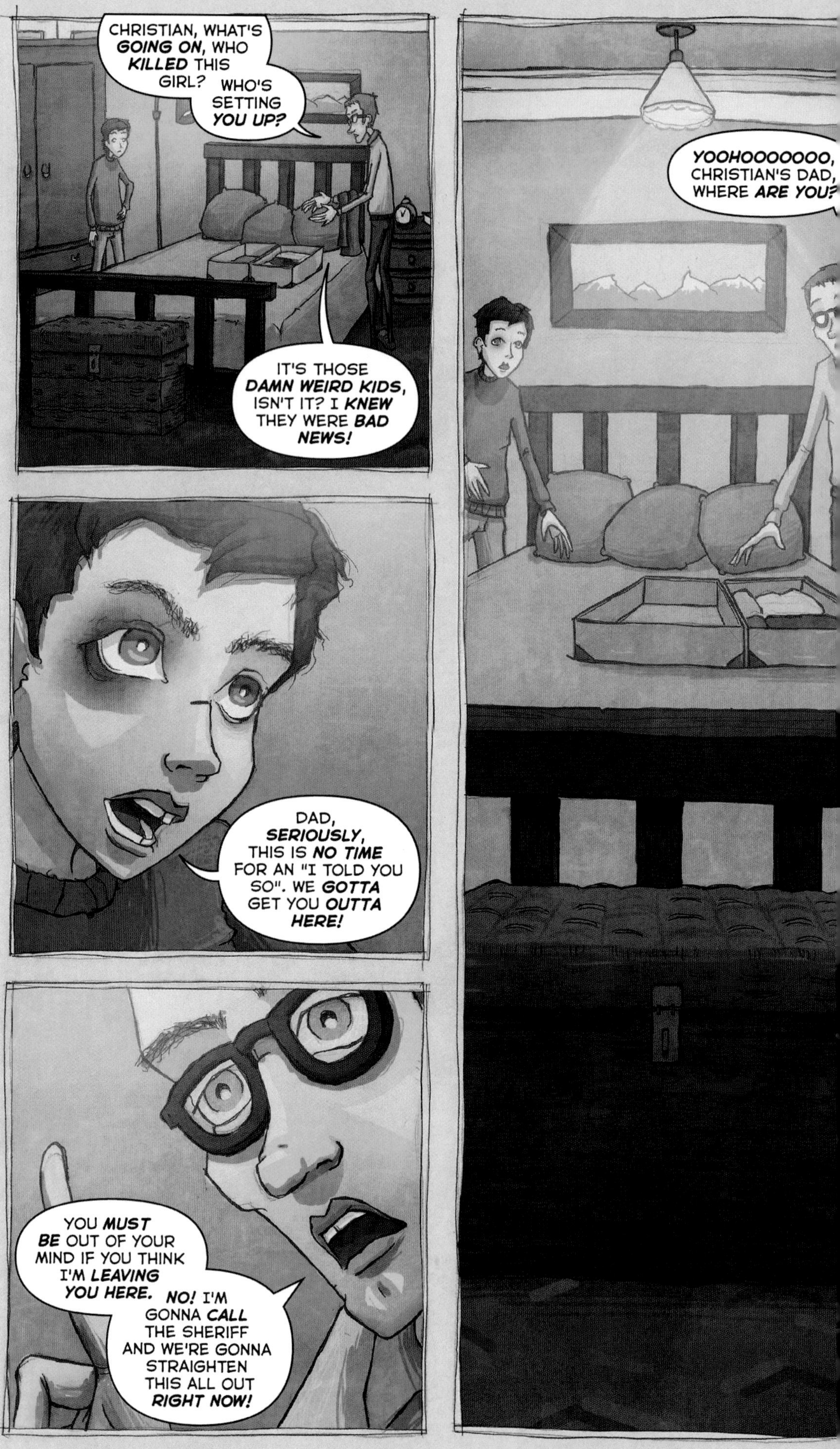
CHRISTIAN, WHAT'S GOING ON, WHO KILLED THIS GIRL?
WHO'S SETTING YOU UP?
IT'S THOSE DAMN WEIRD KIDS, ISN'T IT? I KNEW THEY WERE BAD NEWS!
DAD, SERIOUSLY, THIS IS NO TIME FOR AN "I TOLD YOU SO". WE GOTTA GET YOU OUTTA HERE!
YOU MUST BE OUT OF YOUR MIND IF YOU THINK I'M LEAVING YOU HERE.
NO! I'M GONNA CALL THE SHERIFF AND WE'RE GONNA STRAIGHTEN THIS ALL OUT RIGHT NOW!
YOOHOOOOOOO, CHRISTIAN'S DAD, WHERE ARE YOU?

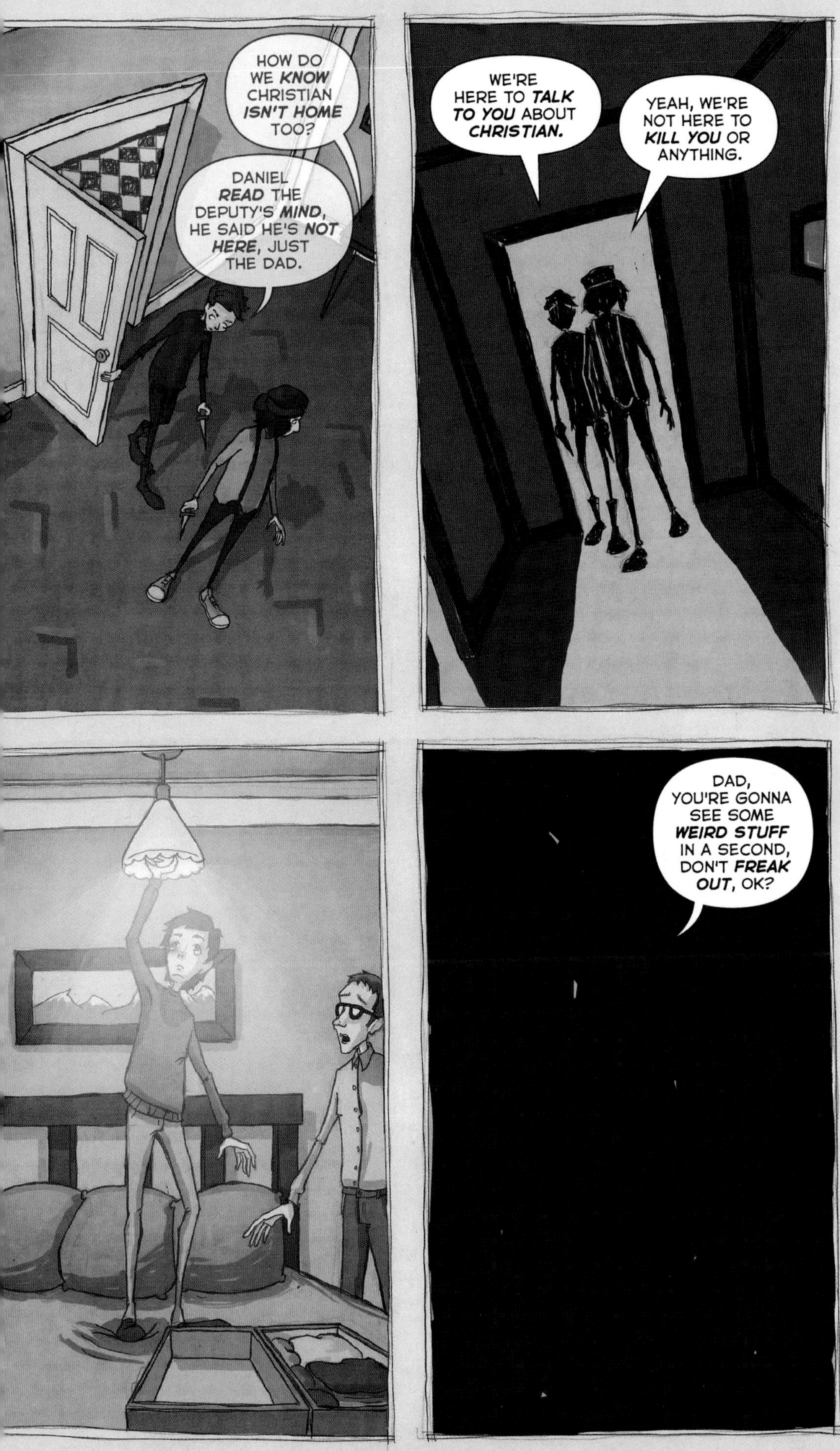
HOW DO WE KNOW CHRISTIAN ISN'T HOME TOO?
DANIEL READ THE DEPUTY'S MIND, HE SAID HE'S NOT HERE, JUST THE DAD.
WE'RE HERE TO TALK TO YOU ABOUT CHRISTIAN.
YEAH, WE'RE NOT HERE TO KILL YOU OR ANYTHING.
DAD, YOU'RE GONNA SEE SOME WEIRD STUFF IN A SECOND, DON'T FREAK OUT, OK?

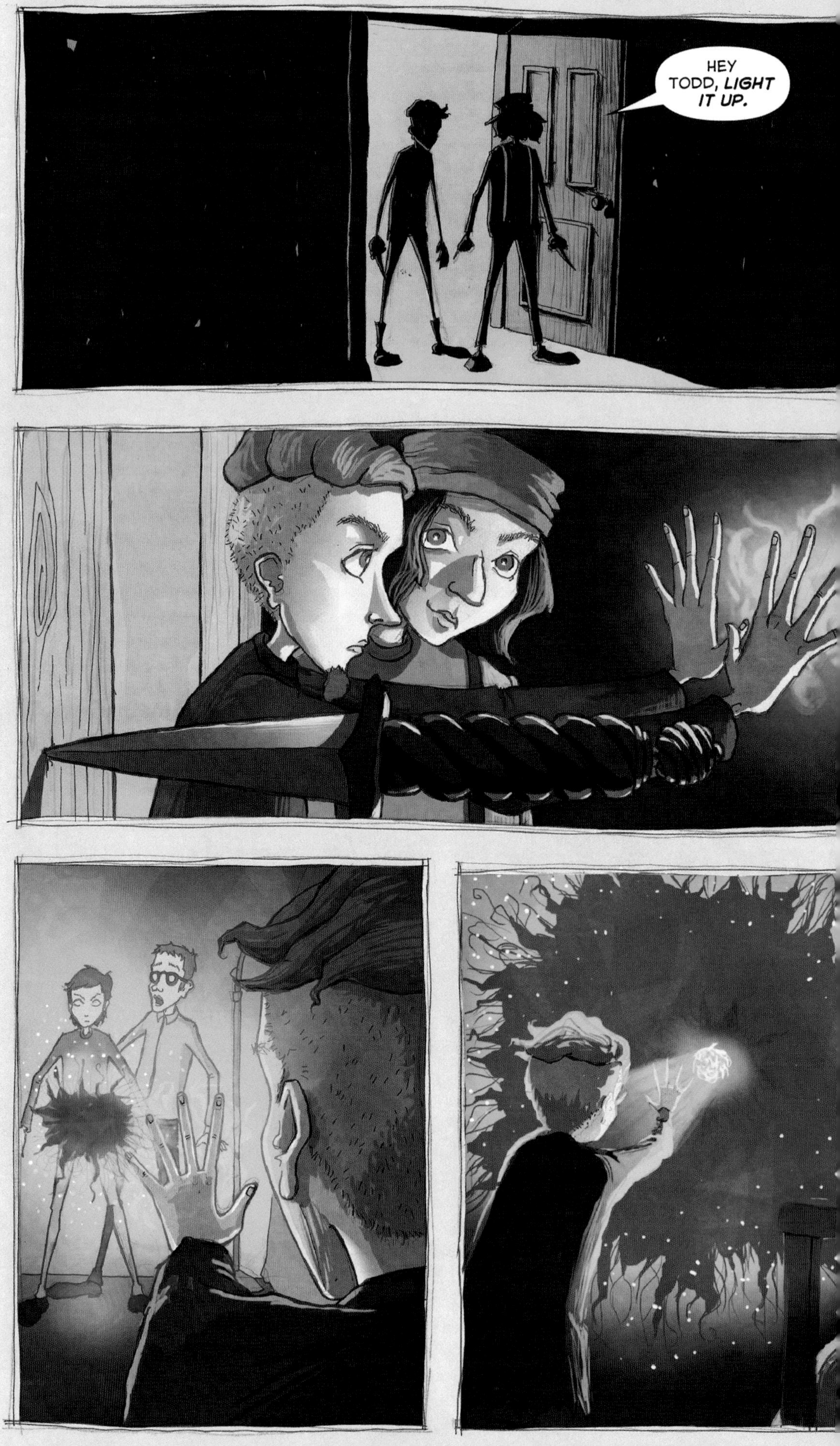
HEY TODD, LIGHT IT UP.

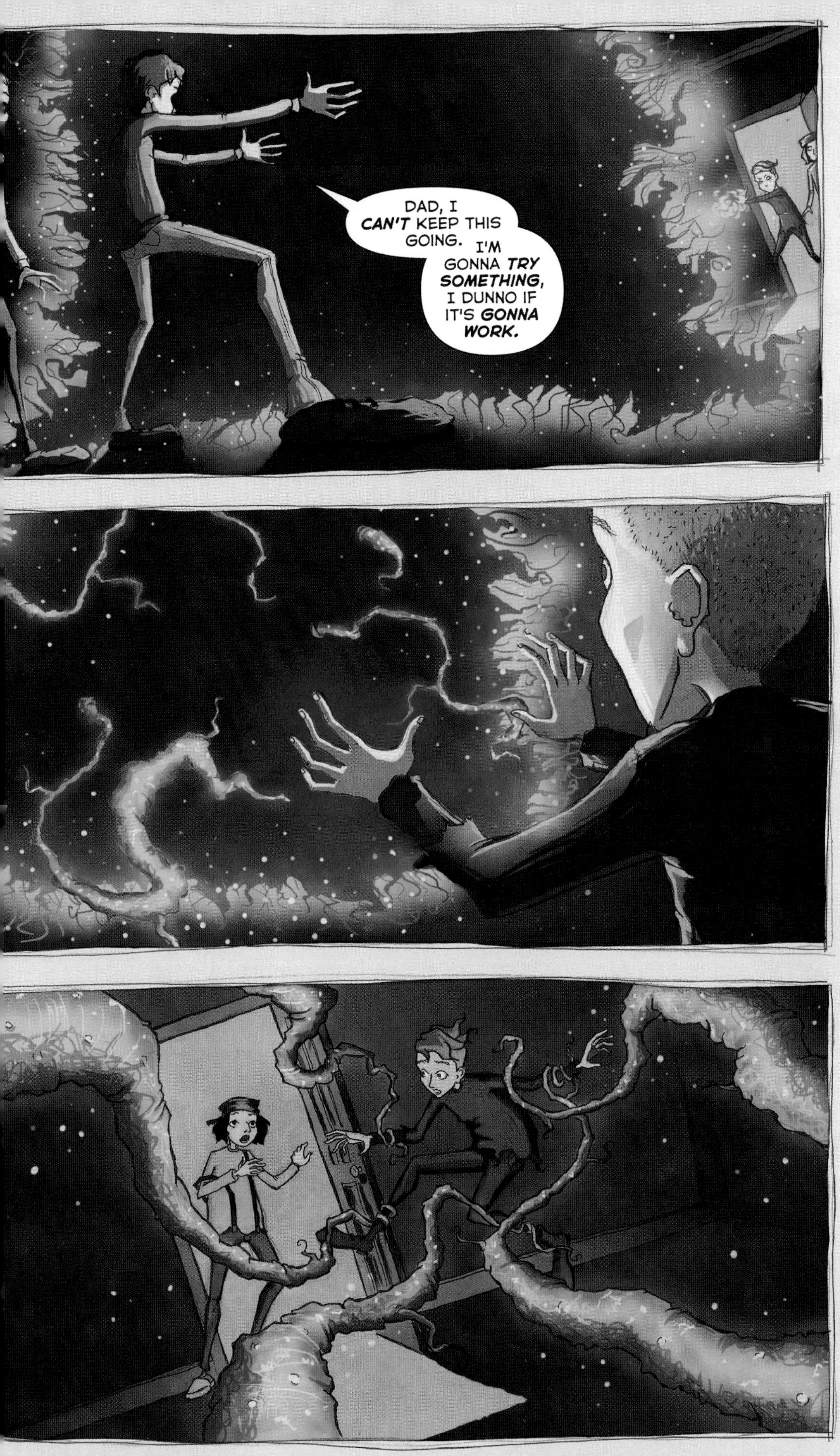
DAD, I CAN'T KEEP THIS GOING.
I'M GONNA TRY SOMETHING, I DUNNO IF IT'S GONNA WORK.

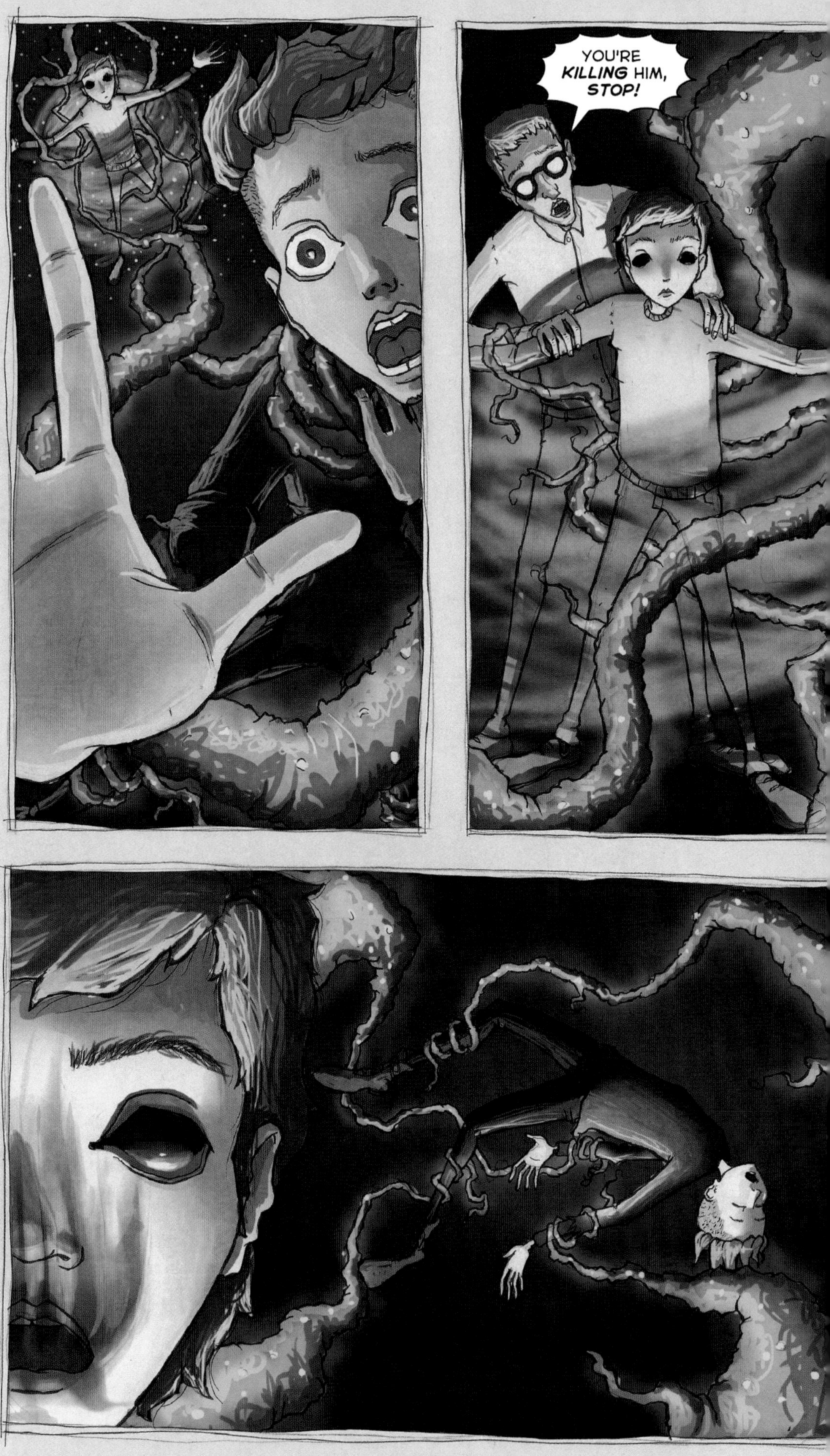
YOU'RE KILLING HIM, STOP!

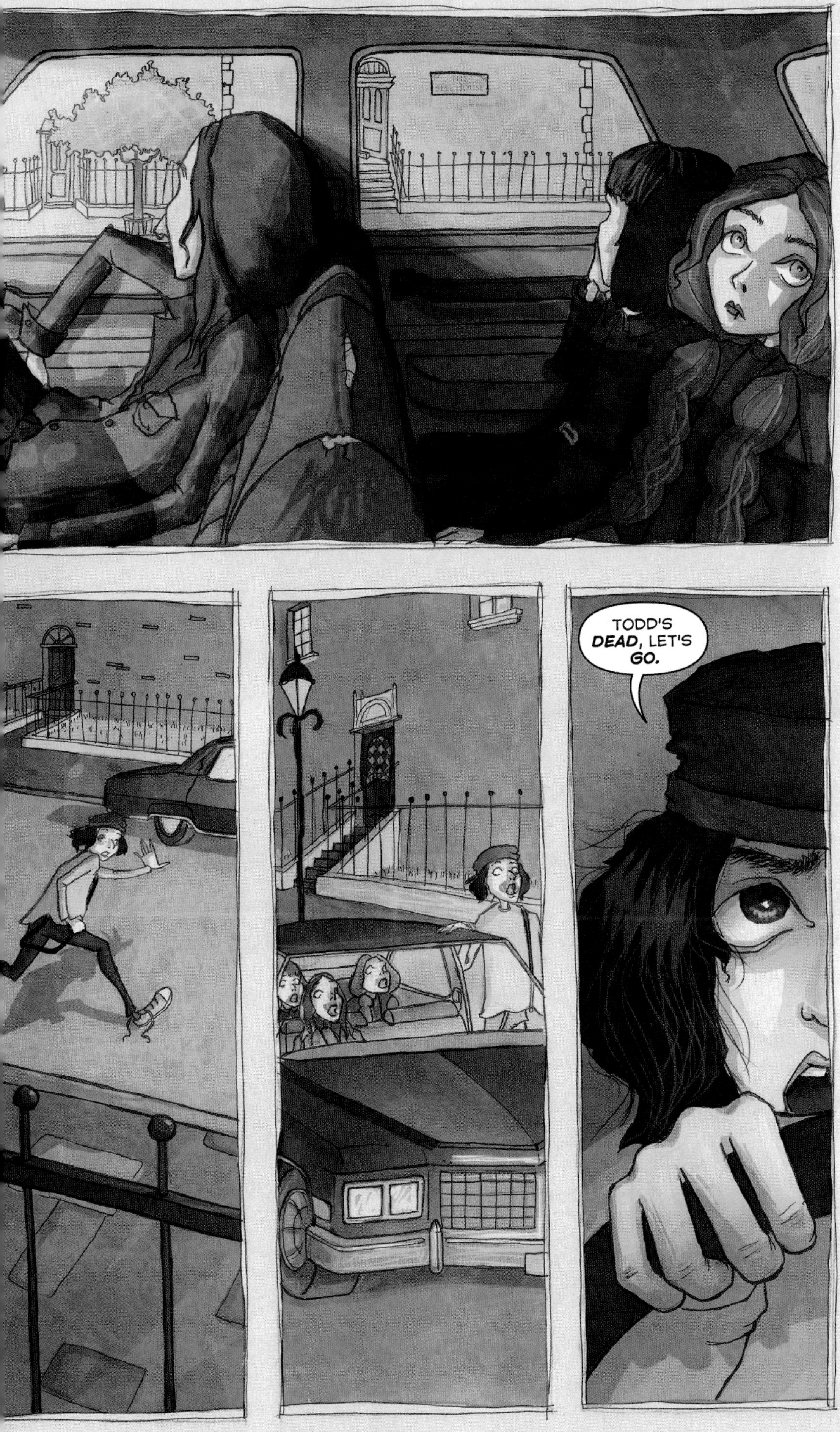
TODD'S **DEAD**, LET'S **GO.**

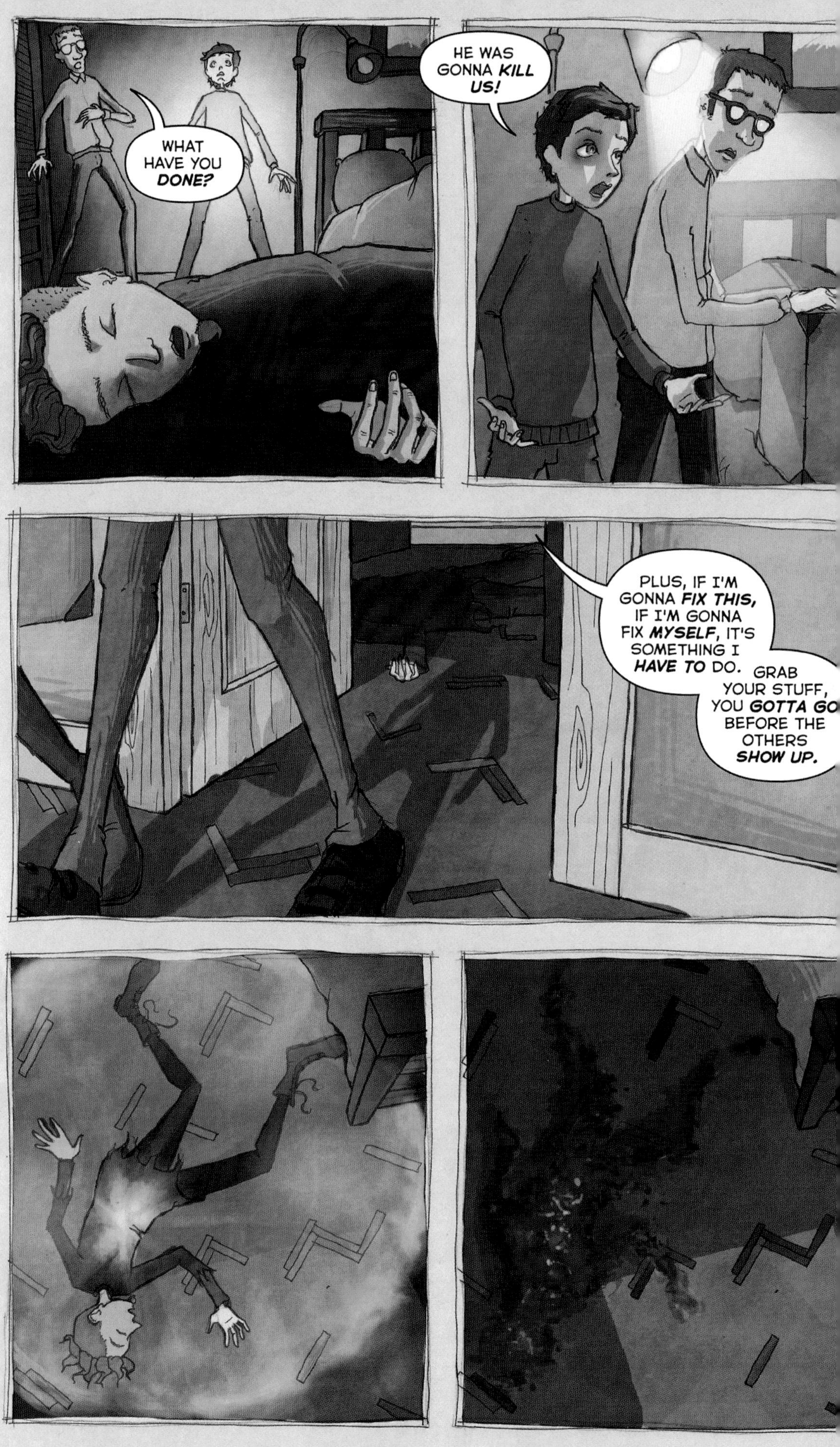
WHAT HAVE YOU DONE?
HE WAS GONNA KILL US!
PLUS, IF I'M GONNA FIX THIS, IF I'M GONNA FIX MYSELF, IT'S SOMETHING I HAVE TO DO.
GRAB YOUR STUFF, YOU GOTTA GO BEFORE THE OTHERS SHOW UP.

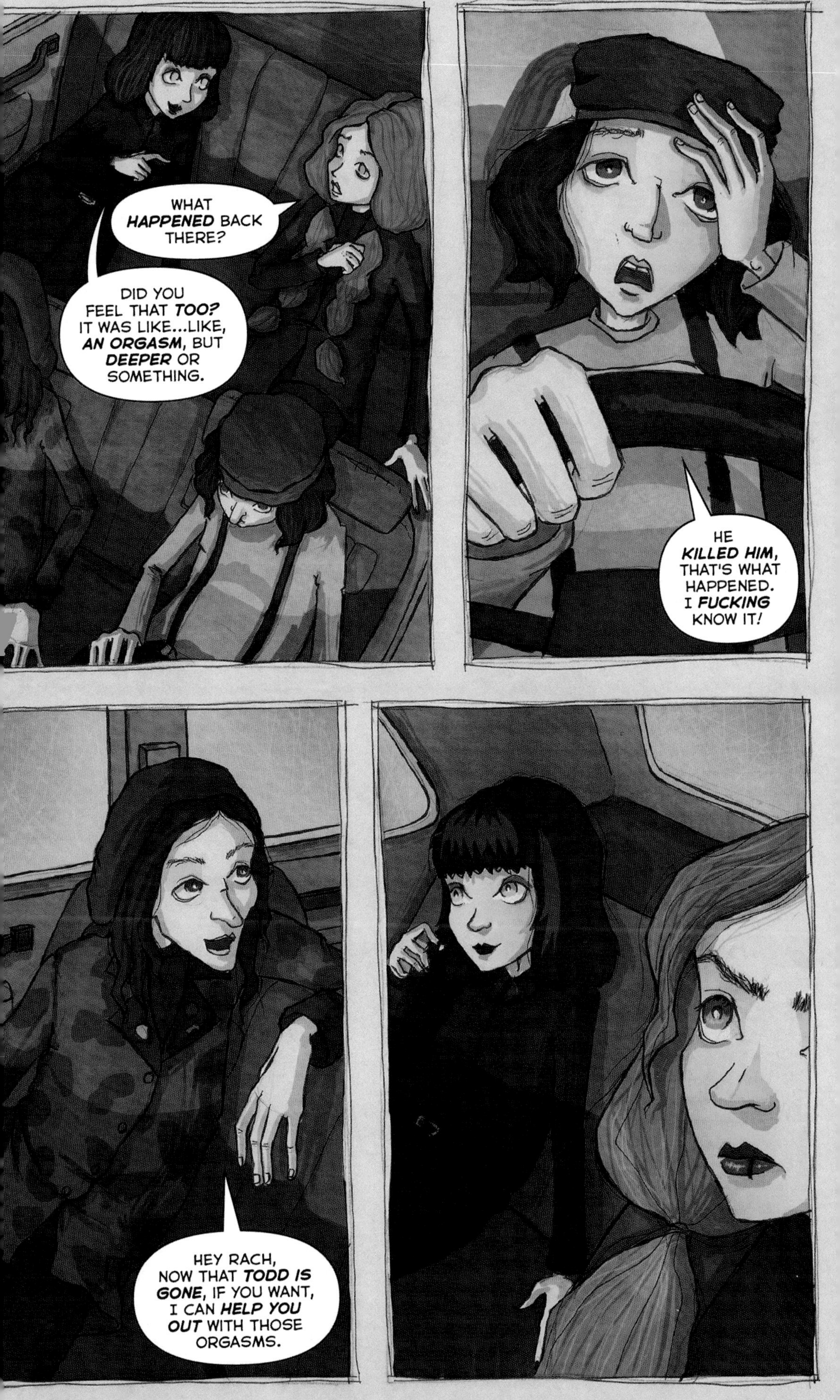
WHAT *HAPPENED* BACK THERE?
DID YOU FEEL THAT *TOO?* IT WAS LIKE...LIKE, *AN ORGASM*, BUT *DEEPER* OR SOMETHING.
HE *KILLED HIM*, THAT'S WHAT HAPPENED. I *FUCKING* KNOW IT!
HEY RACH, NOW THAT *TODD IS GONE*, IF YOU WANT, I CAN *HELP YOU OUT* WITH THOSE ORGASMS.

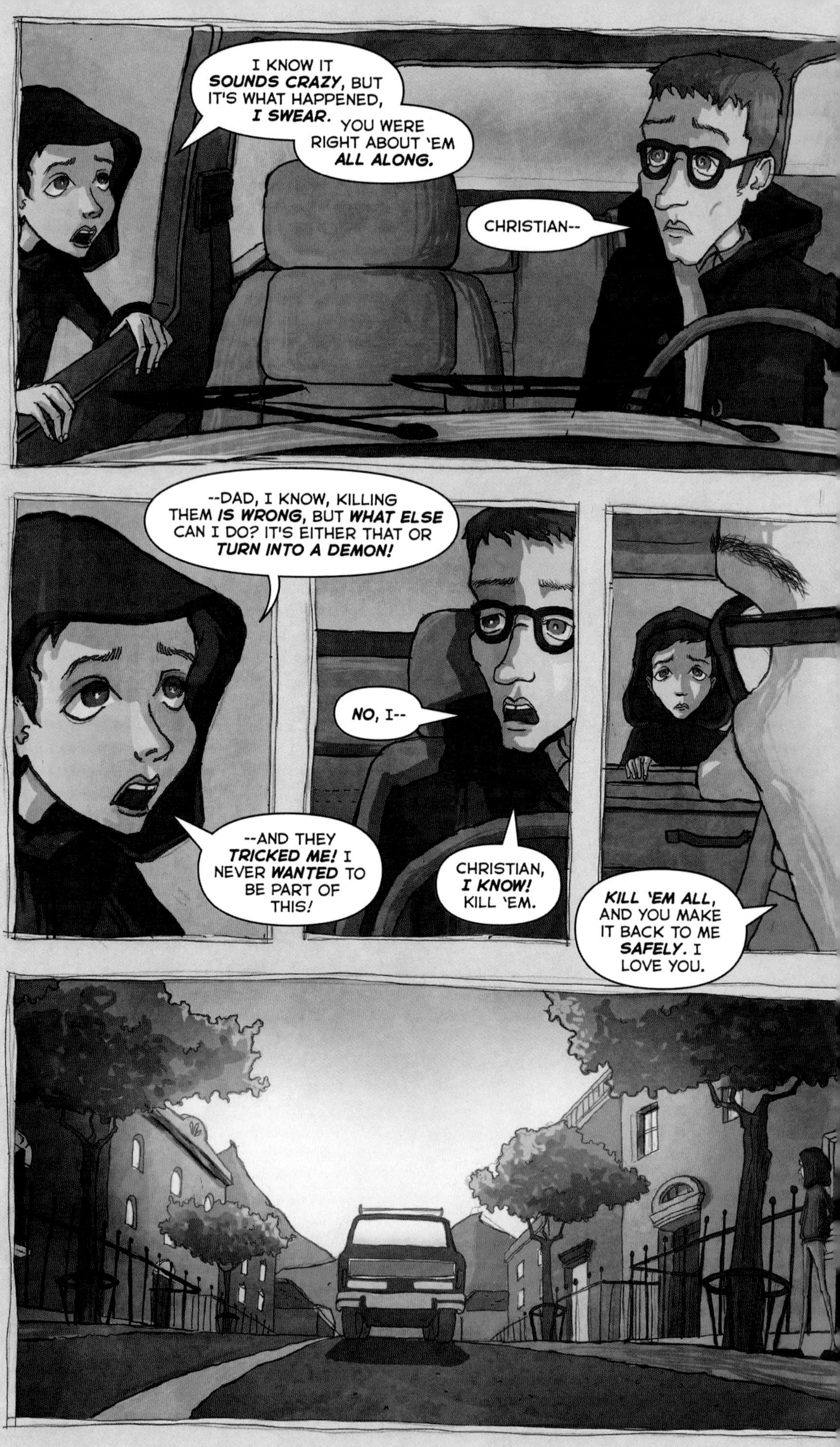
I KNOW IT SOUNDS CRAZY, BUT IT'S WHAT HAPPENED, I SWEAR.
YOU WERE RIGHT ABOUT 'EM ALL ALONG.
CHRISTIAN--
--DAD, I KNOW, KILLING THEM IS WRONG, BUT WHAT ELSE CAN I DO? IT'S EITHER THAT OR TURN INTO A DEMON!
NO, I--
--AND THEY TRICKED ME! I NEVER WANTED TO BE PART OF THIS!
CHRISTIAN, I KNOW! KILL 'EM.
KILL 'EM ALL, AND YOU MAKE IT BACK TO ME SAFELY. I LOVE YOU.

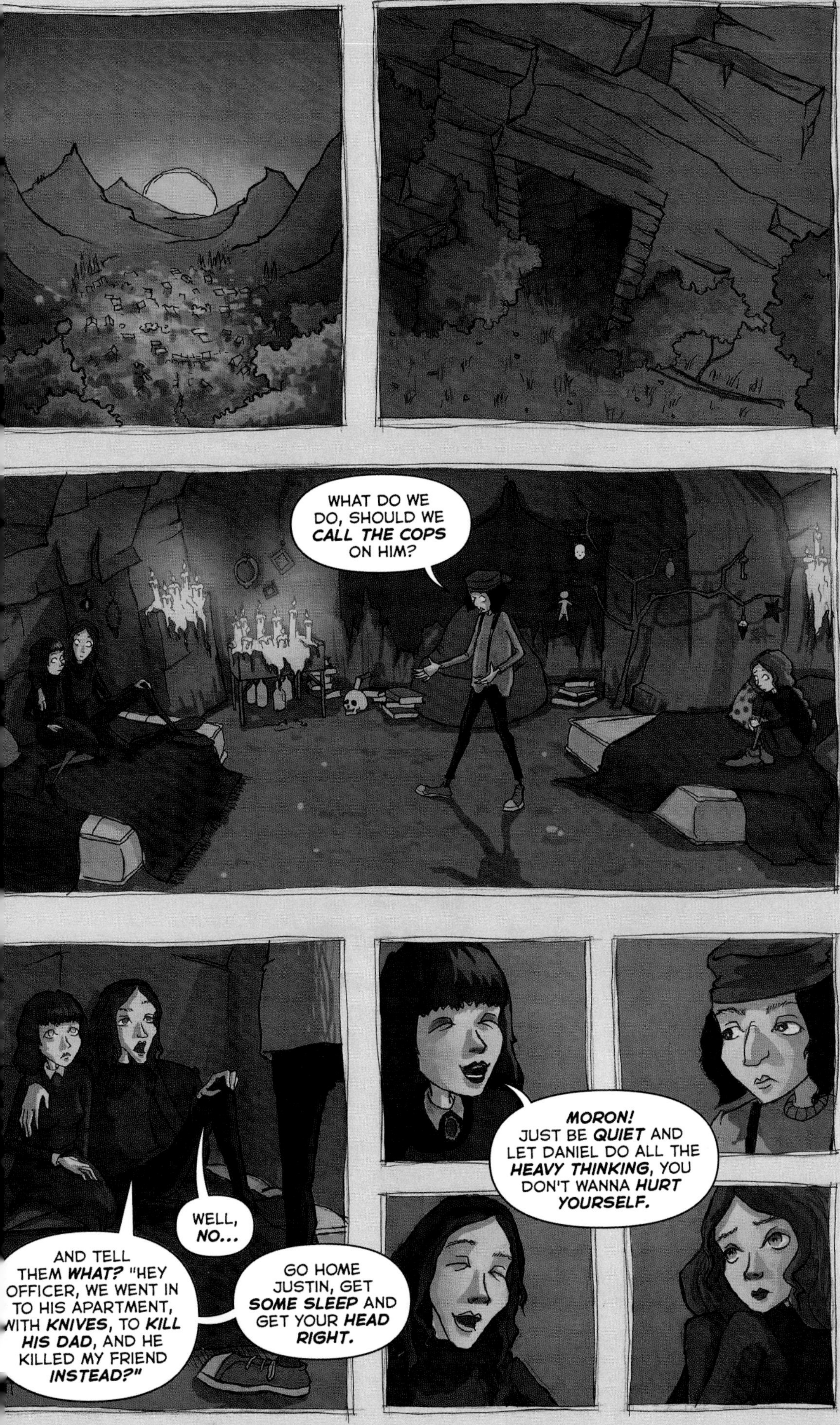

WHAT DO WE DO, SHOULD WE *CALL THE COPS* ON HIM?
WELL, *NO...*
AND TELL THEM *WHAT?* "HEY OFFICER, WE WENT IN TO HIS APARTMENT, WITH *KNIVES,* TO *KILL HIS DAD,* AND HE KILLED MY FRIEND *INSTEAD?"*
GO HOME JUSTIN, GET *SOME SLEEP* AND GET YOUR *HEAD RIGHT.*
MORON! JUST BE *QUIET* AND LET DANIEL DO ALL THE *HEAVY THINKING,* YOU DON'T WANNA *HURT YOURSELF.*

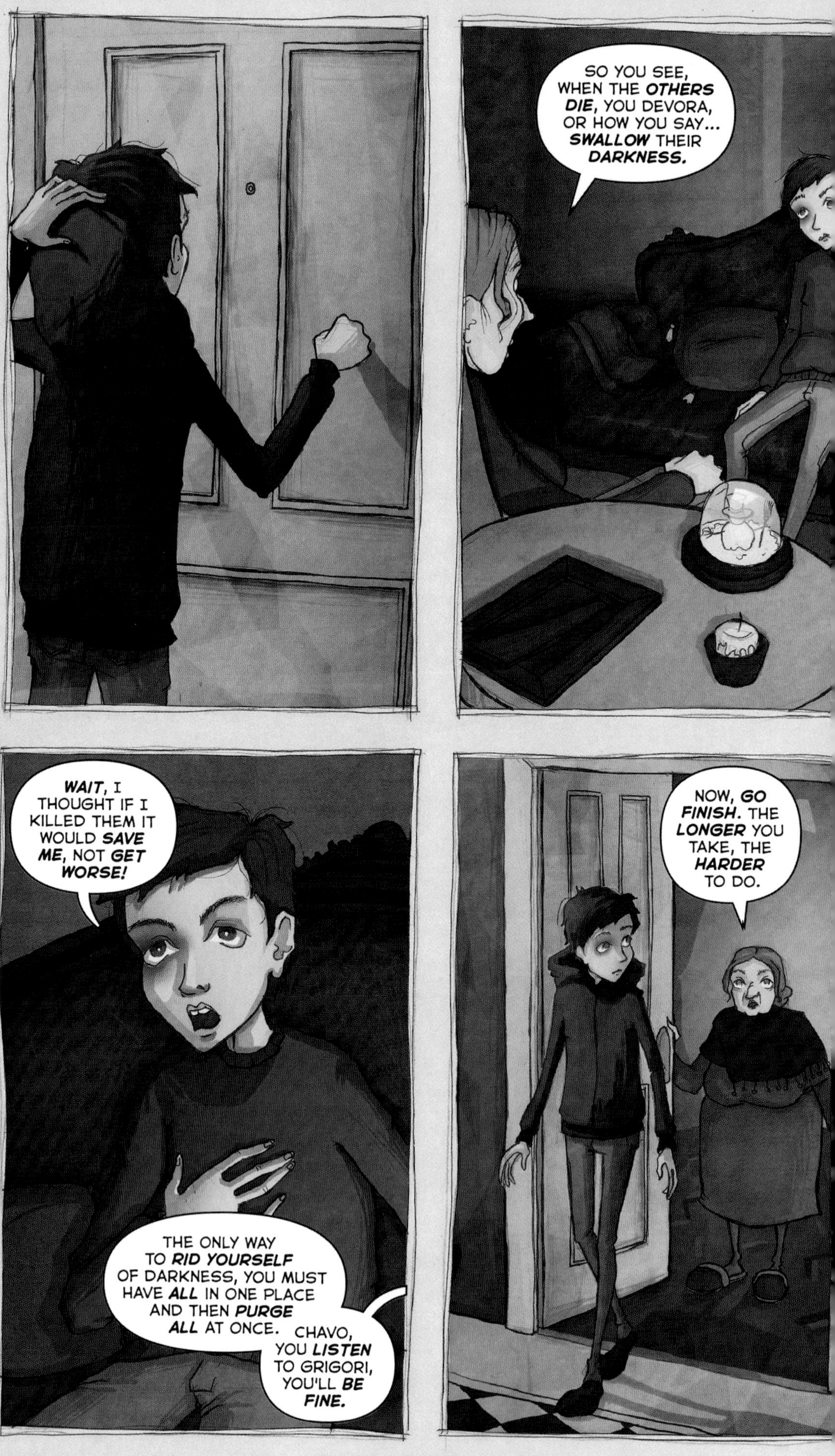
SO YOU SEE, WHEN THE OTHERS DIE, YOU DEVORA, OR HOW YOU SAY... SWALLOW THEIR DARKNESS.
WAIT, I THOUGHT IF I KILLED THEM IT WOULD SAVE ME, NOT GET WORSE!
THE ONLY WAY TO RID YOURSELF OF DARKNESS, YOU MUST HAVE ALL IN ONE PLACE AND THEN PURGE ALL AT ONCE.
CHAVO, YOU LISTEN TO GRIGORI, YOU'LL BE FINE.
NOW, GO FINISH. THE LONGER YOU TAKE, THE HARDER TO DO.

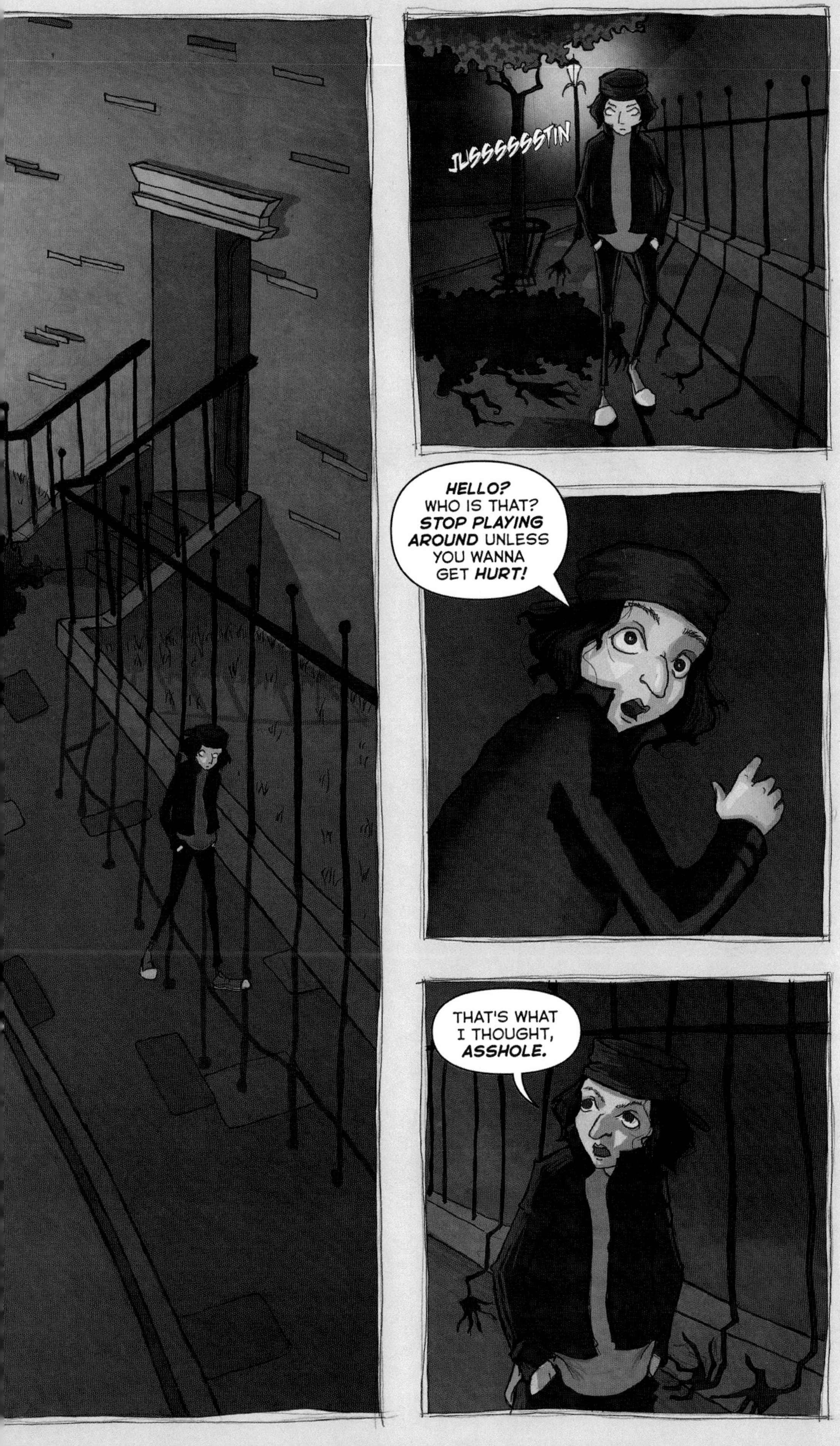
JUSSSSSSTIN
HELLO? WHO IS THAT? STOP PLAYING AROUND UNLESS YOU WANNA GET HURT!
THAT'S WHAT I THOUGHT, ASSHOLE.

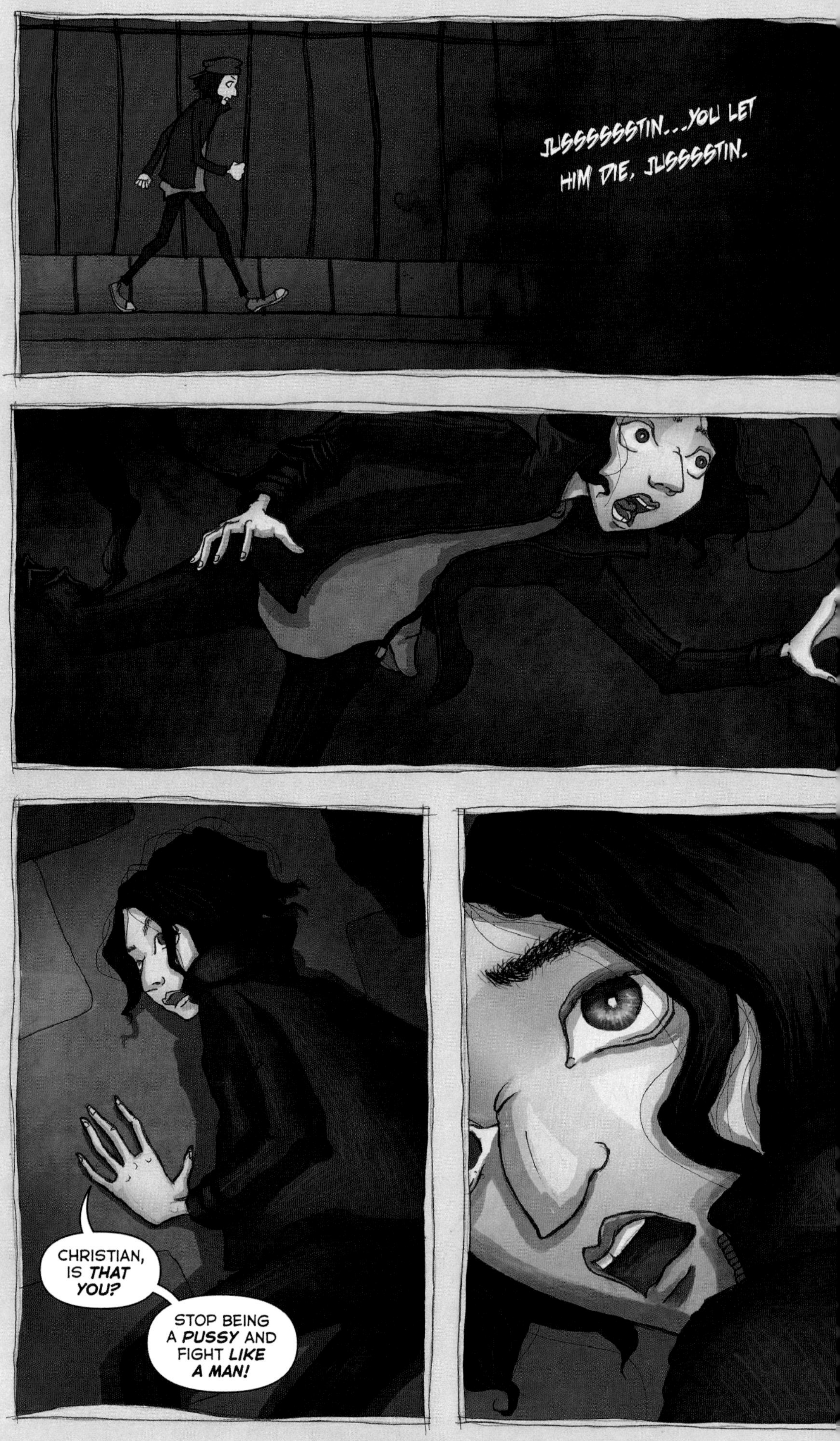
JUSSSSSSTIN...YOU LET HIM DIE, JUSSSSTIN.
CHRISTIAN, IS THAT YOU?
STOP BEING A PUSSY AND FIGHT LIKE A MAN!

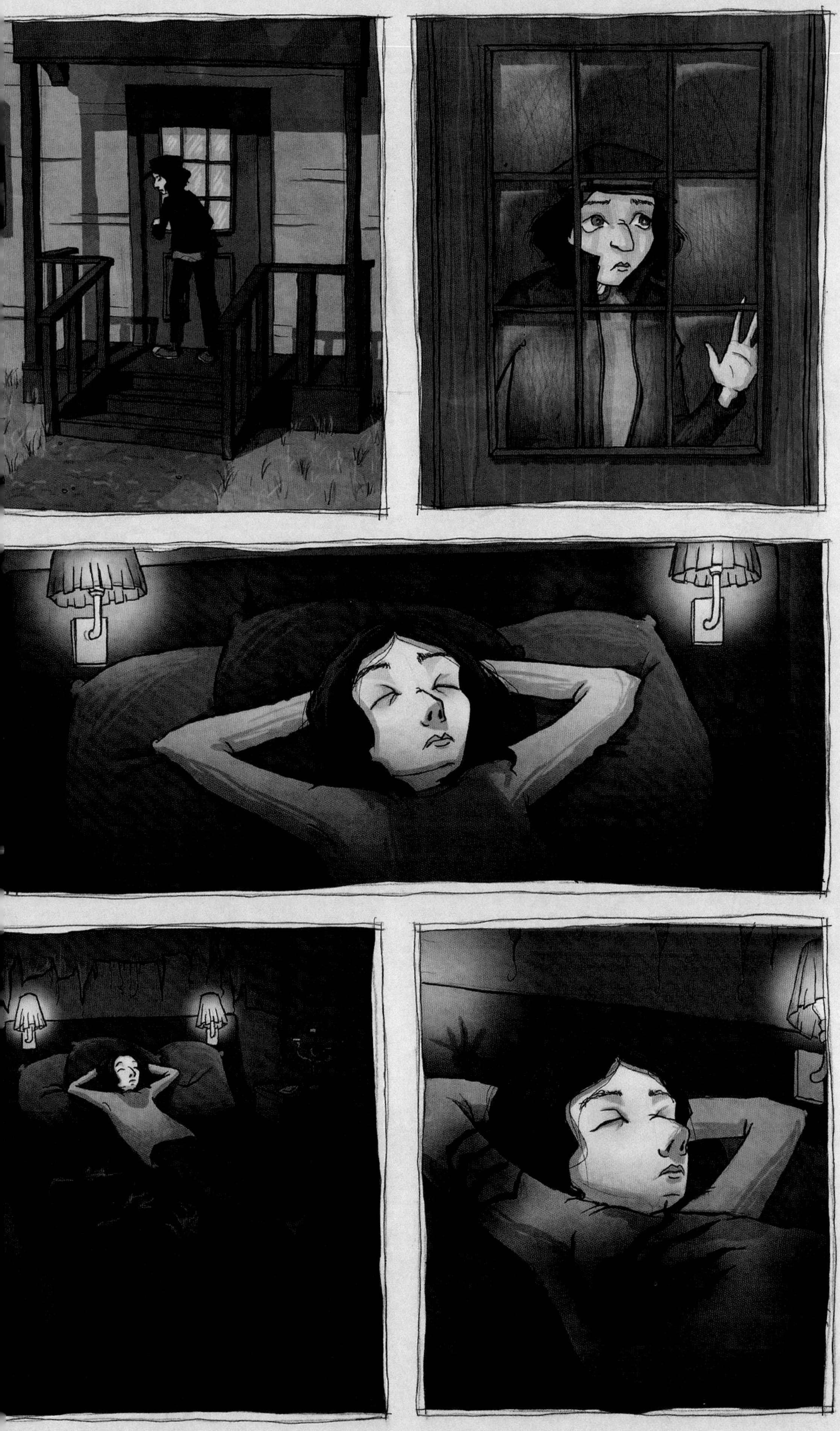

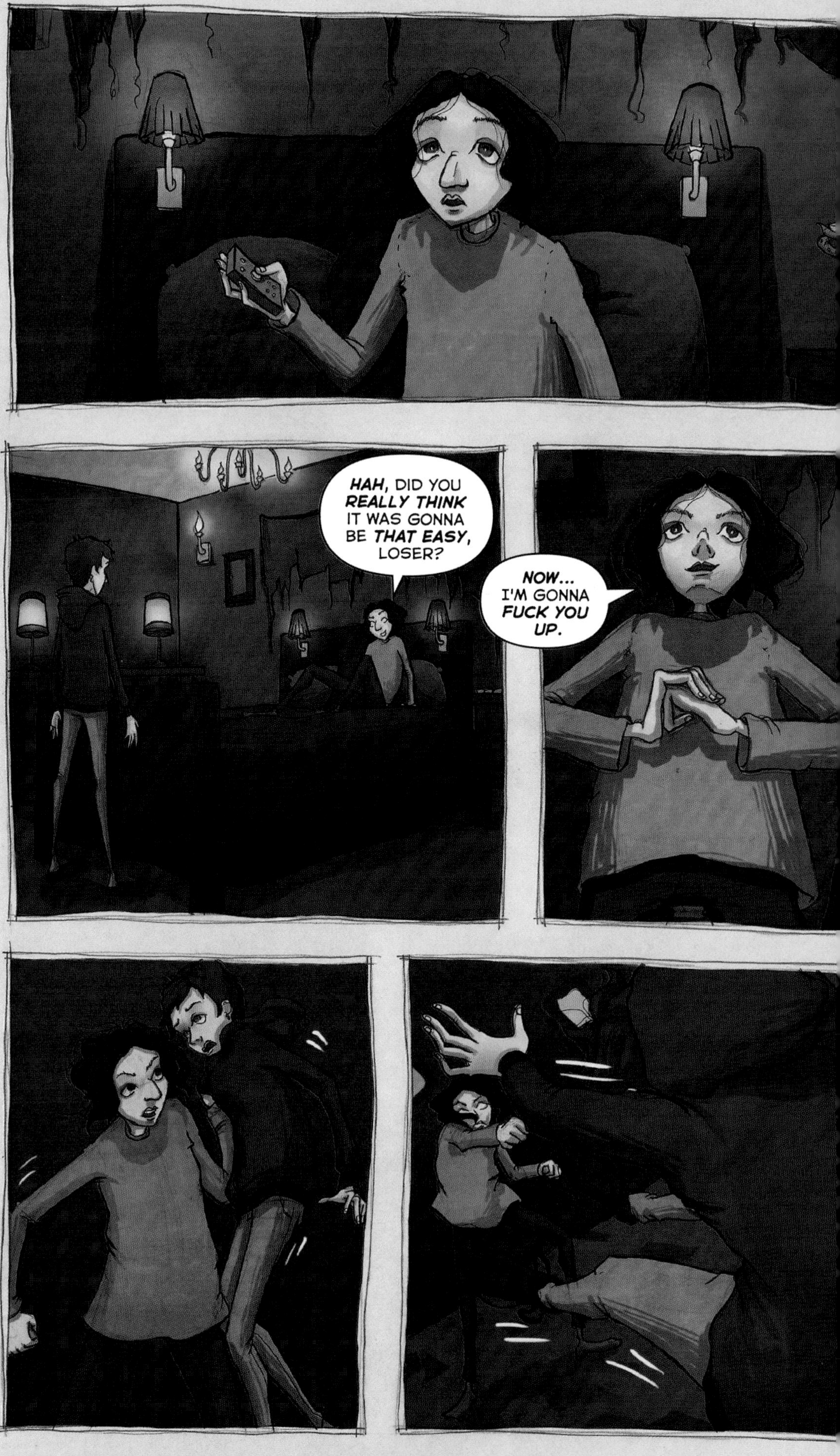
HAH, DID YOU REALLY THINK IT WAS GONNA BE THAT EASY, LOSER?
NOW... I'M GONNA FUCK YOU UP.

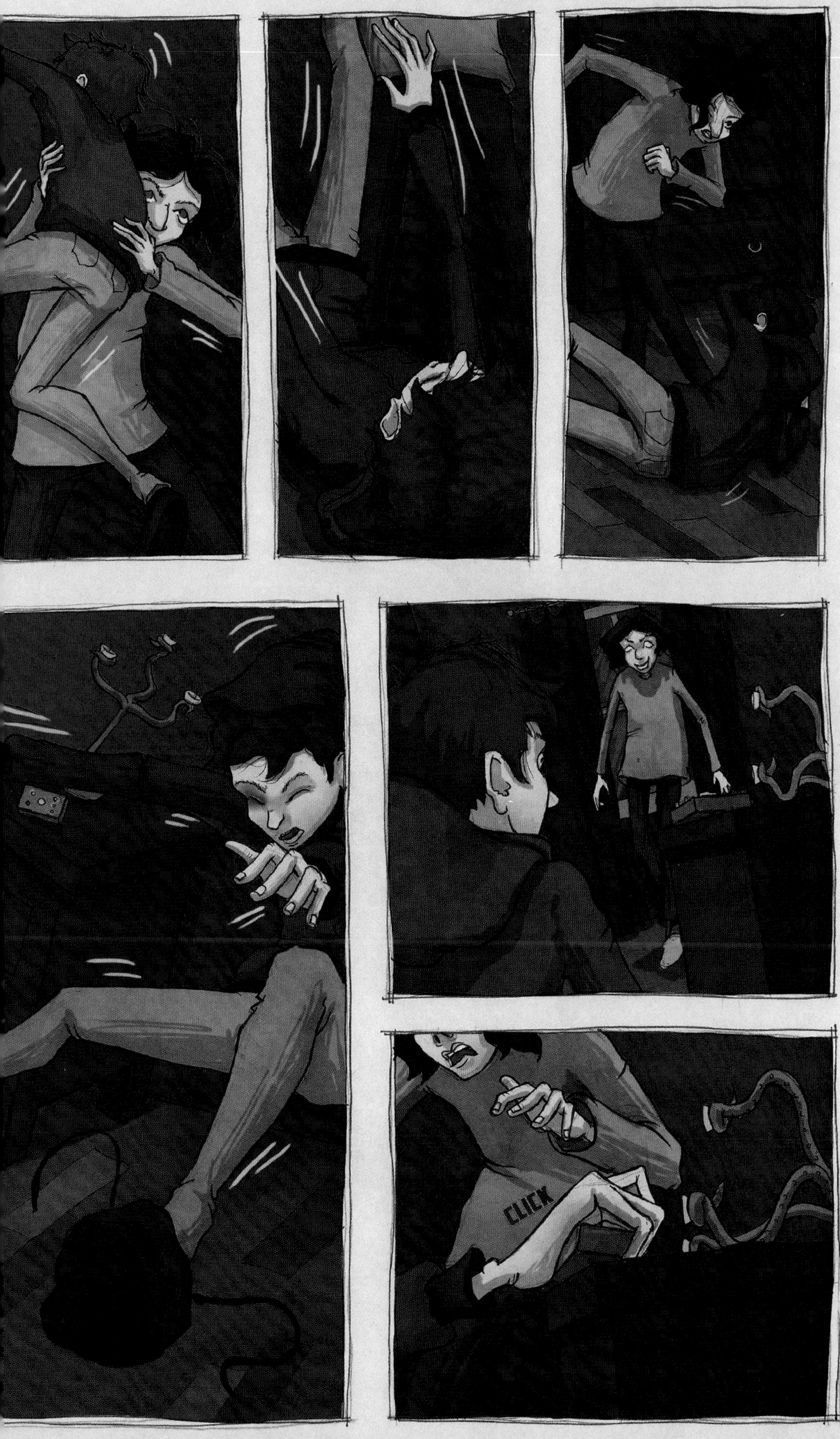
CLICK

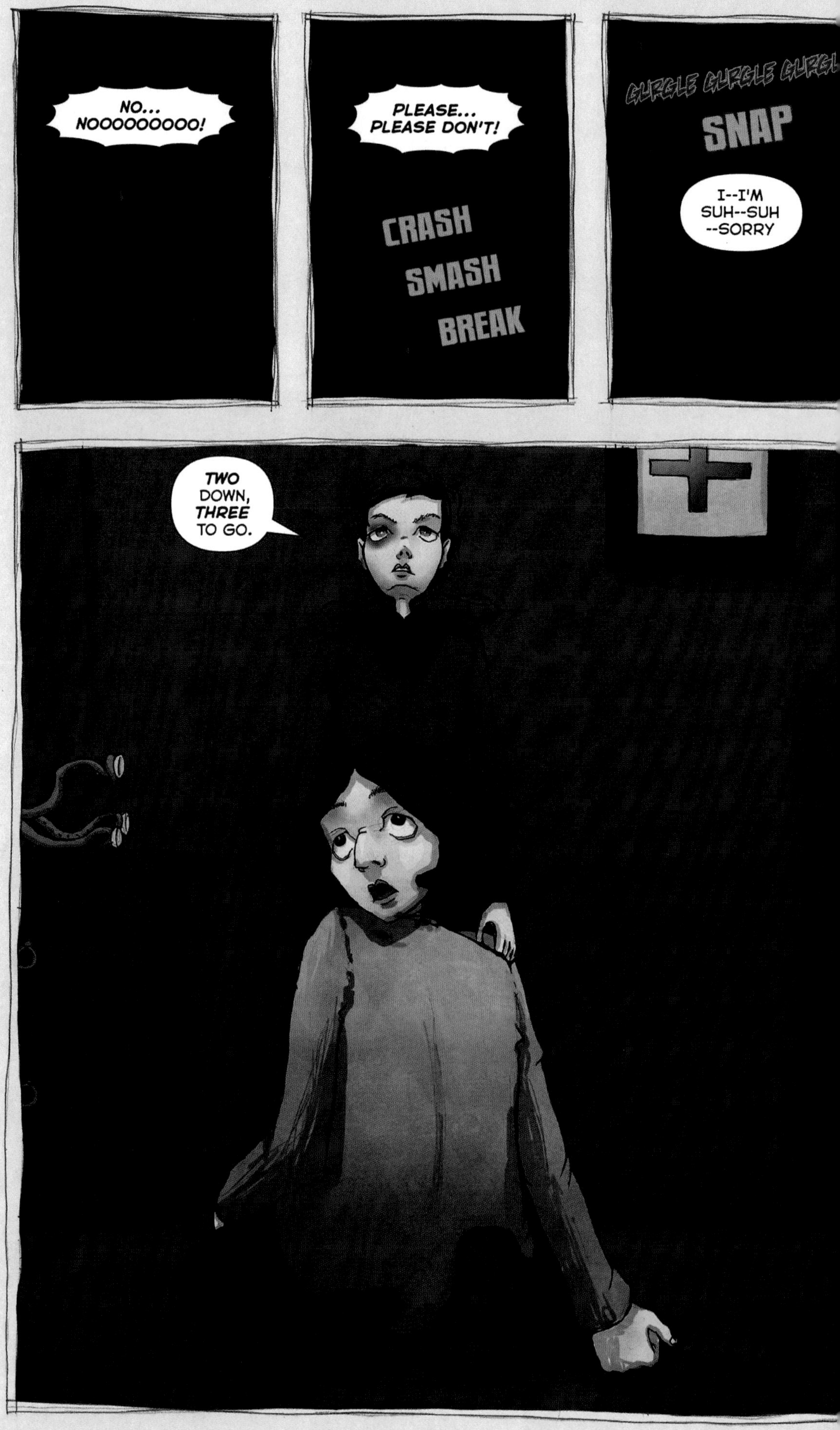
NO... NOOOOOOOOO!
PLEASE... PLEASE DON'T!
CRASH
SMASH
BREAK
GURGLE GURGLE GURGL
SNAP
I--I'M SUH--SUH --SORRY
TWO DOWN, THREE TO GO.

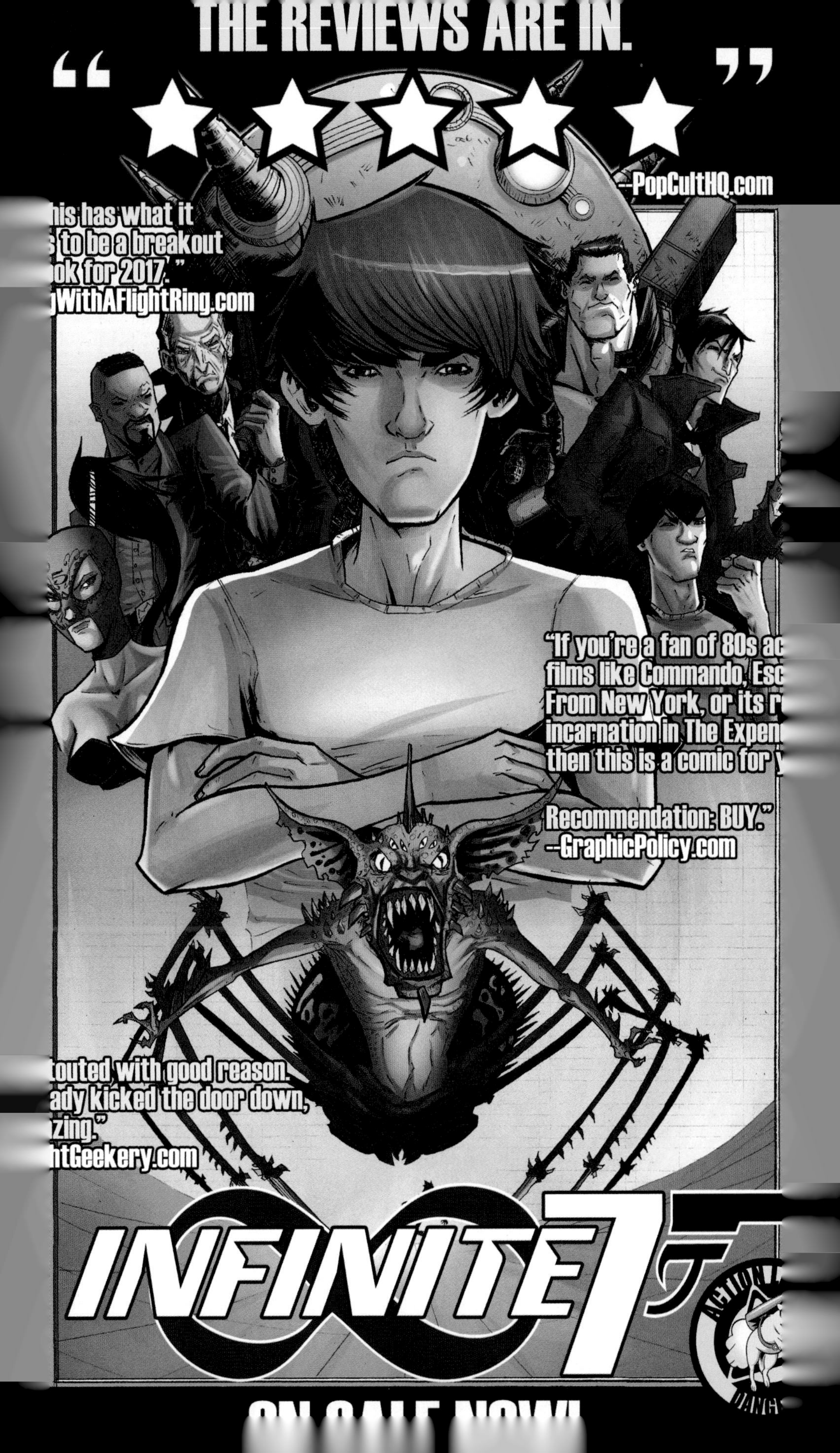

THE REVIEWS ARE IN.
“★★★★★”
--PopCultHQ.com
his has what it
s to be a breakout
ok for 2017.”
WithAFlightRing.com
“If you're a fan of 80s ac
films like Commando, Esc
From New York, or its r
incarnation in The Expen
then this is a comic for y
Recommendation: BUY.”
--GraphicPolicy.com
touted with good reason.
ady kicked the door down,
zing.”
ntGeekery.com
INFINITE 7
ON SALE NOW!

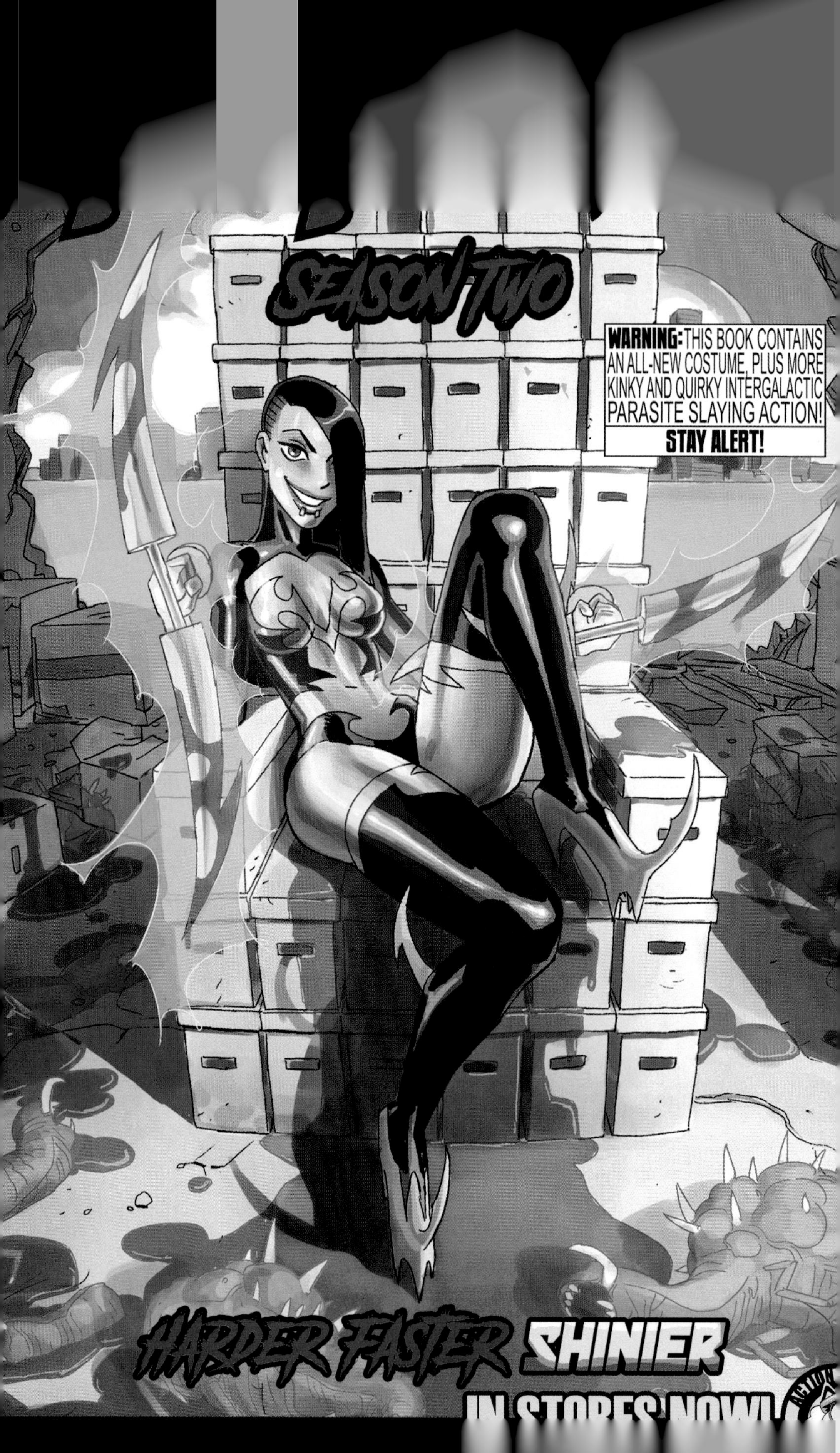
SEASON TWO
WARNING: THIS BOOK CONTAINS AN ALL-NEW COSTUME, PLUS MORE KINKY AND QUIRKY INTERGALACTIC PARASITE SLAYING ACTION!
STAY ALERT!
HARDER FASTER SHINIER
IN STORES NOW!

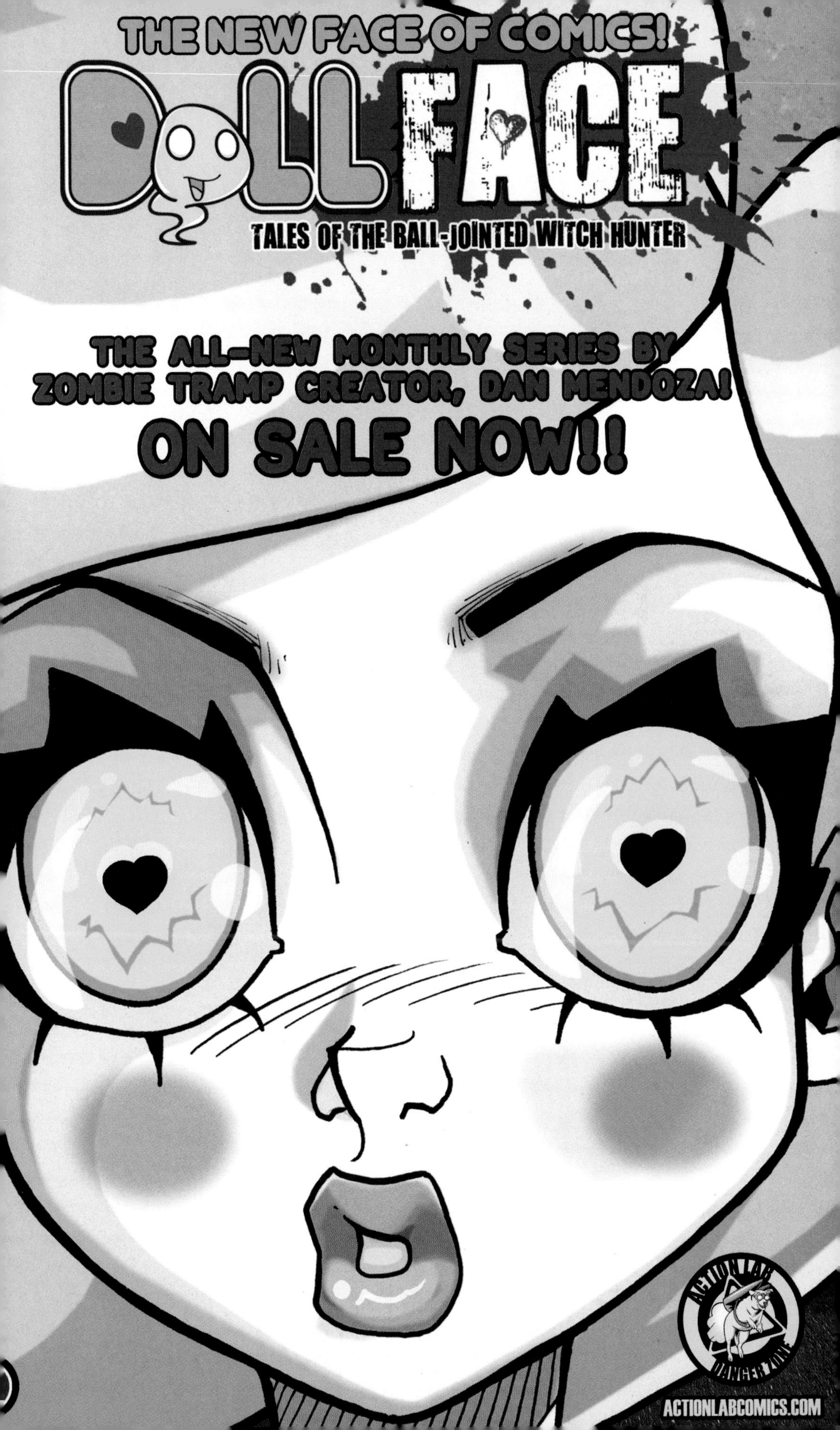

THE NEW FACE OF COMICS!
DOLL FACE
TALES OF THE BALL-JOINTED WITCH HUNTER
THE ALL-NEW MONTHLY SERIES BY ZOMBIE TRAMP CREATOR, DAN MENDOZA!
ON SALE NOW!!
ACTION LAB DANGER ZONE
ACTIONLABCOMICS.COM

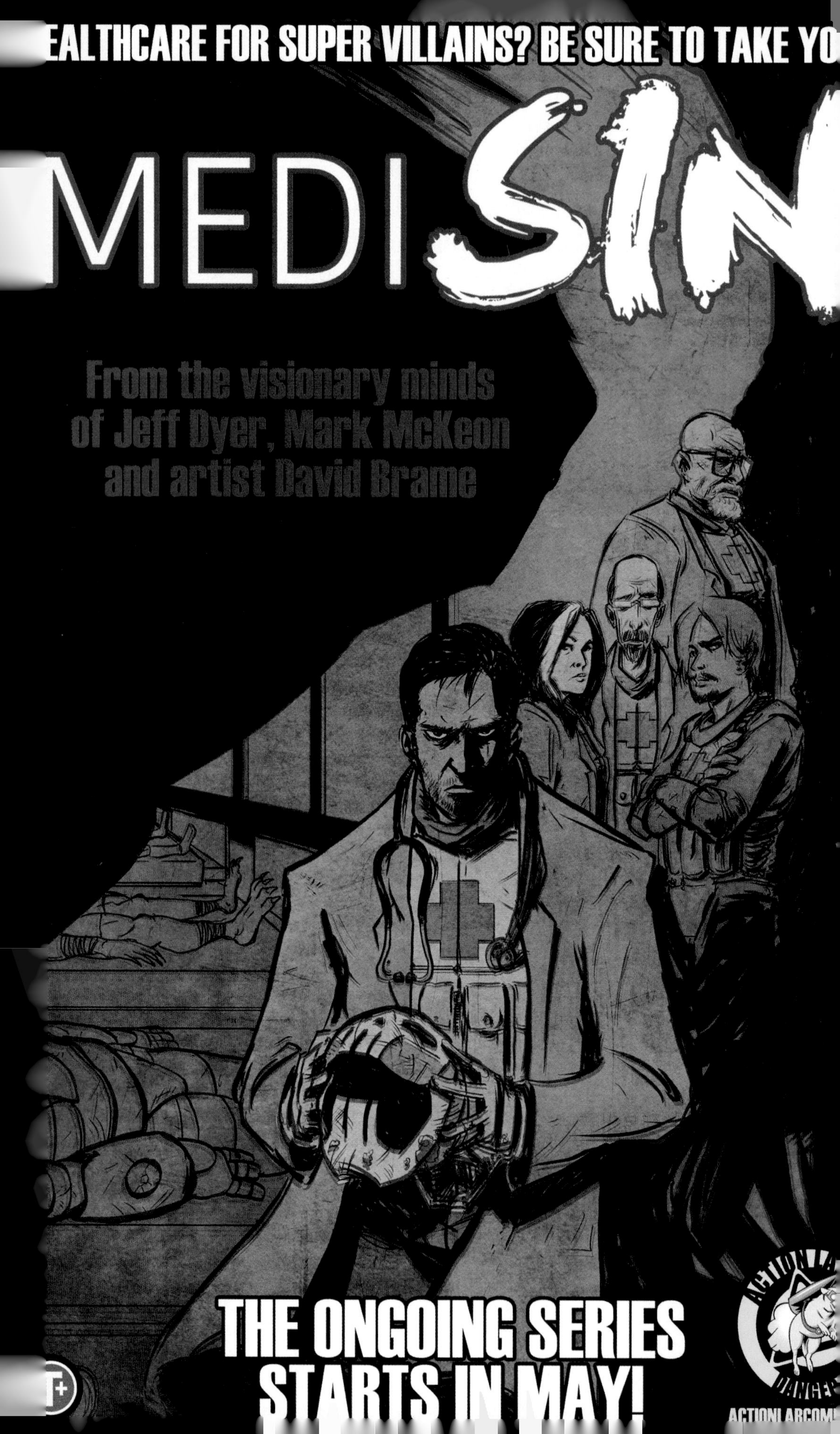
EALTHCARE FOR SUPER VILLAINS? BE SURE TO TAKE YO
MEDISIN
From the visionary minds of Jeff Dyer, Mark McKeon and artist David Brame
THE ONGOING SERIES STARTS IN MAY!

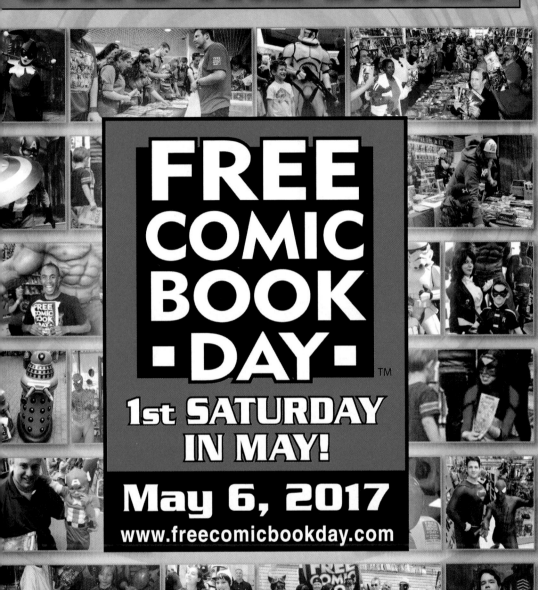

SAVE THE DATE!

FREE COMIC BOOK ·DAY·™

1st SATURDAY IN MAY!

May 6, 2017
www.freecomicbookday.com

FREE COMICS FOR EVERYONE!

Details @ www.freecomicbookday.com

 /freecomicbook   @freecomicbook   @freecomicbookday

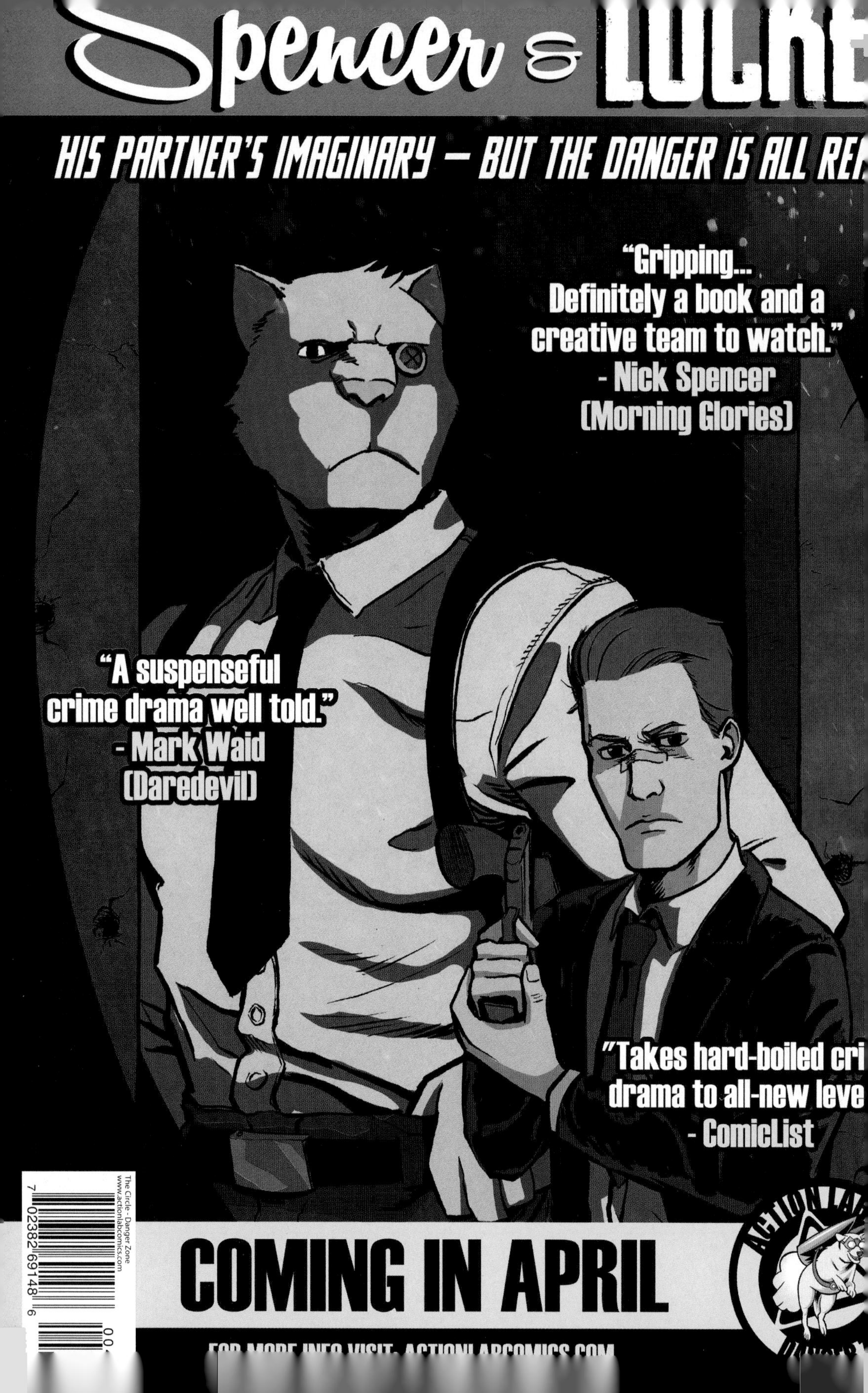
Spencer & LOCKE
HIS PARTNER'S IMAGINARY — BUT THE DANGER IS ALL
"Gripping... Definitely a book and a creative team to watch."
- Nick Spencer (Morning Glories)
"A suspenseful crime drama well told."
- Mark Waid (Daredevil)
"Takes hard-boiled cri
drama to all-new leve
- ComicList
The Circle - Danger Zone
www.actionlabcomics.com
COMING IN APRIL
FOR MORE INFO VISIT: ACTIONLABCOMICS.COM

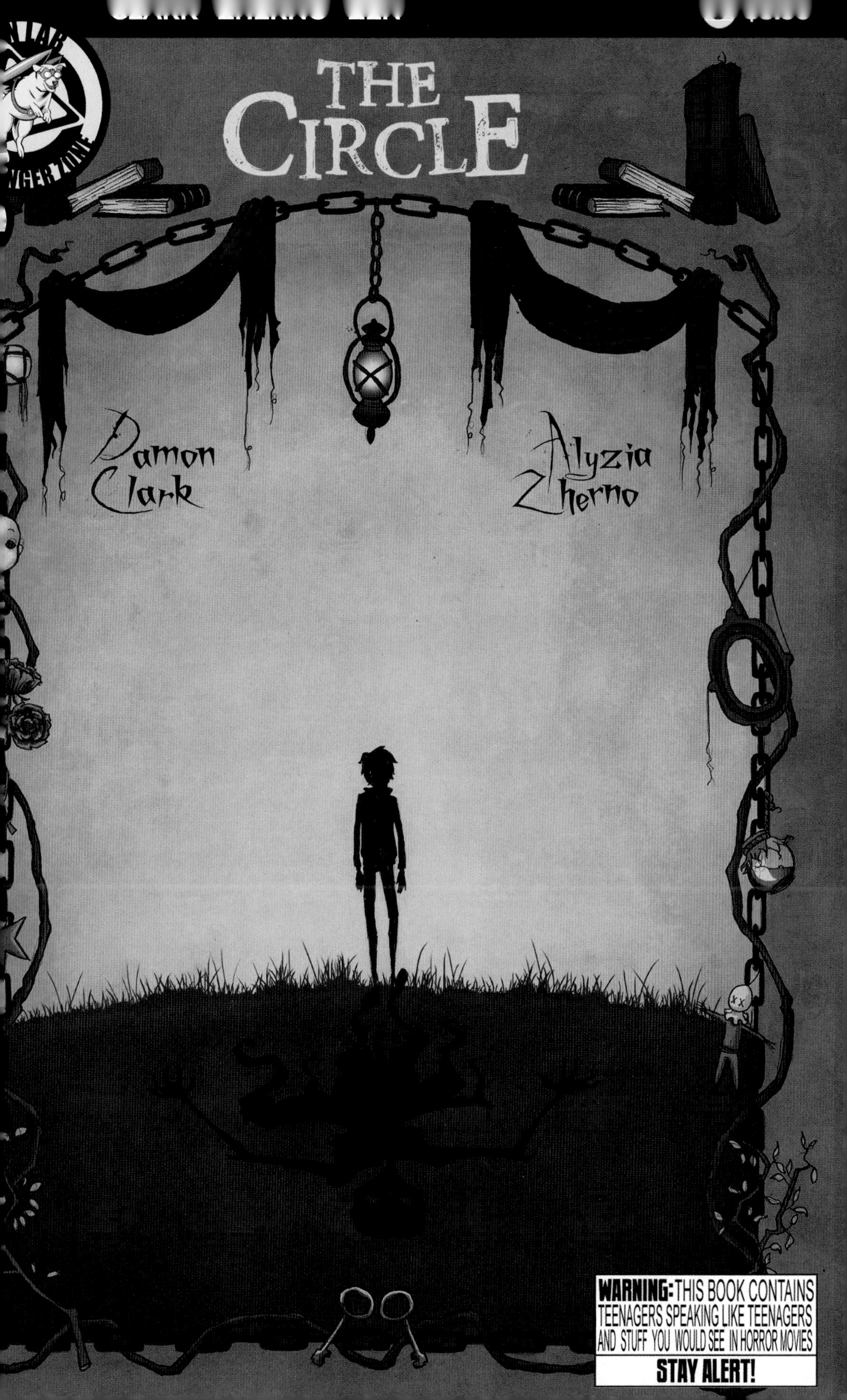
THE CIRCLE
Damon Clark
Alyzia Zherno
WARNING: THIS BOOK CONTAINS TEENAGERS SPEAKING LIKE TEENAGERS AND STUFF YOU WOULD SEE IN HORROR MOVIES
STAY ALERT!

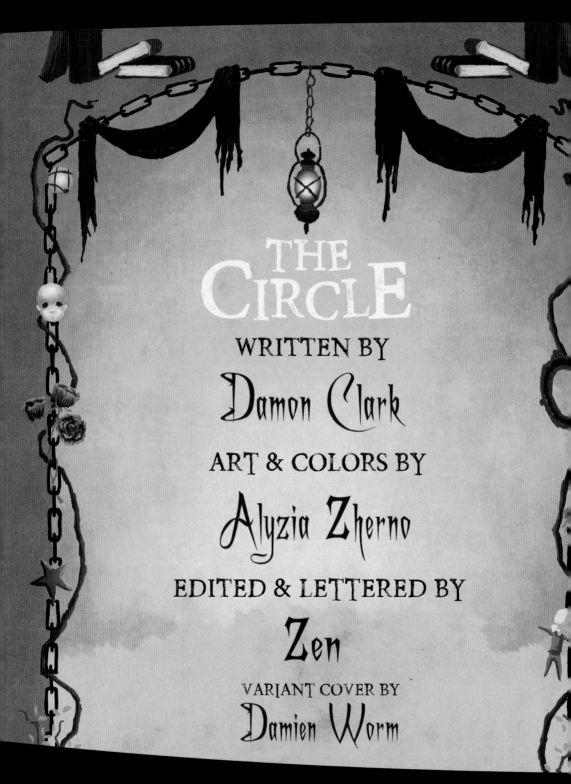

THE CIRCLE

WRITTEN BY
Damon Clark

ART & COLORS BY
Alyzia Zherno

EDITED & LETTERED BY
Zen

VARIANT COVER BY
Damien Worm

JASON MARTIN - PUBLISHER
DAVE DWONCH - PRESIDENT OF MARKETING
SHAWN GABBORIN - EDITOR IN CHIEF
NICOLE D'ANDRIA - MARKETING DIRECTOR/EDITOR
JIM DIETZ - SOCIAL MEDIA MANAGER
SCOTT BRADLEY - CFO
BRYAN SEATON - CEO

THE CIRCLE #5 April 2017.
Copyright Damon Clark and Alyzia Zherno, 2017.
Published by Action Lab Comics.
All rights reserved.

Christian

Daniel

Phoebe

Todd

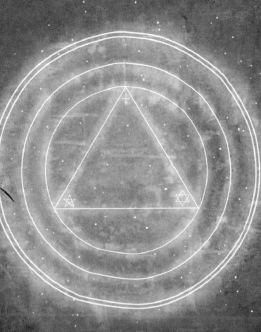

Rachel

Justin

Thomas

Chad & Brett

Trisha

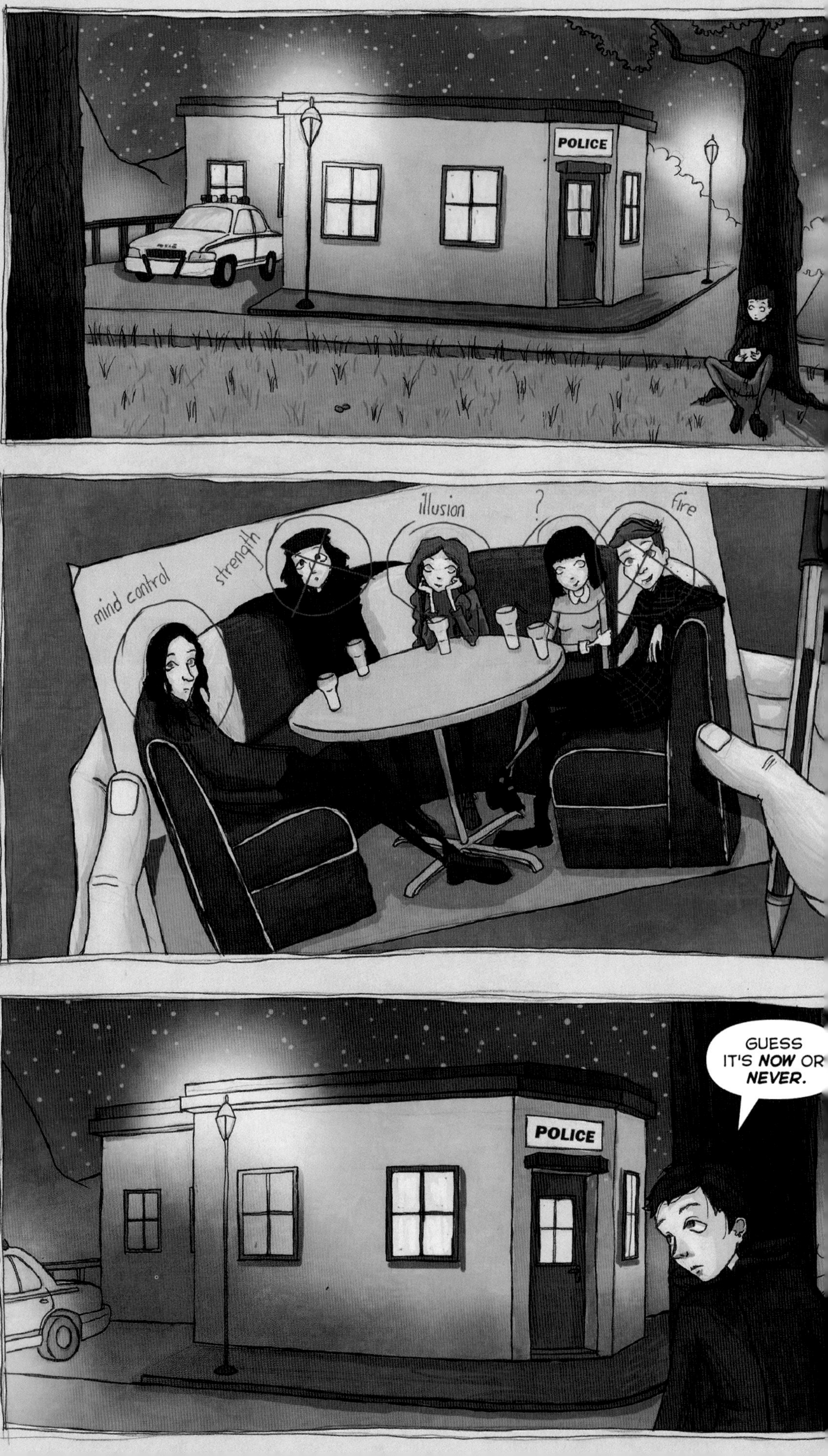

POLICE
mind control
strength
illusion
?
fire
POLICE
GUESS IT'S *NOW* OR *NEVER*.

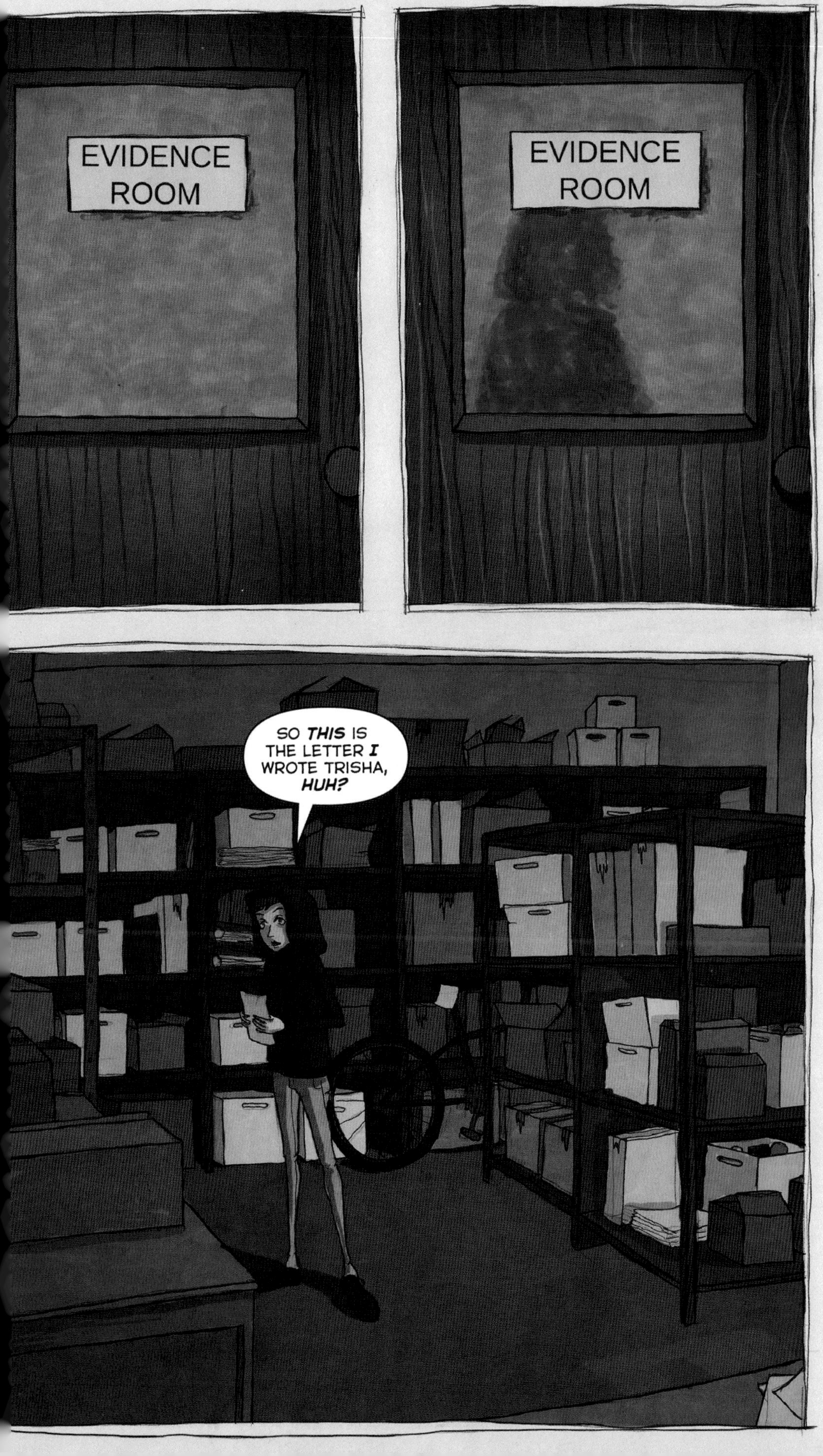
EVIDENCE ROOM
EVIDENCE ROOM
SO THIS IS THE LETTER I WROTE TRISHA, HUH?

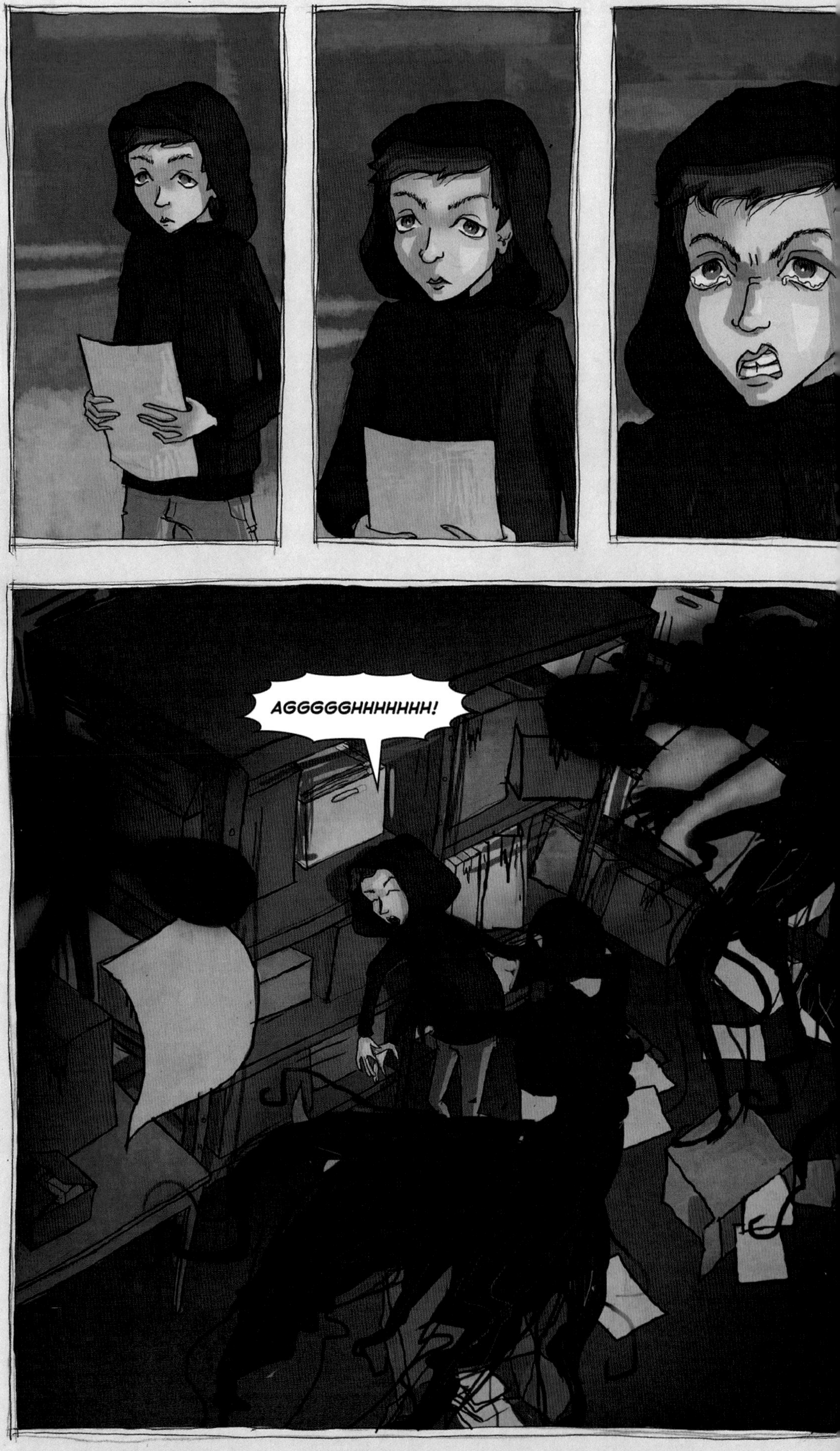
AGGGGGHHHHHHH!

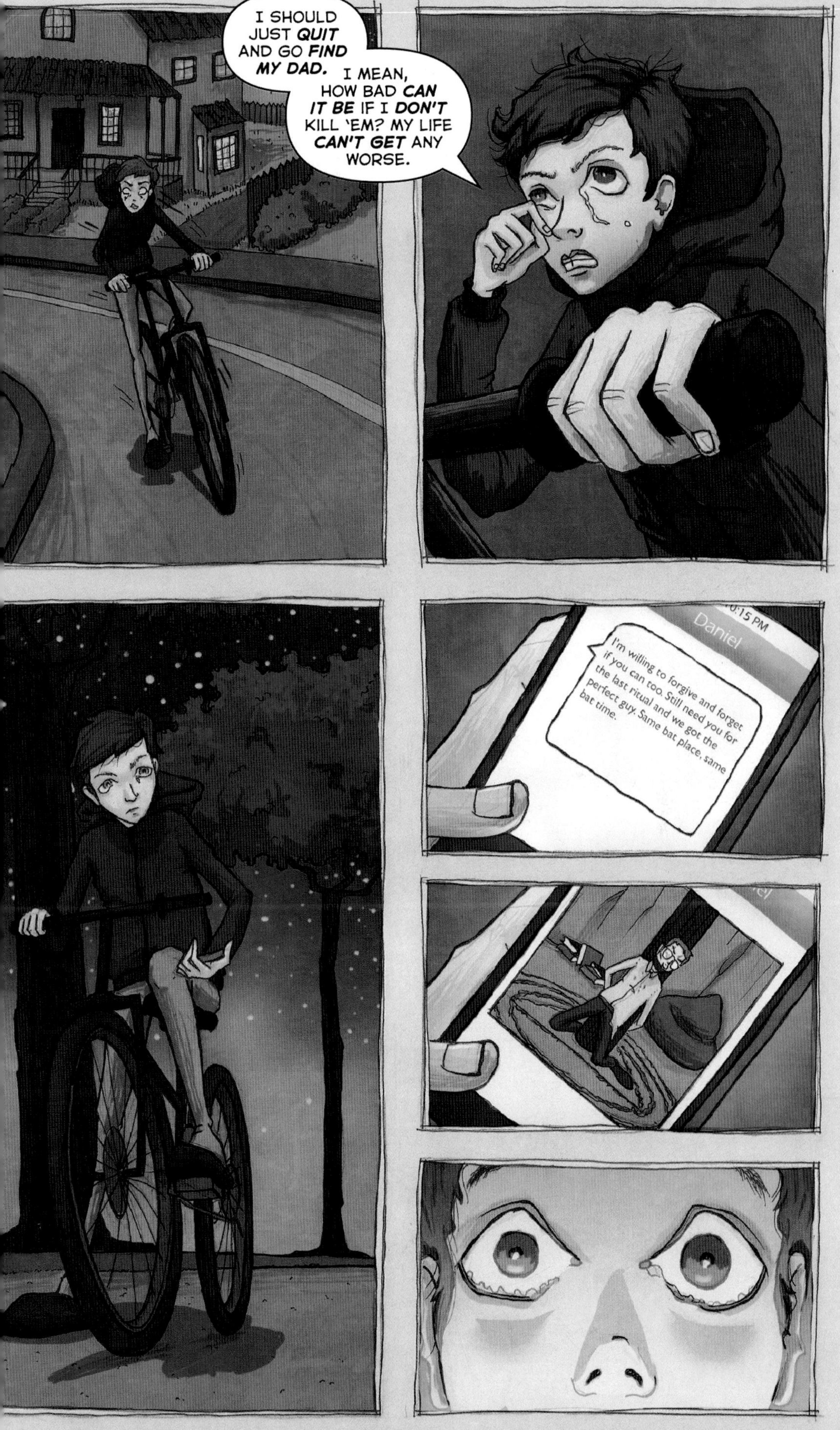
I SHOULD JUST QUIT AND GO FIND MY DAD.
I MEAN, HOW BAD CAN IT BE IF I DON'T KILL 'EM? MY LIFE CAN'T GET ANY WORSE.
Daniel
I'm willing to forgive and forget if you can too. Still need you for the last ritual and we got the perfect guy. Same bat place, same bat time.

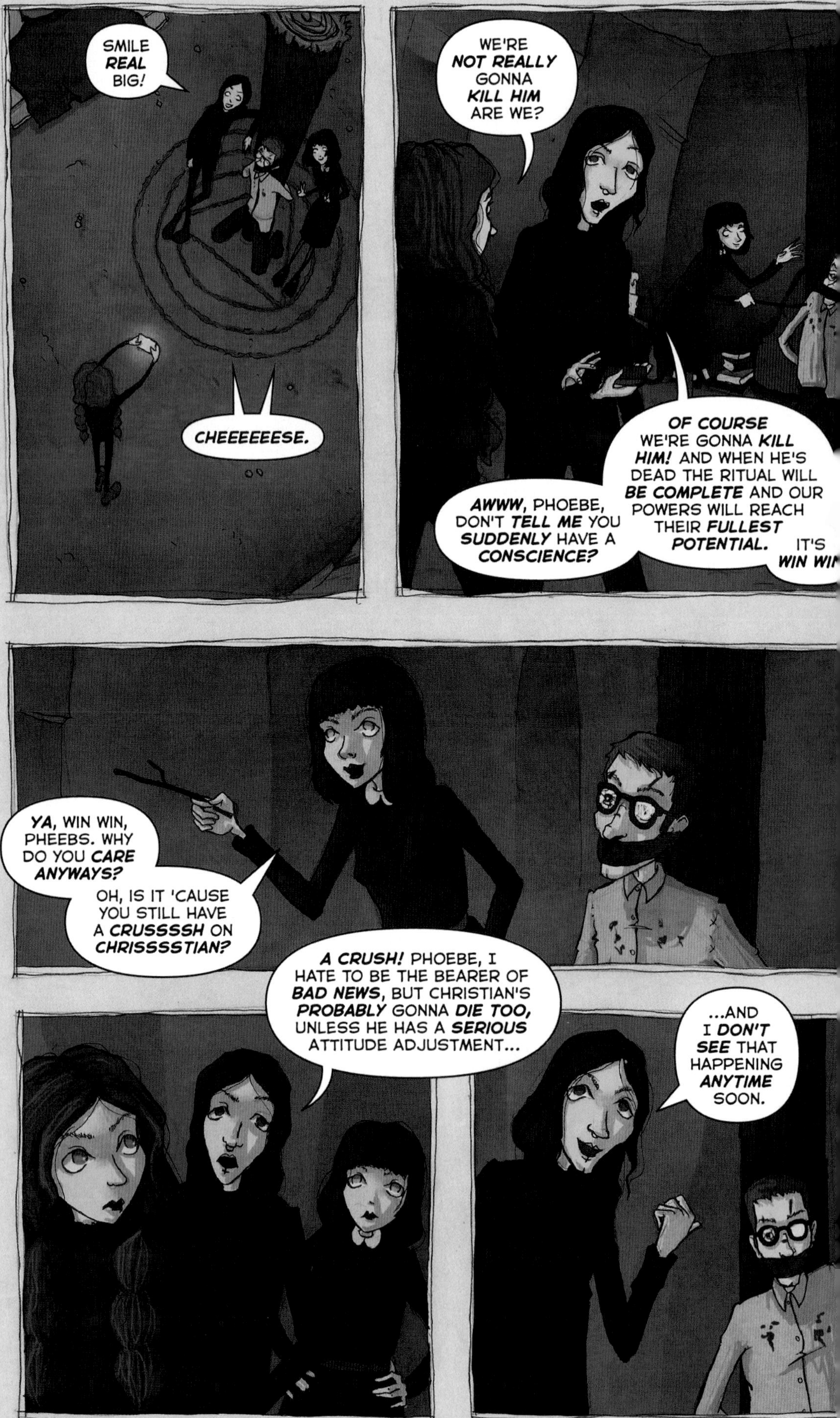
SMILE REAL BIG!
CHEEEEEEESE.
WE'RE NOT REALLY GONNA KILL HIM ARE WE?
AWWW, PHOEBE, DON'T TELL ME YOU SUDDENLY HAVE A CONSCIENCE?
OF COURSE WE'RE GONNA KILL HIM! AND WHEN HE'S DEAD THE RITUAL WILL BE COMPLETE AND OUR POWERS WILL REACH THEIR FULLEST POTENTIAL.
IT'S
YA, WIN WIN, PHEEBS. WHY DO YOU CARE ANYWAYS?
OH, IS IT 'CAUSE YOU STILL HAVE A CRUSSSSH ON CHRISSSSTIAN?
A CRUSH! PHOEBE, I HATE TO BE THE BEARER OF BAD NEWS, BUT CHRISTIAN'S PROBABLY GONNA DIE TOO, UNLESS HE HAS A SERIOUS ATTITUDE ADJUSTMENT...
...AND I DON'T SEE THAT HAPPENING ANYTIME SOON.

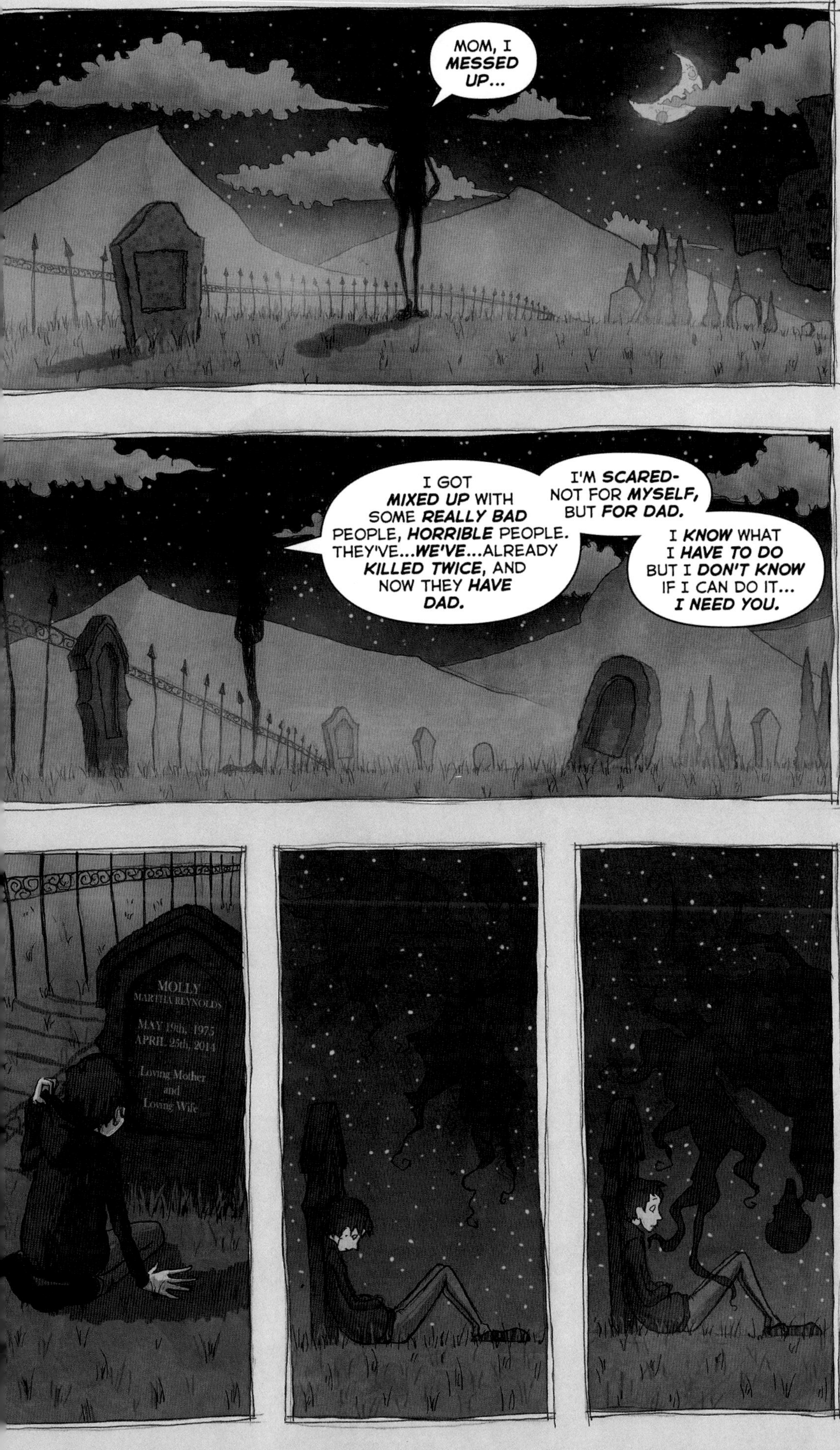
MOM, I MESSED UP...
I GOT MIXED UP WITH SOME REALLY BAD PEOPLE, HORRIBLE PEOPLE. THEY'VE...WE'VE...ALREADY KILLED TWICE, AND NOW THEY HAVE DAD.
I'M SCARED- NOT FOR MYSELF, BUT FOR DAD.
I KNOW WHAT I HAVE TO DO BUT I DON'T KNOW IF I CAN DO IT... I NEED YOU.
MOLLY
MARTHA REYNOLDS
MAY 19th, 1975
APRIL 25th, 2014
Loving Mother and Loving Wife

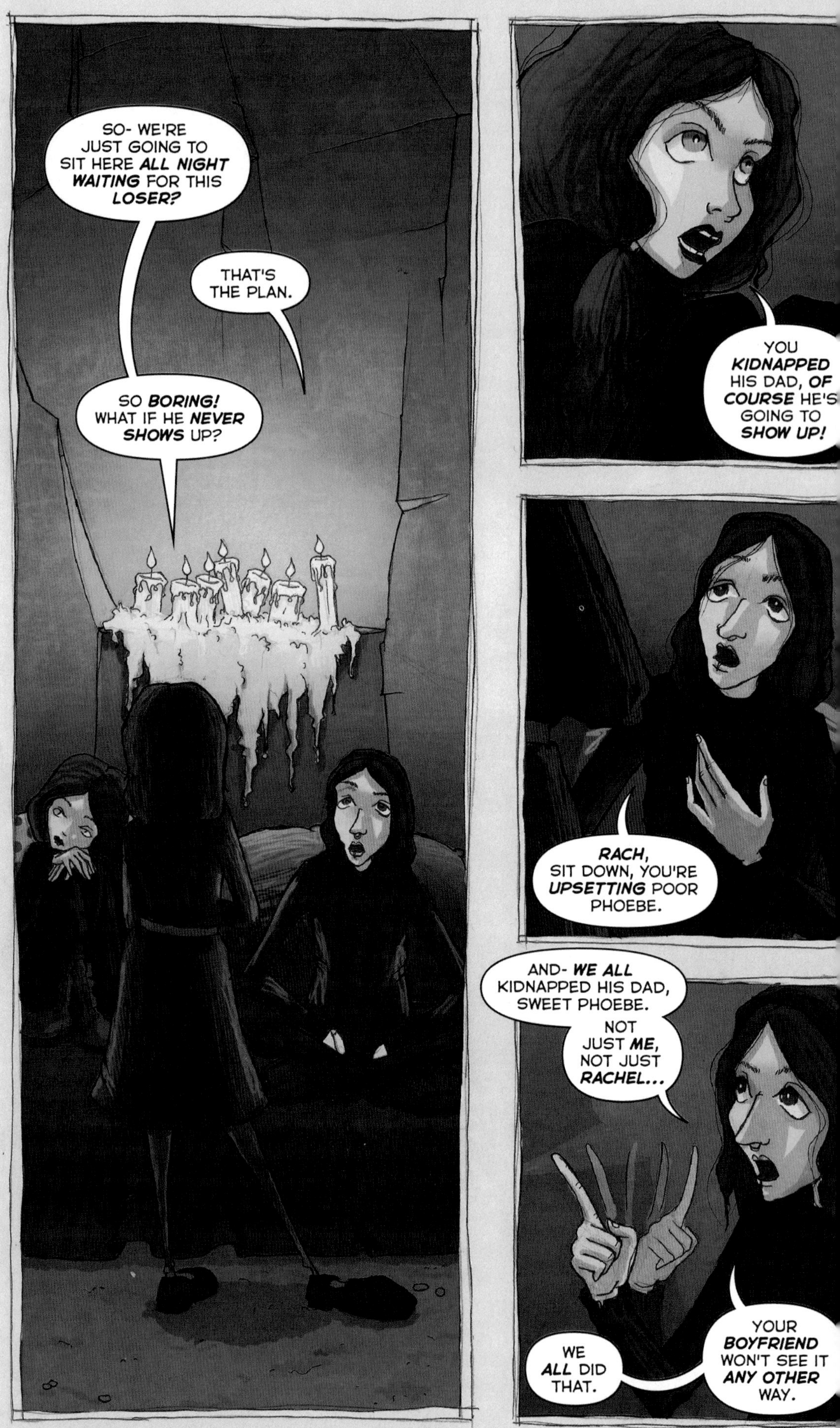
SO- WE'RE JUST GOING TO SIT HERE ALL NIGHT WAITING FOR THIS LOSER?
THAT'S THE PLAN.
SO BORING! WHAT IF HE NEVER SHOWS UP?
YOU KIDNAPPED HIS DAD, OF COURSE HE'S GOING TO SHOW UP!
RACH, SIT DOWN, YOU'RE UPSETTING POOR PHOEBE.
AND- WE ALL KIDNAPPED HIS DAD, SWEET PHOEBE.
NOT JUST ME, NOT JUST RACHEL...
WE ALL DID THAT.
YOUR BOYFRIEND WON'T SEE IT ANY OTHER WAY.

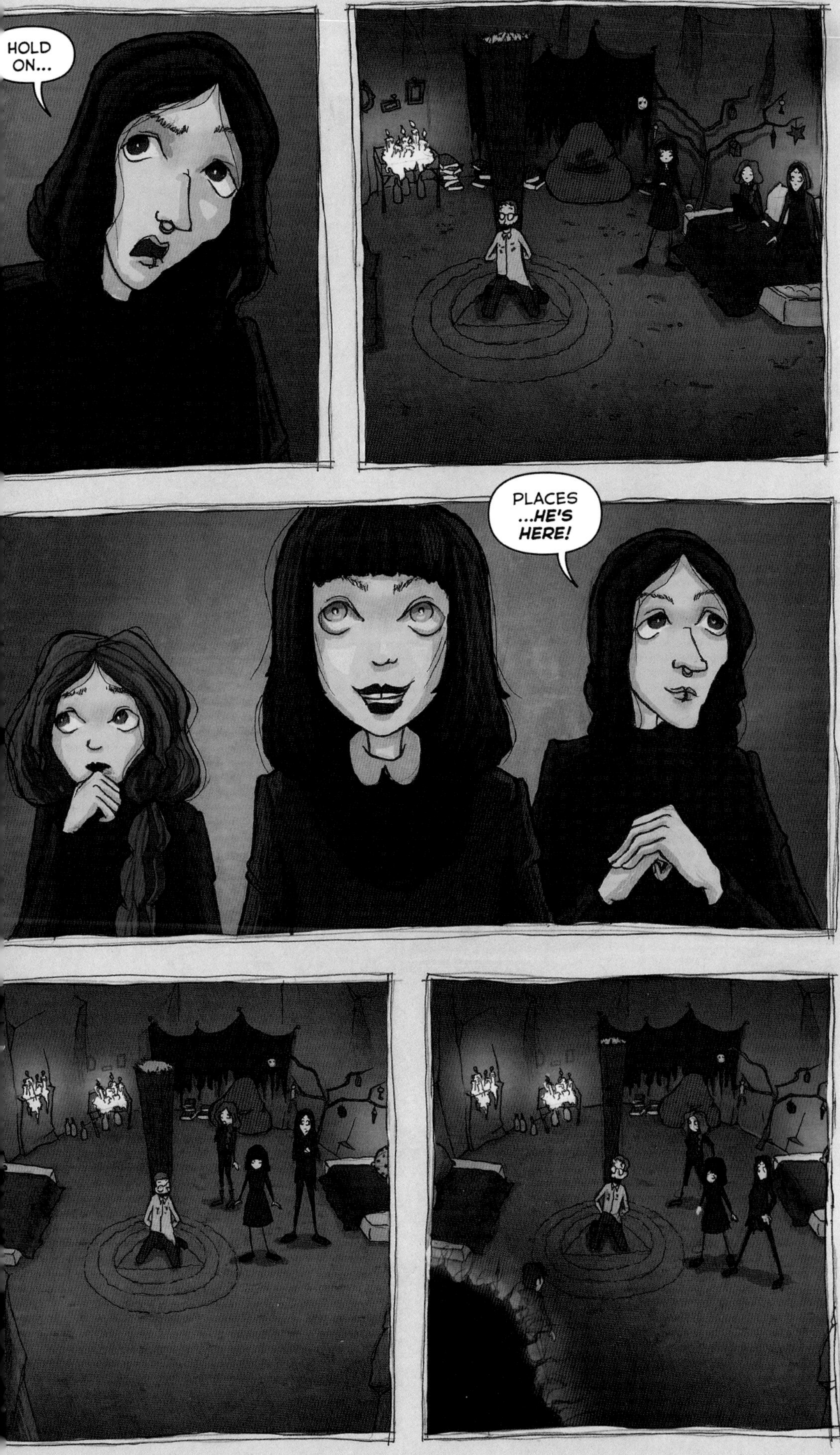
HOLD ON...
PLACES ...HE'S HERE!

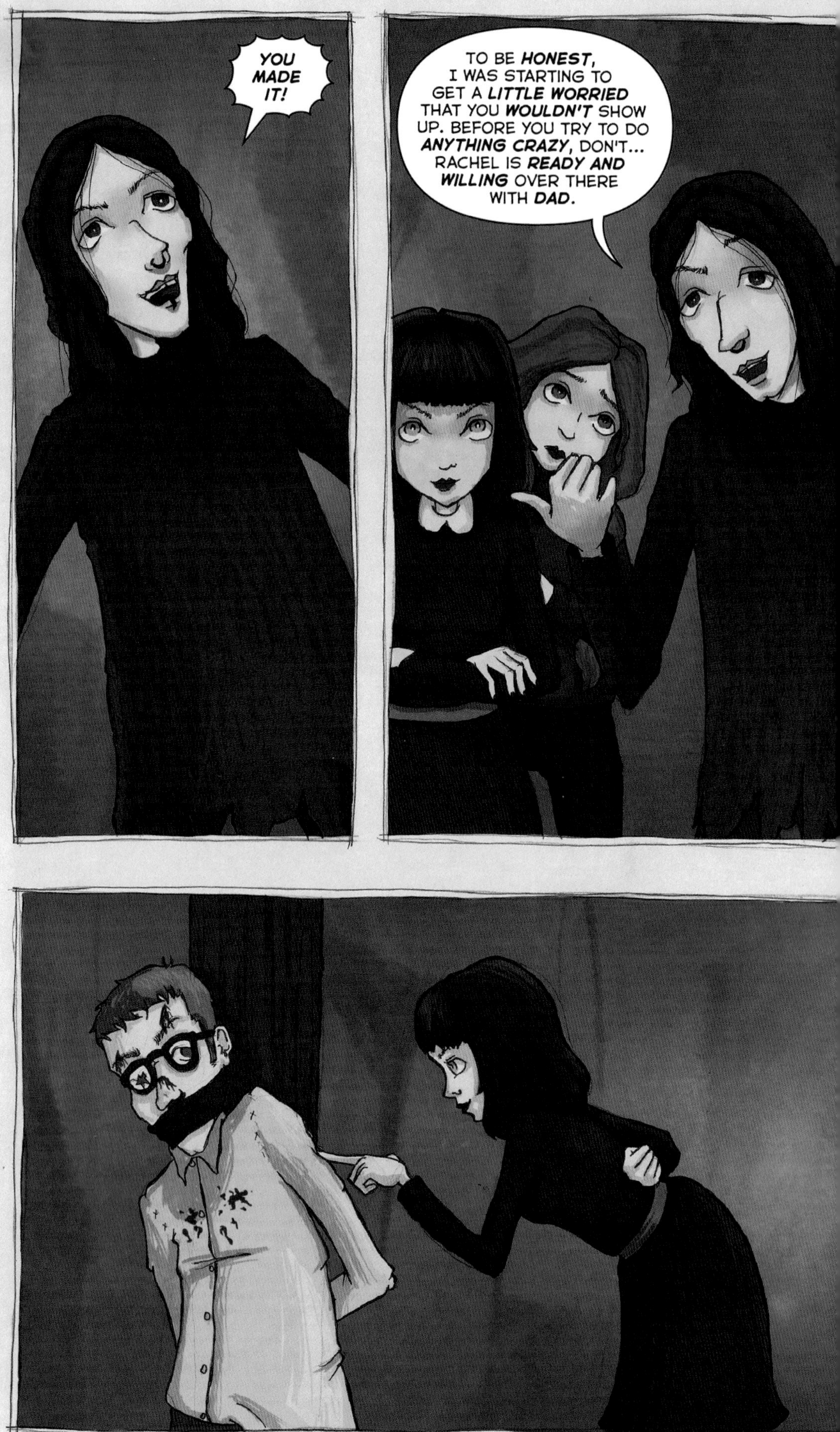
YOU MADE IT!
TO BE HONEST, I WAS STARTING TO GET A LITTLE WORRIED THAT YOU WOULDN'T SHOW UP. BEFORE YOU TRY TO DO ANYTHING CRAZY, DON'T... RACHEL IS READY AND WILLING OVER THERE WITH DAD.

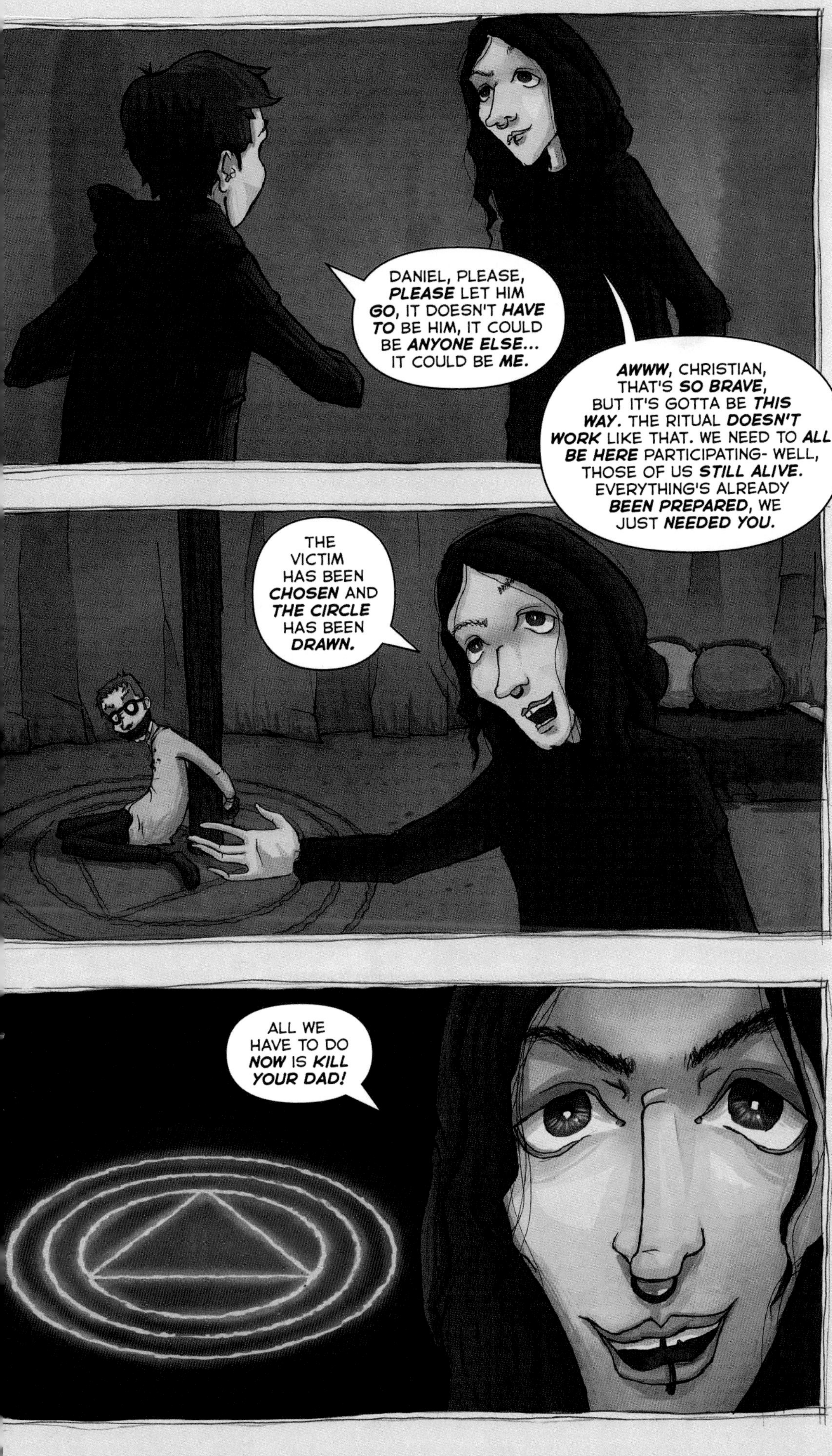
DANIEL, PLEASE, PLEASE LET HIM GO, IT DOESN'T HAVE TO BE HIM, IT COULD BE ANYONE ELSE... IT COULD BE ME.
AWWW, CHRISTIAN, THAT'S SO BRAVE, BUT IT'S GOTTA BE THIS WAY. THE RITUAL DOESN'T WORK LIKE THAT. WE NEED TO ALL BE HERE PARTICIPATING- WELL, THOSE OF US STILL ALIVE. EVERYTHING'S ALREADY BEEN PREPARED, WE JUST NEEDED YOU.
THE VICTIM HAS BEEN CHOSEN AND THE CIRCLE HAS BEEN DRAWN.
ALL WE HAVE TO DO NOW IS KILL YOUR DAD!

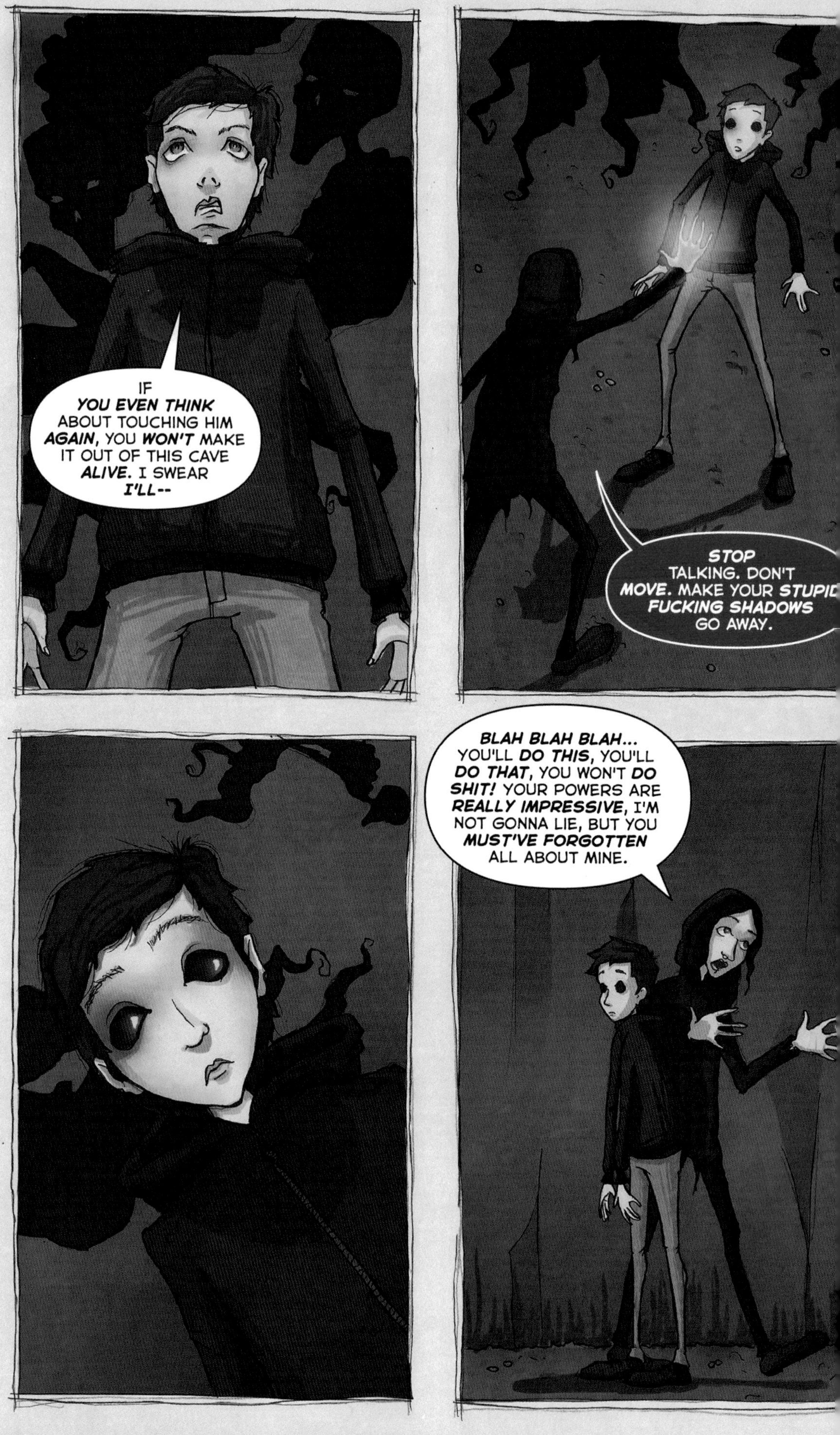
IF YOU EVEN THINK ABOUT TOUCHING HIM AGAIN, YOU WON'T MAKE IT OUT OF THIS CAVE ALIVE. I SWEAR I'LL--
STOP TALKING. DON'T MOVE. MAKE YOUR STUPID FUCKING SHADOWS GO AWAY.
BLAH BLAH BLAH... YOU'LL DO THIS, YOU'LL DO THAT, YOU WON'T DO SHIT! YOUR POWERS ARE REALLY IMPRESSIVE, I'M NOT GONNA LIE, BUT YOU MUST'VE FORGOTTEN ALL ABOUT MINE.

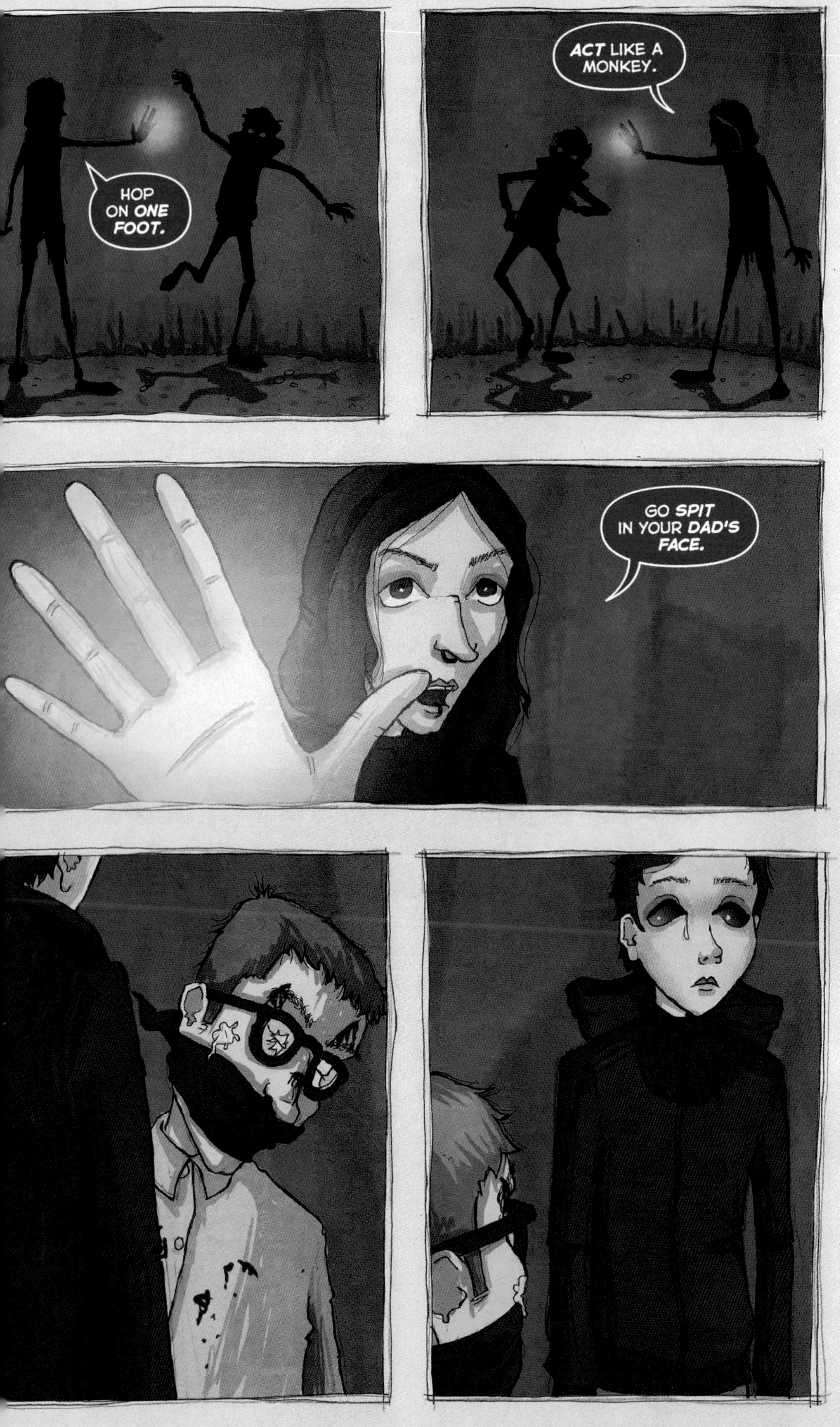
HOP ON ONE FOOT.
ACT LIKE A MONKEY.
GO SPIT IN YOUR DAD'S FACE.

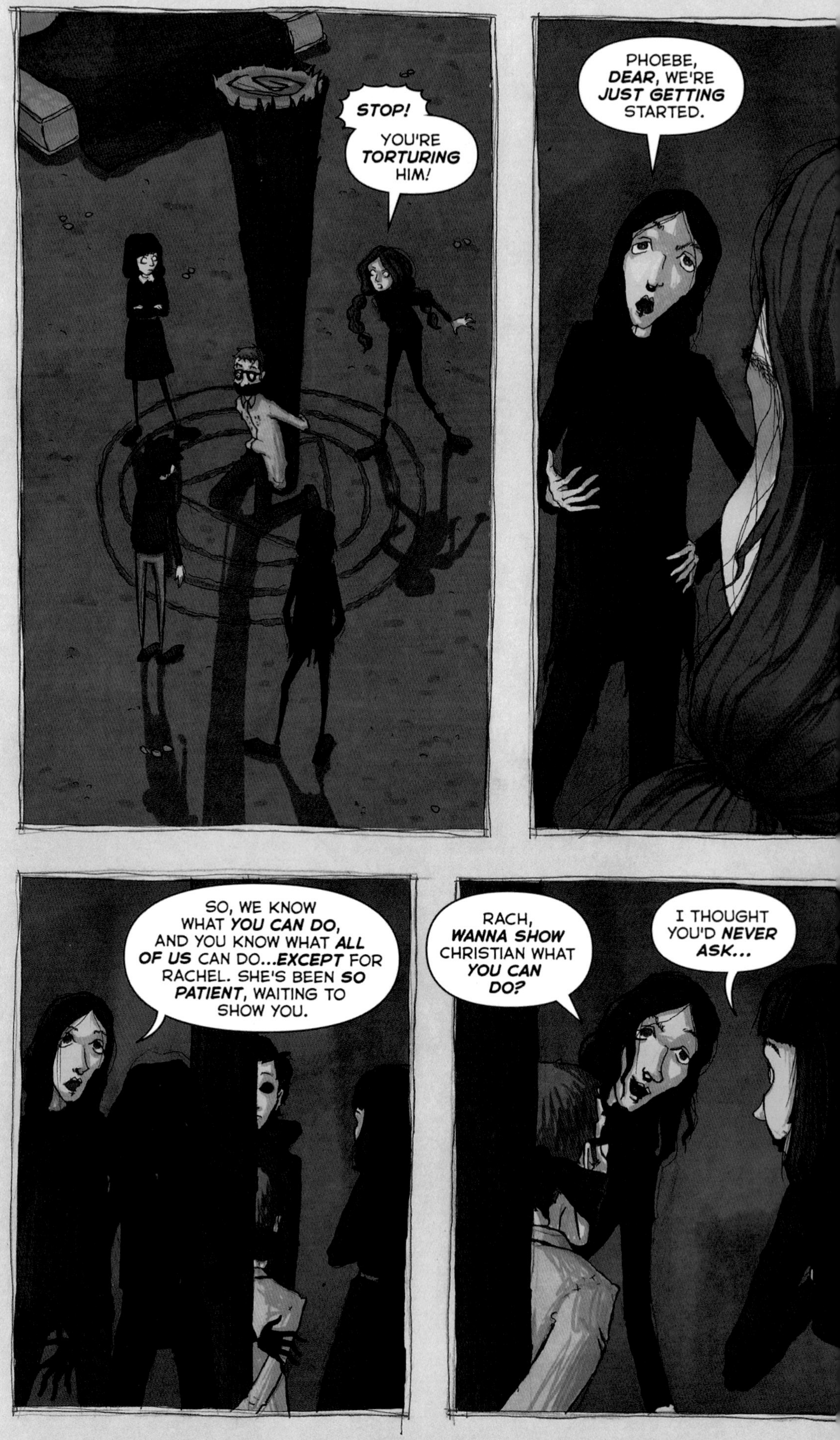
STOP!
YOU'RE TORTURING HIM!
PHOEBE, DEAR, WE'RE JUST GETTING STARTED.
SO, WE KNOW WHAT YOU CAN DO, AND YOU KNOW WHAT ALL OF US CAN DO...EXCEPT FOR RACHEL. SHE'S BEEN SO PATIENT, WAITING TO SHOW YOU.
RACH, WANNA SHOW CHRISTIAN WHAT YOU CAN DO?
I THOUGHT YOU'D NEVER ASK...

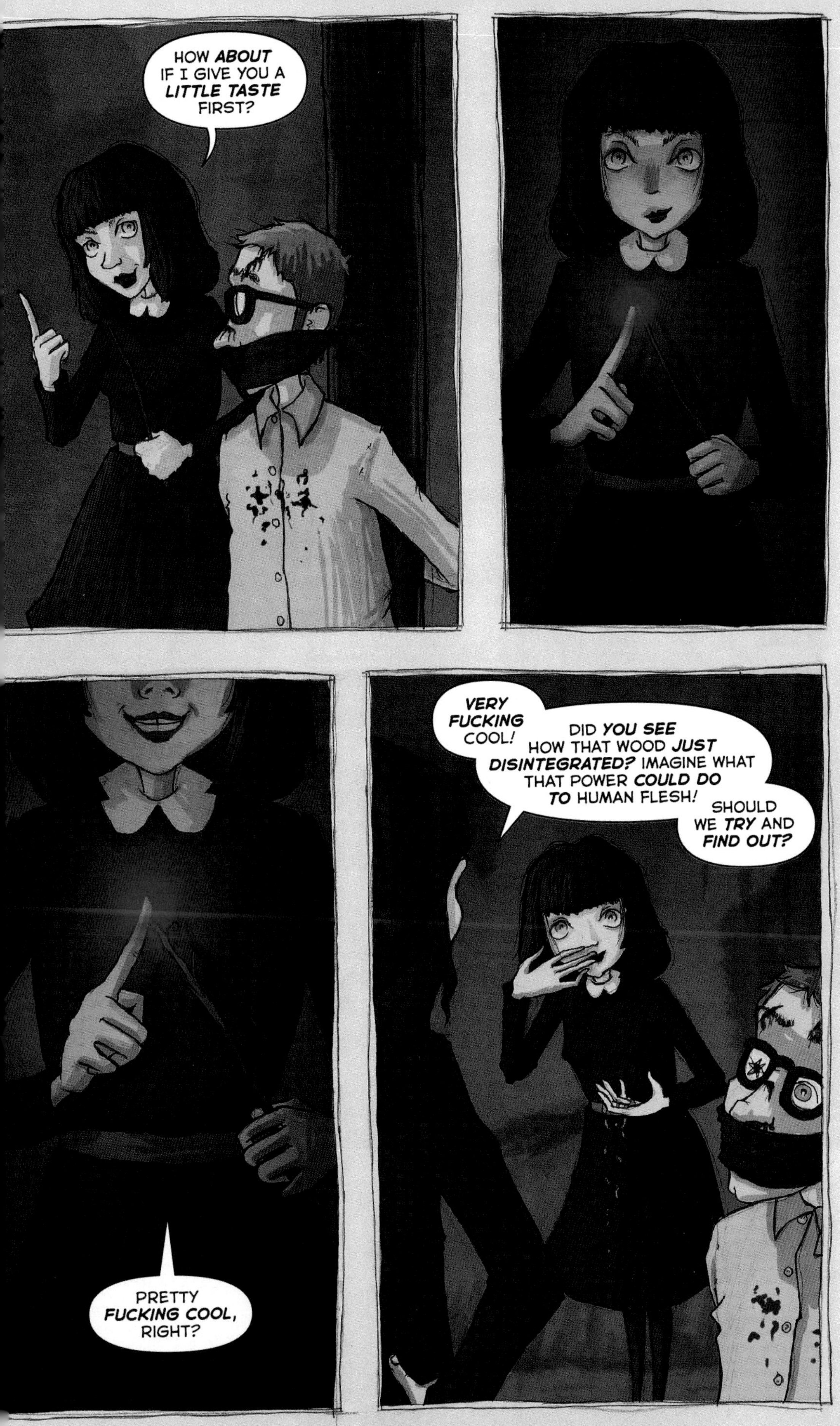

HOW ABOUT IF I GIVE YOU A LITTLE TASTE FIRST?
PRETTY FUCKING COOL, RIGHT?
VERY FUCKING COOL!
DID YOU SEE HOW THAT WOOD JUST DISINTEGRATED? IMAGINE WHAT THAT POWER COULD DO TO HUMAN FLESH!
SHOULD WE TRY AND FIND OUT?

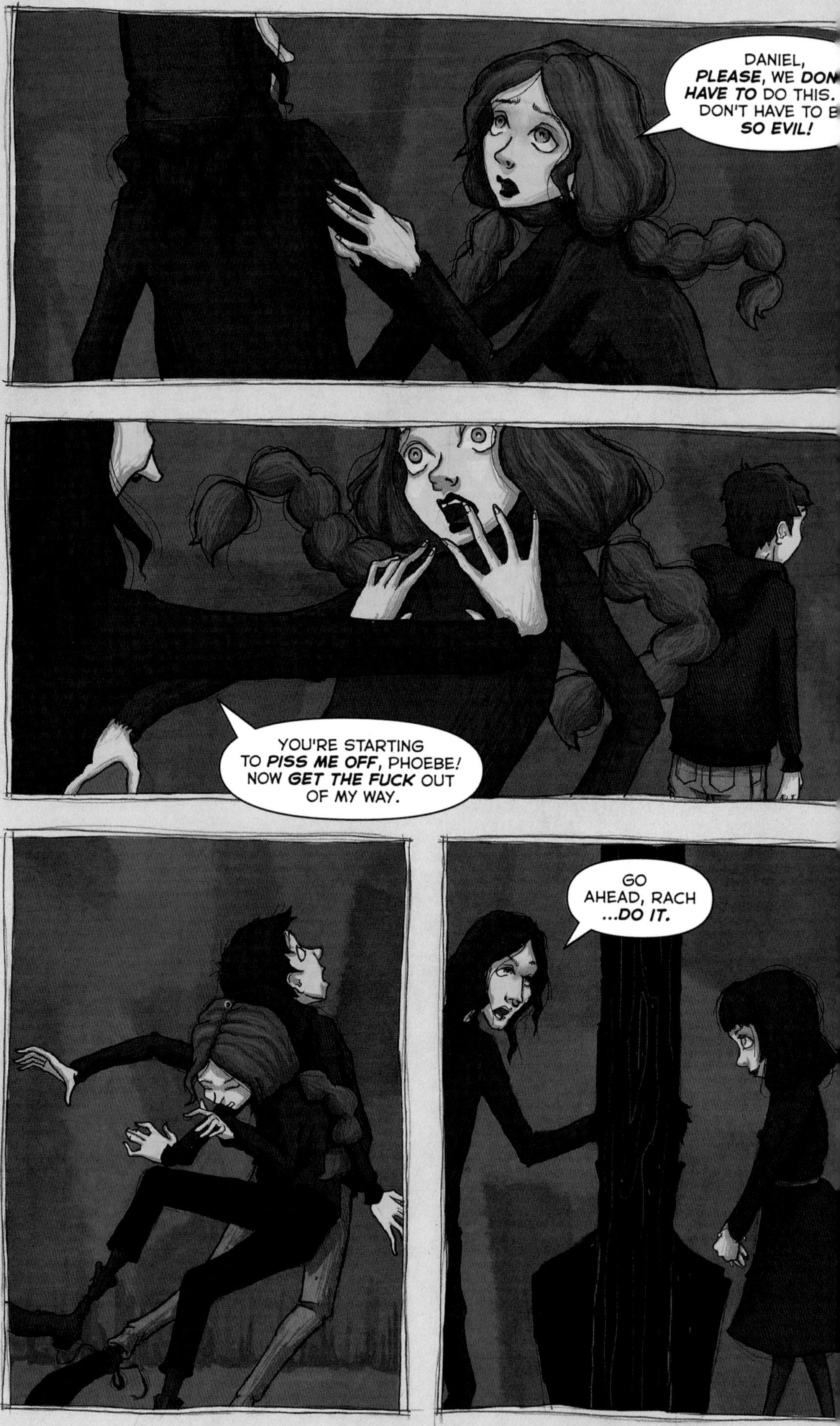
DANIEL, PLEASE, WE DON HAVE TO DO THIS. DON'T HAVE TO B SO EVIL!
YOU'RE STARTING TO PISS ME OFF, PHOEBE! NOW GET THE FUCK OUT OF MY WAY.
GO AHEAD, RACH ...DO IT.

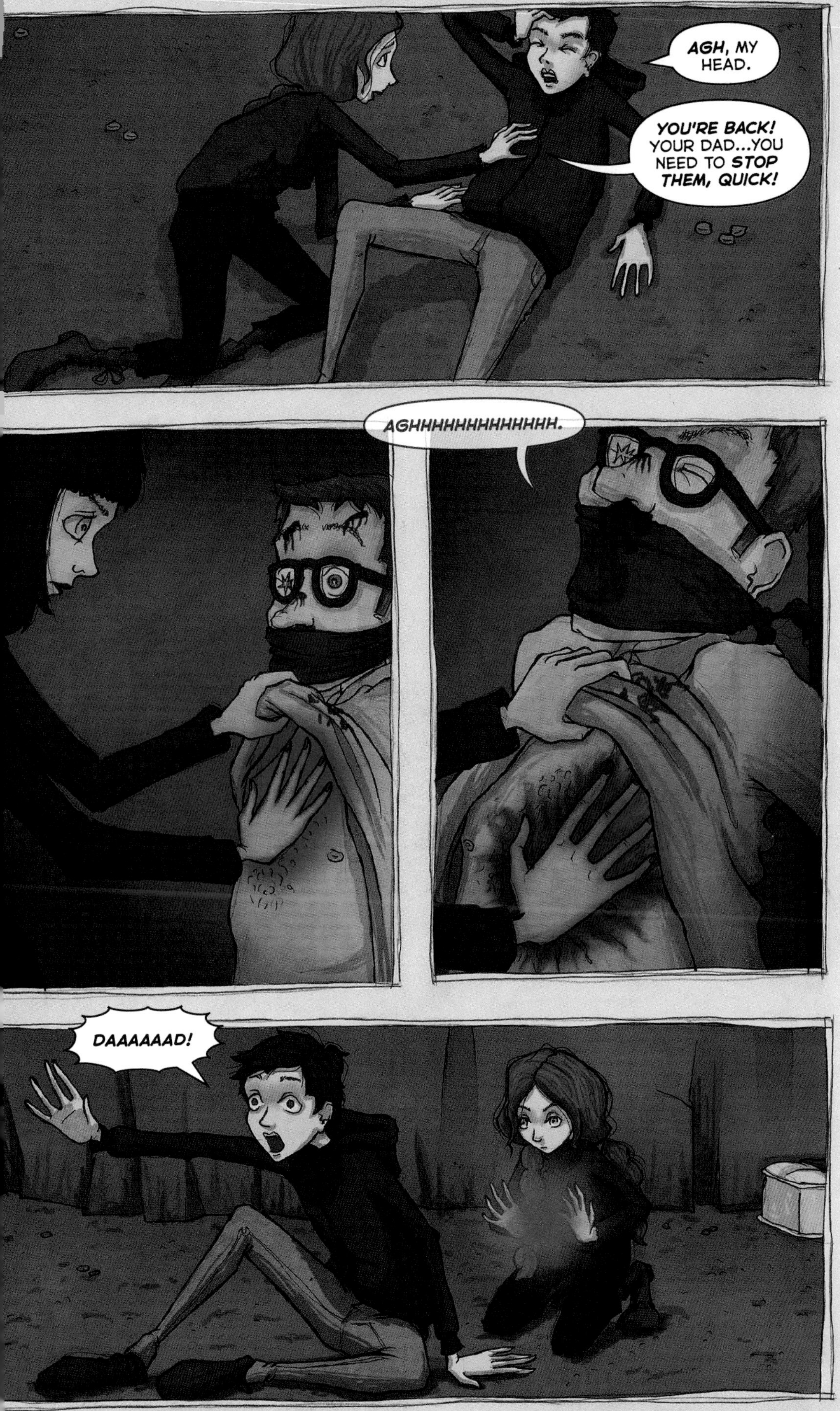
AGH, MY HEAD.
YOU'RE BACK! YOUR DAD...YOU NEED TO STOP THEM, QUICK!
AGHHHHHHHHHHHHH.
DAAAAAAD!

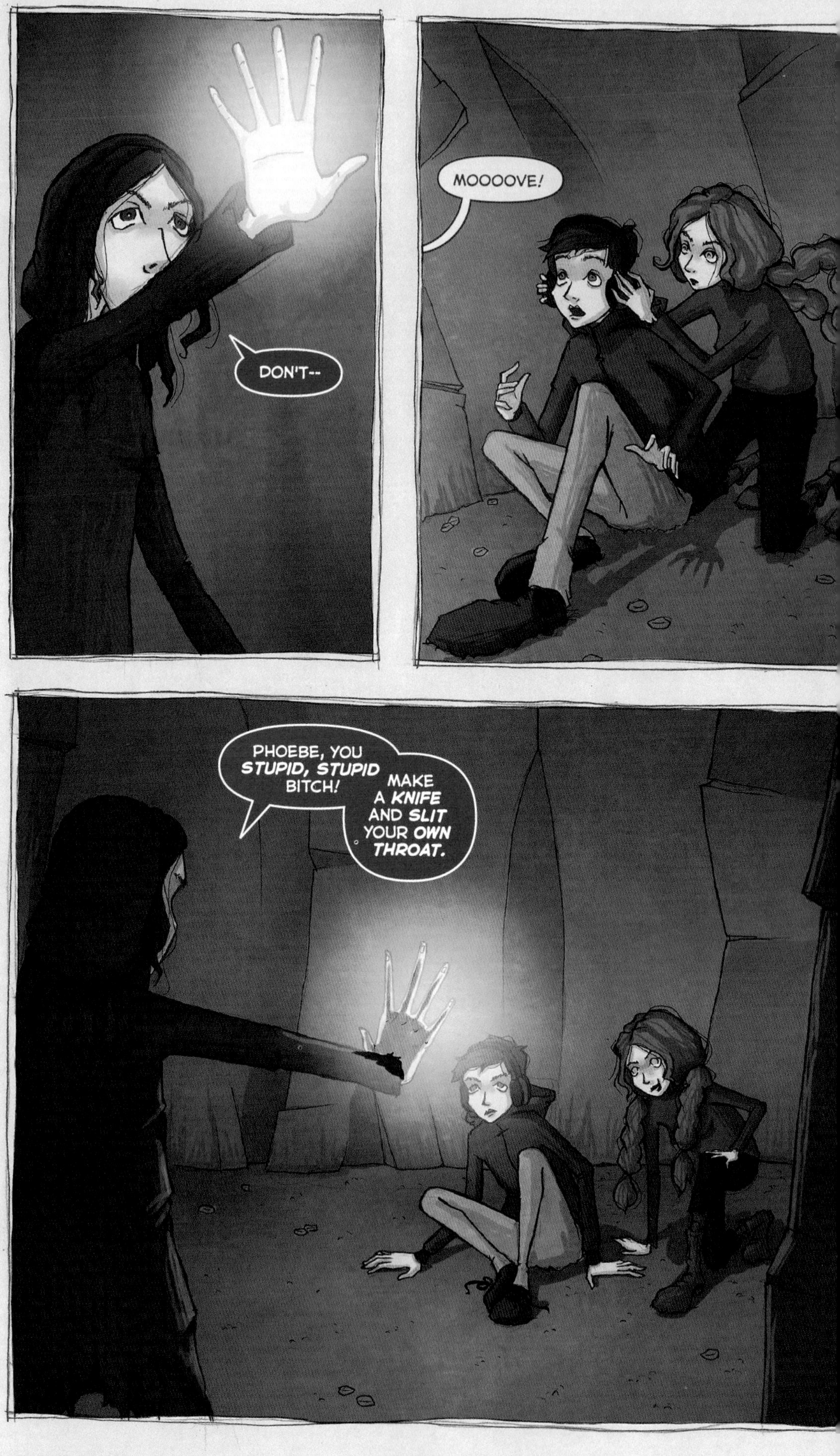
DON'T--
MOOOOVE!
PHOEBE, YOU STUPID, STUPID BITCH!
MAKE A KNIFE AND SLIT YOUR OWN THROAT.

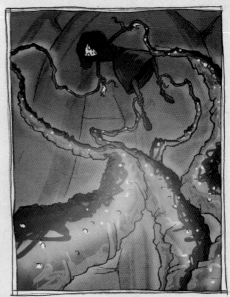

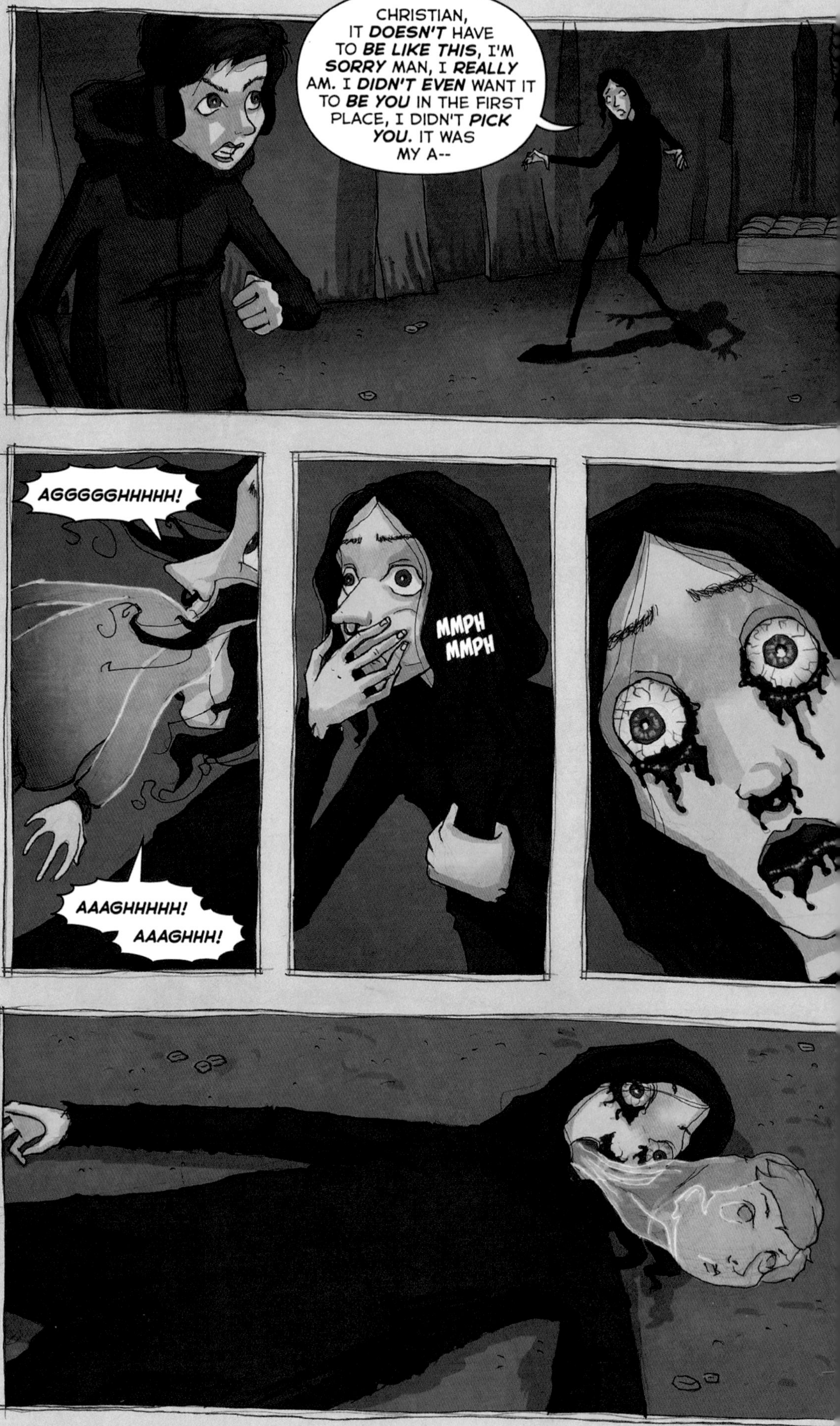
CHRISTIAN, IT DOESN'T HAVE TO BE LIKE THIS, I'M SORRY MAN, I REALLY AM. I DIDN'T EVEN WANT IT TO BE YOU IN THE FIRST PLACE, I DIDN'T PICK YOU. IT WAS MY A--
AGGGGGHHHHH!
AAAGHHHHH!
AAAGHHH!
MMPH MMPH

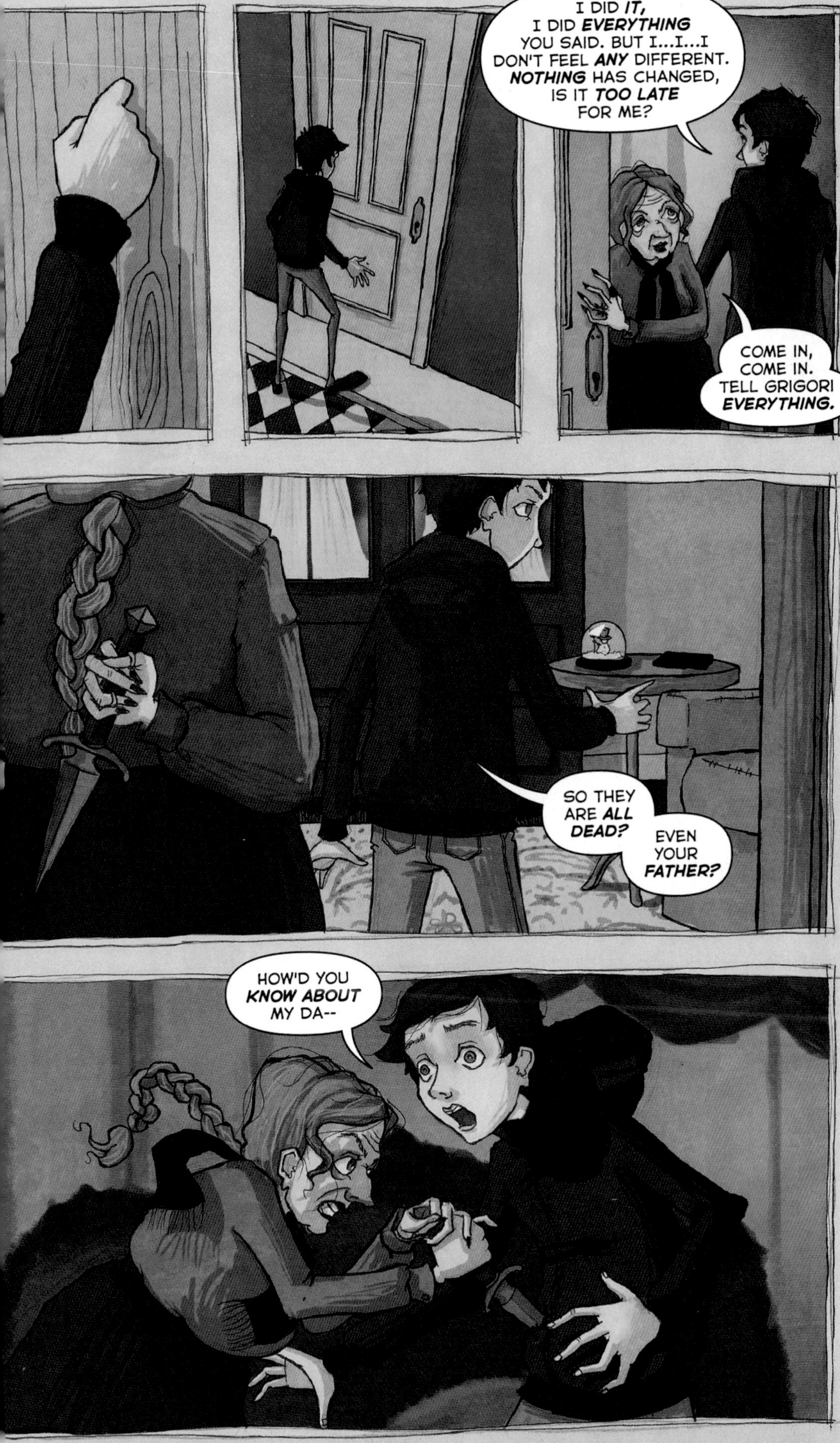
I DID IT, I DID EVERYTHING YOU SAID. BUT I...I...I DON'T FEEL ANY DIFFERENT. NOTHING HAS CHANGED, IS IT TOO LATE FOR ME?
COME IN, COME IN. TELL GRIGORI EVERYTHING.
SO THEY ARE ALL DEAD?
EVEN YOUR FATHER?
HOW'D YOU KNOW ABOUT MY DA--

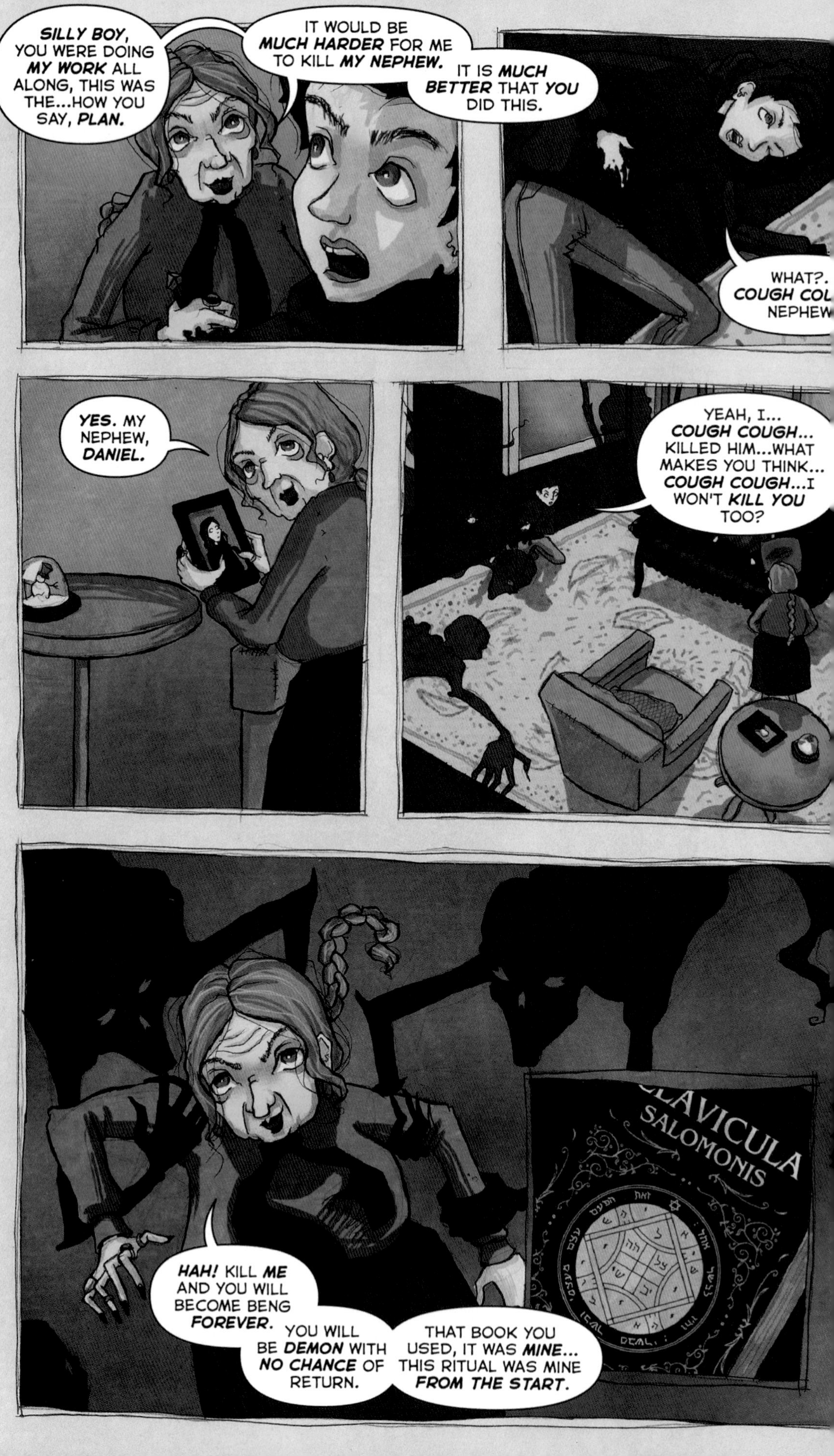
SILLY BOY, YOU WERE DOING MY WORK ALL ALONG, THIS WAS THE...HOW YOU SAY, PLAN.
IT WOULD BE MUCH HARDER FOR ME TO KILL MY NEPHEW.
IT IS MUCH BETTER THAT YOU DID THIS.
WHAT?. COUGH COL NEPHEW
YES. MY NEPHEW, DANIEL.
YEAH, I... COUGH COUGH... KILLED HIM...WHAT MAKES YOU THINK... COUGH COUGH...I WON'T KILL YOU TOO?
CLAVICULA SALOMONIS
HAH! KILL ME AND YOU WILL BECOME BENG FOREVER.
YOU WILL BE DEMON WITH NO CHANCE OF RETURN.
THAT BOOK YOU USED, IT WAS MINE... THIS RITUAL WAS MINE FROM THE START.

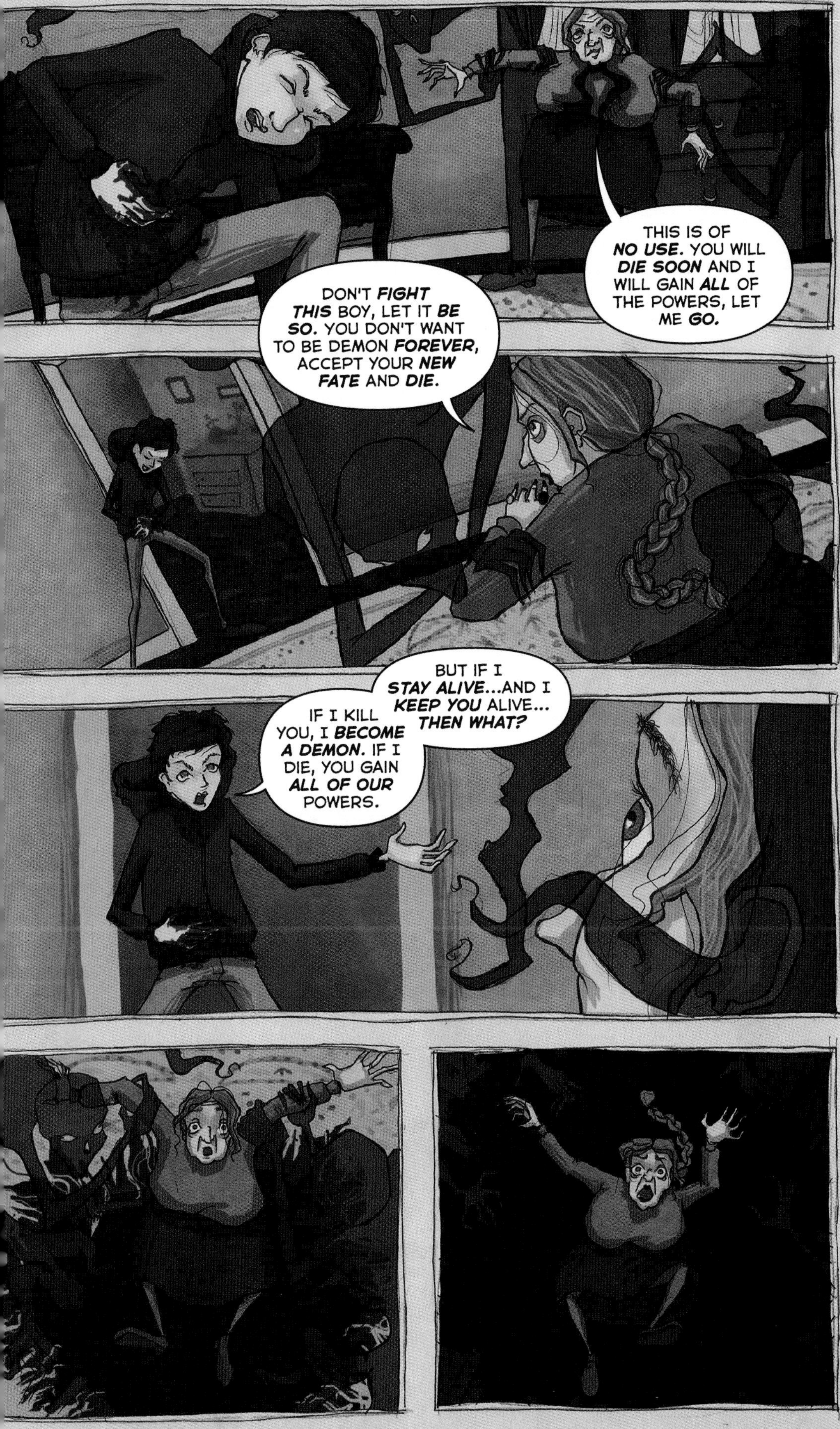
THIS IS OF NO USE. YOU WILL DIE SOON AND I WILL GAIN ALL OF THE POWERS, LET ME GO.
DON'T FIGHT THIS BOY, LET IT BE SO. YOU DON'T WANT TO BE DEMON FOREVER, ACCEPT YOUR NEW FATE AND DIE.
IF I KILL YOU, I BECOME A DEMON. IF I DIE, YOU GAIN ALL OF OUR POWERS.
BUT IF I STAY ALIVE...AND I KEEP YOU ALIVE... THEN WHAT?

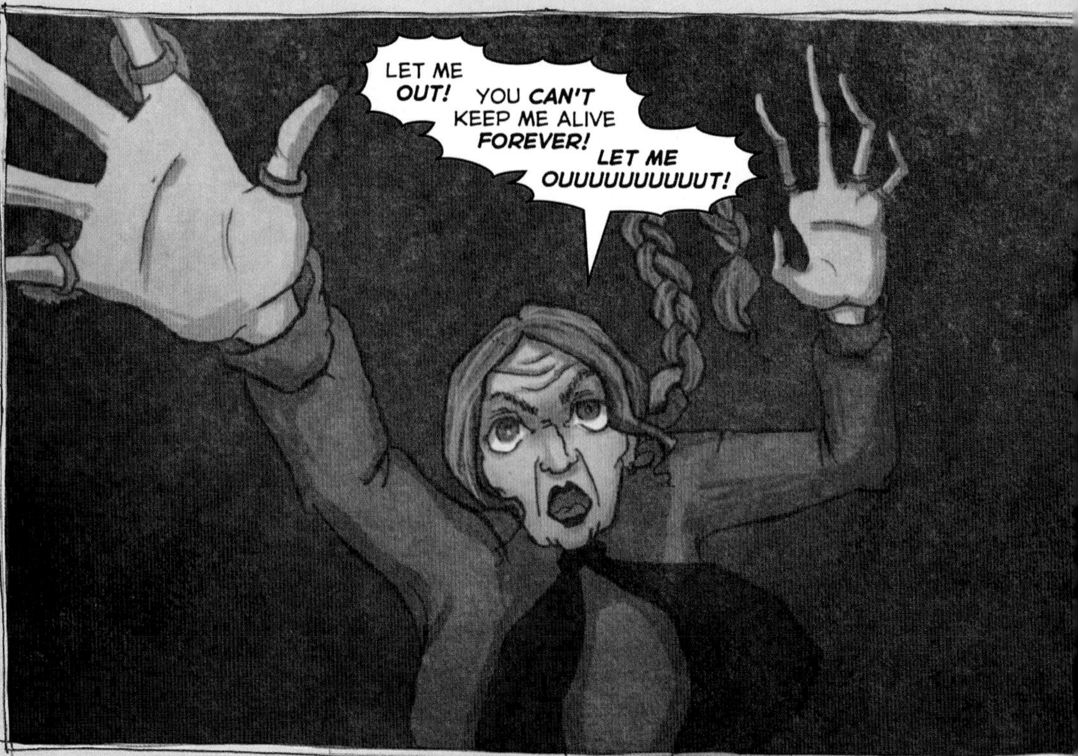
LET ME **OUT!**
YOU **CAN'T** KEEP ME ALIVE **FOREVER!**
LET ME OUUUUUUUUUUT!

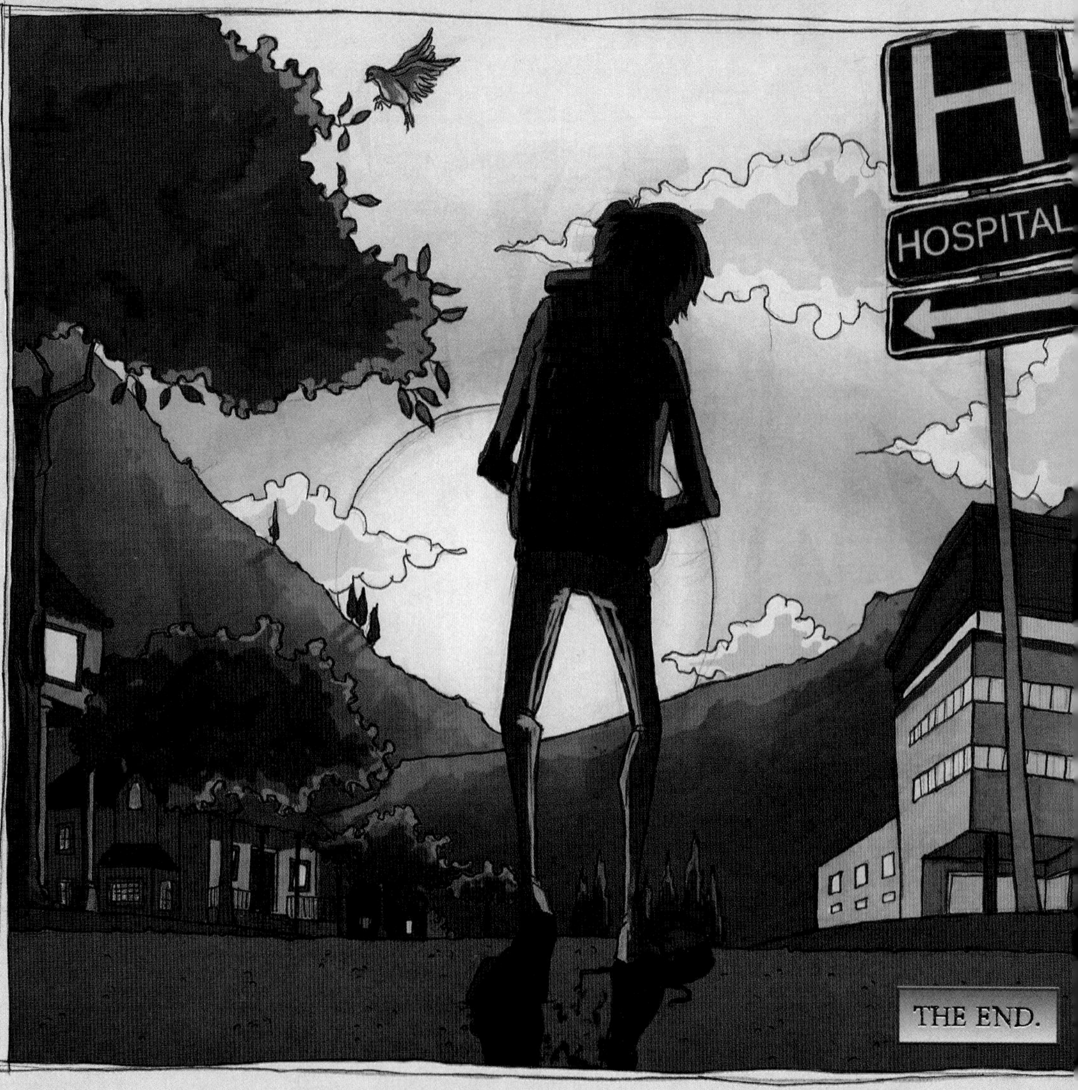
H
HOSPITAL
THE END.